**LABOR AND EMPLOYMENT
RELATIONS ASSOCIATION SERIES**

The Evolution of Workplace Dispute Resolution: International Perspectives

Edited by

Ariel C. Avgar
Deborah Hann
J. Ryan Lamare
David Nash

The Evolution of Workplace Dispute Resolution: International Perspectives. Copyright © 2023 by the Labor and Employment Relations Association. Printed in the United States of America. All rights reserved. No part of the book may be used without written permission, except in the case of brief quotations embodied in critical articles and reviews.

First Edition
ISBN 978-0-913447-27-7
Price: $39.95

LABOR AND EMPLOYMENT RELATIONS ASSOCIATION SERIES
LERA *Proceedings of the Annual Meeting* (published online annually, in the fall)
LERA *Annual Research Volume* (published annually, in the summer/fall)
LERA Online Membership Directory (updated daily, member/subscriber access only)
LERA *Labor and Employment Law News* (published online each quarter)
LERA *Perspectives on Work* (published annually, in the fall)

Information regarding membership, subscriptions, meetings, publications, and general affairs of LERA can be found at the Association website at www.leraweb.org. Members can make changes to their member records, including contact information, affiliations, and preferences, by accessing the online directory at the website or by contacting the LERA national office.

LABOR AND EMPLOYMENT RELATIONS ASSOCIATION
University of Illinois at Urbana-Champaign
School of Labor and Employment Relations
121 Labor and Employment Relations Building
504 East Armory Ave., MC-504
Champaign, IL 61820
Telephone: 217/333-0072   Fax: 217/265-5130
Website: www.leraweb.org
E-mail: LERAoffice@illinois.edu

Acknowledgments

The editors wish to express their deepest gratitude to Emily Smith, Bernadette Tiemann, and Peggy Currid for the tremendous support and guidance they provided throughout the entire research volume process.

Contents

Chapter 1: Introduction
The Evolution of Workplace Dispute Resolution:
International Perspectives 1
Ariel C. Avgar, Deborah Hann, J. Ryan Lamare, and David Nash

Chapter 2
Up for the Challenge? Alternative Dispute Resolution at
a Crossroads in the United States 11
Ariel C. Avgar, J. Ryan Lamare, and Katrina Nobles

Chapter 3
Do Firms Practice Conflict Management Strategically?
Survey Evidence from Britain 29
Deborah Hann and David Nash

Chapter 4
Employment Relationship Problems and Workplace Conflict
Management in New Zealand: Reframing Employment Dispute
Resolution Policy, Processes, and Practices.. 49
Gaye Greenwood, Erling Rasmussen, and Yashika Chandhok

Chapter 5
Understanding Workplace Conflict and Its Management in the
Context of COVID-19... 73
Julian Teicher, Bernadine Van Gramberg, and Greg J. Bamber

Chapter 6
Establishment-Level Conflict Management in the Time of the
COVID-19 Pandemic: The Case of Germany 93
Martin Behrens

Chapter 7
COVID-19 and the Resolution of Workplace Conflict:
The Case of Ireland 115
Paul Teague, William Roche, and Denise Currie

Chapter 8
Engaging Managers with Online Learning in a Context of
COVID-19 Uncertainty: Challenges and Opportunities 137
*Rita Neves, Paul Latreille, Richard Saundry, Peter Urwin,
and Fatima Maatwk*

About the Contributors 161

LERA Executive Board Members 2023–2024 167

CHAPTER 1

Introduction
The Evolution of Workplace Dispute Resolution: International Perspectives

Ariel C. Avgar
Cornell University

Deborah Hann
Cardiff University

J. Ryan Lamare
University of Illinois Urbana-Champaign

David Nash
Cardiff University

In 1999, LERA published a research volume titled Employment Dispute Resolution and Worker Rights, edited by Adrienne Eaton and Jeffery Keefe. It provided an important review of central themes about the implementation of various dispute resolution practices and processes in union and nonunion US organizations. It has served as a valuable resource for both researchers and practitioners in the dispute resolution field, and its chapters have been cited extensively. In what follows, we introduce a new LERA research volume that complements previous volumes on the subject, highlights new developments from the past two decades, and broadens the focus on international developments in this area.

Conflicts and disputes are powerful and consequential dynamics in all organizations. As a result, many organizations invest considerable efforts in designing and assessing effective methods for addressing workplace conflict. Research conducted over the past two decades has documented a diverse array of strategies and approaches deployed by organizations. Some organizations rely on traditional managerial authority and litigation-focused approaches to manage conflict, while an increasing number of firms have experimented with conflict resolution models that aim to address conflict at more informal levels and with a proactive rather than reactive goal. These approaches have a host of implications for workers, managers, and organizations. During this period, a substantial body of research has been amassed, providing empirical evidence that both describes new models and documents the outcomes associated with different organizational strategies.

This volume focuses on the intersections between institutions and actors in shaping innovative conflict management practices, showcasing scholarship from various countries, including Australia, New Zealand, the United States, Ireland, Germany, and the United Kingdom. The intention of the volume is to synthesize a global body of research on conflict management undertaken by labor and employment relations scholars and to assess the current state of employment relations research in this area. In doing so, this volume seeks to provide a roadmap for where research in this area has been and where it should now be headed.

Of particular interest is the volume's focus on international dispute resolution developments. With some important exceptions, research in the dispute resolution domain has been lacking in international and comparative perspectives. Much emphasis has been placed on advancements in specific countries, often using the United States as a reference point but with limited attention given to converging and diverging patterns and trends. This volume addresses this gap by including chapters on a number of different countries and using these insights to begin developing a systematic understanding of national dispute resolution differences and their associated consequences for workers and employers.

A second point of note is that this volume arrives at a time of significant turbulence in the conflict management field. Many scholars and practitioners face critical dilemmas about how to effectively resolve workplace disputes while maintaining a balance between efficiency and equity in these processes. Binding dispute resolution practices have come under increasing pressure, especially in the United States. Globally, there are significant concerns about the degree to which workplace conflict is underpinned by strategic thinking or whether it is simply a product of reactive forces implemented in an ad hoc and haphazard manner.

Finally, the tumult of the global pandemic has risked pushing workplace conflict systems to a breaking point. Several chapters in this volume address the conflict management responses researchers have observed in relation to the pandemic—both broadly (across systems, institutions, and countries) and narrowly (within a single system, institution, or country).

We hope that the volume makes an important contribution to the study of dispute resolution and serves as a useful resource for LERA members, both scholars and practitioners. In what follows in this introduction, we cover two broad topics. First, we provide a more detailed motivation for this research volume and explain why a volume of this nature matters given the changing landscape of dispute resolution. Then we detail the specific contributions of each chapter and underscore their value to LERA scholars and practitioners.

THE CHANGING LANDSCAPE OF WORKPLACE DISPUTE RESOLUTION

Interest in research on conflict resolution at work and in organizations has blossomed in recent years for a variety of reasons. This interest has increased for at least two key reasons. First, private mechanisms for resolving conflicts have become more ubiquitous and widespread at companies. These mechanisms were once a relatively niche aspect of workplace activities, typically involving grievances and, occasionally, interest disputes covering discrete groups of employees. Second, research into organizational adoption of alternative dispute resolution (ADR) practices has increasingly emphasized strategic choice, potentially mirroring the shift in thinking that occurred in the field of human resource management in the late 20th century. Concurrent with these shifts, we have seen growing public scrutiny around the privatization of conflict and its implications for employee access to justice, as well as societal concerns about equity and voice.

Additionally, conflict resolution systems have come under intense pressure as a result of several exogenous crises over the past decade, including the Global Financial Crisis, and, most recently, the COVID-19 pandemic. These crises reinforced and unearthed many traditional sources of conflict while also introducing new types of disputes into workplaces. This volume is intended to engage with and speak to all of these broad shifts and to inform scholars and practitioners about them.

For much of the 20th century, the mechanisms regulating workplace conflicts were constrained and overseen in several ways. In the United States, conflicts were handled at either the collective level via union grievance processes or at the individual level through public courts. In other countries, disputes were often managed via the use of public agencies such as tribunals and commissions. However, during the latter portion of the 20th century, conflict resolution practices underwent a substantial restructuring within the United States and around the world. These changes were multifaceted and complex, but they generally corresponded to a shift away from public goods and public agencies in many countries as a result of deregulatory pressures, growing emphasis on neoliberalism, and a broad decline in reliance on and protection of collective actors—namely, unions and the state. In the conflict resolution sphere, with some exceptions, this shift most prominently manifested in the rise of private, organizationally derived and oriented mechanisms for resolving conflicts—and the conceptualization of the individual rather than collective groups as a key user of these systems.

This reconceptualization of conflict as a more individual, private matter was initially met with a mixture of skepticism and optimism by conflict management scholars. Under a deregulated and organizationally oriented approach to conflict, many scholars saw potential for innovative solutions to long-standing problems facing individuals who were previously denied access to public spaces for voicing their workplace concerns and rights. ADR presented employers and employees with an opportunity to identify conflict at an early stage, resolve it using interest-based methods, and potentially prevent future conflicts from arising.

Despite recognizing the potential for positive change, many others expressed substantial concerns about the outsized influence that employers would have under a deregulated workplace conflict management process and about the ensuing power imbalances that might result from such an approach to handling disputes. While the proposed efficiency gains and innovations derived from relatively affordable and low-barrier-to-entry systems were attractive, they were counterbalanced against various equity concerns regarding the extent to which employers might benefit implicitly or explicitly from them at the expense of employees. These concerns were especially pronounced for practices such as so-called forced arbitration, which resulted in outcomes that were binding on employees and mandatory as a condition of employment.

In addition to significant equity challenges to ADR, those in the field have also expressed concerns, albeit to a lesser degree, about the rise of private ADR systems. In particular, the emergence of forced arbitration has led to concerns about the lack of public scrutiny of potentially malfeasant employers. While ADR scholars have focused primarily on evaluating the efficiency claims of these systems in contrast to evidence demonstrating equity and voice issues, activists and nonacademics have begun challenging the confidential nature of these systems. This shift coincides with the rise of the #MeToo movement in the United States and the growing concern that these systems should not be allowed to relegate fundamental US civil rights violations—particularly workplace sexual harassment and assault—to private forums.

Outside the US context, private ADR structures and systems have emerged as a relatively recent phenomenon, embedded within substantially different institutional and legal contexts. Private conflict resolution mechanisms frequently operate alongside long-standing state-based and collective options. However, there is increasing evidence of a global shift in conflict resolution, potentially mirroring that which occurred in the United States, as evidenced by the weakening of unions and public agencies and their replacement with more individualized and private options. The changing global landscape of conflict management has affected not only so-called liberal market economies such as the United Kingdom, Ireland, New Zealand, and Australia, which share many similar political economy characteristics with the United States, but also countries such as Germany, which has long been considered a stronghold of collective rights and coordination among labor, management, and the state. Overall, this global shift away from public conflict options and toward the private ADR space has been less clearly well supported by key institutions, such as the courts, in most countries relative to the situation in the United States, but it reflects an important set of global developments that have received comparatively less attention in the conflict management field.

Beyond questions about the extent to which various ADR mechanisms can balance efficiency interests with equity concerns, conflict management researchers and scholars are increasingly exploring whether private conflict management systems are undergoing a strategic turn mirroring that which was witnessed in both the fields of labor relations and human resource management in the late 20th century. In the United States, private conflict management practices at firms were frequently created in response to litigation threats, aligning ADR more closely with a company's legal rather than human resource concerns. However, ADR has recently expanded to include an array of interest-based interventions designed to empower and improve relationships rather than simply serving as an alternative to litigation.

As a result, scholarship on workplace dispute resolution has begun to explore the extent to which ADR and human resources (HR) are linked at companies that have more fully integrated approaches to conflict management. Emerging evidence thus far suggests that a strategic turn may indeed be unfolding, positioning ADR practices alongside other strategic human resource endeavors rather than as a purely reactive set of practices designed to reduce litigation threats. Outside the United States, the extent to which ADR has taken a strategic turn and become aligned with a firm's human resource practices is even less understood, with many scholars in the conflict resolution field asserting that this area of research requires significant examination. Preliminary evidence suggests that globally, ADR may be less strategic and more fragmented and ad hoc. However, it also tends to function less as a litigation substitute and more as a distinct set of practices outside the public or human resource realms.

Ultimately, the evolving landscape of ADR has raised questions about the extent to which private dispute resolution practices and systems can effectively handle a wide variety disputes and remain resilient to broader employment shocks and turmoil. Conflict systems involving collective actors and public agencies tend to be viewed as highly stable and robust—with the ability to adapt to changing circumstances because of their inherent pluralism and the power balances among various actors in the system. However, with the rise of private and individualized ADR, the degree to which a more unitarist system can adjust to unforeseen events in a way that protects equity and voice remains uncertain. The COVID-19 pandemic in early 2020 presented a particularly stark test of these systems. In addition to expanding our understanding of ADR's international scope and its strategic (or ad hoc) nature, a key goal of this volume is to explore the extent to which exogenous shocks, such as the global pandemic, have fundamentally reshaped conflict management in organizations and societies and to assess the responsiveness of the systems to such events.

THE CONTRIBUTIONS WITHIN THIS VOLUME

Each of the chapters within this research volume is designed to both complement and expand on the current understanding of workplace conflict and its resolution locally and globally, and they speak to the tensions and questions highlighted in the preceding section. In this section, we briefly highlight key findings and the contributions to the field.

The United States at an Individual-Rights Conflict Crossroads

Chapter 2, by Avgar, Lamare, and Nobles, "Up for the Challenge? Alternative Dispute Resolution at a Crossroads in the United States" focuses on the changing nature of work and conflict within the United States, which has the most widespread and well-documented use and system of dispute resolution described in this volume. The United States presents an interesting starting point for this volume because it has commonly served as a bellwether for trends and innovations in conflict management practices, both positive and negative. This chapter therefore provides a useful reference point for the remainder of the book, as well as a potential contrast to the other countries covered in the volume.

For many decades, workplace dispute resolution in the United States was considered a stable system. However, this perspective has undergone significant change in recent years. In this chapter, the authors examine the current pressures facing the US dispute resolution system, specifically questioning the extent to which core assumptions underpinning ADR in the United States remain valid, given a series of profound shifts in both work and conflict within organizations.

Scholars have spent the past several decades examining the increasing shift to private methods of dispute resolution and the implication these have for individual employees and the workplace as a system. Because this privatized system led to a greater focus on individual employment contracts as opposed to collectively bargained contracts, new conflicts and issues arose, resulting in highly varied practices and outcomes associated with these conflicts.

In recent years, these systems have come under increasing scrutiny, with major questions and concerns being voiced. In Chapter 2, the authors discuss several of these issues in detail, including the changing nature of work, the expansion of new organizational forums and nontraditional employment, the rise of the platform economy, the introduction of new technology, and the increase in remote work during the COVID-19 pandemic. They also examine how and whether traditional ADR methods and mechanisms can withstand these changes.

In addition to new issues arising, the authors of Chapter 2 consider the evolving balance between individual and collective voices through the growth of worker centers and collectives, as well as social justice organizations. The examples described of unrest and tension impacting the field lead directly to variations in reactive versus strategic approaches across neutrals, companies, and industries, further leading to a system in flux searching for a solid foundation on which to stand.

The Relationship Between Conflict, Human Resources Strategy, and Managerial Practices in the United Kingdom

In Chapter 3, "Do Firms Practice Conflict Management Strategically? Survey Evidence from Britain," Hann and Nash extend the nascent application of strategic thinking in conflict resolution, moving beyond the United States and traditional industrial relations scholarship to focus on human resource functions within the United Kingdom. The authors examine the growing interest in whether the approaches of organizations to conflict management is strategic or simply pragmatic. Although much has been written on the spread of ADR, little attention has been paid to how these practices relate to wider organizational strategic objectives, particularly as articulated through HR policies. Drawing on nationwide UK survey data, Hann and Nash evaluate whether there is evidence of linkages between policies and approaches to conflict management and firms' broader strategies at different levels.

The authors seek to determine whether internal logics within organizations' approaches to conflict align with their wider practices in terms of both strategy and implementation. They find that conflict management is weakly linked to human resource strategies, with the important exception of employee voice. Additionally, the authors show that there are stark differences in the stated policies within organizations and their actual use of dispute resolution practices.

The authors interpret these outcomes in two meaningful and compelling ways. The first conclusion is that the lack of consistency between conflict management and overarching human resource strategy may be intentional. Disentangling a firm's approach to disputes from its wider strategies provides greater flexibility to intervene in specific and nuanced conflicts as deemed appropriate, without having to force the intervention to fit within the organization's overall strategic vision or broad work policies. Second, this way of thinking about conflict vis-à-vis human resource strategy offers an important counterpoint to existing research that highlights and expects consistency between stated policies and their implementations as a key mechanism for perceptions of organizational justice.

Reframing Workplace Conflict Resolution and Employment Relationship Disputes in New Zealand

In Chapter 4, "Employment Relationship Problems and Workplace Conflict Management in New Zealand: Reframing Employment Dispute Resolution Policy, Processes, and Practice," Greenwood, Rasmussen, and Chandhok show how workplace conflict resolution in New Zealand has benefited from well-established and effective processes within official employment institutions. Unlike in the United States and similar contexts, in New Zealand the state has historically played a substantial role in providing not only traditional but also ADR processes such as negotiation, conciliation, arbitration, mediation, and facilitation. These institutional processes have dominated research and debates about conflict resolution in the New Zealand context. However, reflecting global trends, a shift toward early informal resolution and less institutional, less legalistic management of employment relationship problems can reduce barriers to conflict resolution. To provide such early, low-cost, and nonlegalistic forms of resolution as promoted by employment relations legislation, new approaches to workplace conflict resolution processes are required. The authors argue for a fundamental shift in institutional provision of ADR services and reframe processes for early resolution of conflict.

The authors assert that the employment relationship is more complex and dynamic than the historical construct of employer–employee–union relationships. Their research findings suggest that escalation to formal disputes in New Zealand can be attributed to the influence of positional legalism on institutional and workplace interventions and a lack of attention to the workplace context where conflict emerges. Positioning their chapter at the intersection of both private conflict resolution mechanisms and institutional service provisions, the authors identify how and why complexity in the employment relationship and traditional interventions can lead to escalation of complaints to formal disputes.

Finally, the authors reframe traditional approaches to negotiation and mediation as opportunities for early collaborative sense-making. They argue that attention to reflective, collaborative sense-making is fundamental to the early resolution of complex employment relationship problems.

Workplace Conflict in the Context of the COVID-19 Pandemic

Four chapters in this volume deal directly with the effects of the COVID-19 pandemic on conflict management structures and practices. In "Understanding Workplace Conflict and Its Management in the Context of COVID-19" (Chapter 5), Teicher, Van Gramberg, and Bamber assert that COVID-19 has given rise to a range of novel workplace conflicts that should be considered in conjunction with frames of reference. The chapter builds on insights from frames of reference and applies them to conflict management systems and practices in response to COVID-19, highlighting how workplace ADR systems operate in response to work changes following the pandemic's onset. The chapter concentrates on the various sources of conflict resulting from the pandemic and particularly emphasizes issues arising from some workers being required to continue working in the physical workplace while others were able to work remotely.

To understand these conflicts and their attempted resolution, the authors revisit frames of reference, especially the neopluralist conception, to understand the participation of diverse actors in these disputes. The authors also highlight the challenge in analyzing the atypically interventionist role of the state during the pandemic, which stands outside the liberal democratic model. The chapter focuses on examples drawn from Anglo-American liberal market economies rather than discussing any one particular institutional context. This approach provides a fertile ground for international comparison and analysis regarding the extent to which neoliberal ideology shapes the responses of state actors.

The second chapter focusing specifically on COVID-19 drills down into discrete mechanisms for resolving workplace disputes following the pandemic's onset. In Chapter 6, "Establishment-Level Conflict Management in the Time of the COVID-19 Pandemic: The Case of Germany," Behrens, highlights the role of works councils as a conflict resolution mechanism. He notes that works councils are at the core of what is known as the German dual system of labor relations. In Germany, collective bargaining is conducted primarily at the industry level in negotiations between unions and powerful employer associations, while the regulation of basic work standards—such as the distribution of working time, health and safety, further training, and work organization—is subject to negotiations between plant management and works councils.

Drawing on a large-scale study of German works councils, Behrens empirically investigates whether and how works councils contribute to resolve work-related conflicts under the severe conditions caused by the pandemic. The pandemic caused labor market disruptions at an unprecedented scale, and Behrens treats the event as akin to a stress test for interest representation at the establishment level. Two broad perspectives were tested with evidence. The first, known as crisis corporatism, is informed by earlier experiences during the Global Financial Crisis and assumes that, at times of severe economic pressure, key actors tend to avoid conflict in an effort to guarantee a firm's economic survival. In contrast, a second perspective suggests that it is mostly employers who have strategically used the COVID-19 crisis as a window of opportunity to transform employment relations in their favor. This strategy might be associated with increased levels of establishment-level conflict. In examining both perspectives in Germany, the chapter provides an interesting country-specific case that connects to the preceding chapter on broad COVID-19 responses globally.

The third chapter on COVID-19, by Roche, Teague, and Currie, approaches the pandemic from a different angle and considers its impact on the work undertaken by the Irish public dispute resolution body, the Workplace Resolution Commission (WRC), during the time of the pandemic. In Chapter 7, "COVID-19 and the Resolving of Workplace Conflict: The Case of Ireland," the authors offer a unique exploration of how the WRC adapted its work when the pandemic occurred and examine how and to what degree this dispute resolution body was able to deliver its important services under unanticipated circumstances. COVID-19 occurred five years after the creation of the WRC, by which time many of the initial challenges had been addressed. The authors explore the obstacles faced by a dispute resolution agency in delivering its important services during a period of disruptive organizational change. The question whether there was a shift in the nature and volume of conflict as the world of work changed overnight as a result of COVID-19 is explored as well.

The work draws on interviews with key stakeholders inside the WRC, as well as a major private provider, to consider the extent to which some of these changes might be longer term. The authors find some important evidence of disruptive change in the response to the constraints put in place by lockdowns and social distancing. They note that these changes are not long-term revolutions to the way dispute resolution and conflict management are addressed but are simple responses to the environment. In that context, the chapter contributes not only to our understanding of how conflict can be addressed but also importantly informs current industrial relations debates about the potential for disruptive organizational change caused by COVID-19.

In Chapter 8, "Engaging Managers with Online Learning in a Context of COVID-19 Uncertainty: Challenges and Opportunities," Neves, Latreille, Saundry, Urwin, and Maatwk take a different approach and present initial findings from a live project aimed at training line managers in conflict management. This timely, practical project explores the importance of line managers in delivering effective practices around conflict management and dispute resolution. The evidence on the significance of conflict-competent line managers is well established, yet there has been limited systematic training in this area. In their chapter, the authors, in collaboration with the Advisory Conciliation and Arbitration Service (Acas, the UK's public dispute resolution agency) and funded by the Economic and Social Research Council, developed a systematic intervention with the aim of increasing the confidence of line managers in dealing with difficult situations they face. The aim is to reduce organizational cost and increase productivity. The authors explain and review the pilot of this training program, conducted within four organizations.

In addition to contributing to ongoing debates around the best approaches for delivering training in a post-COVID business world, the authors uncover the importance of engagement with the process for creating positive outcomes around conflict confidence. They find that developing training for line managers to address conflict is not enough; organizations need to ensure that it is taken seriously and that adequate space is created for it. If organizations do not prioritize this training explicitly, conflict will continue to drain organizational productivity as line managers struggle to deal with disputes as they arise.

CONCLUSION

This volume encompasses a wide range of topics and advances discussions around conflict, both geographically and thematically. It makes important contributions to the field of knowledge in three key ways. First, it reinforces the argument that there is a growing and sustained shift from traditional public-driven, collective-focused approaches to conflict resolution, even where the state has historically played a key role. The ability of public dispute resolution agencies to adapt to the changing world is highlighted as a key point for wider future discussion. The chapters reveal a tension around equity as new processes emerge to supplant traditional state-sponsored ones. However, the chapters present differing assessments of the extent to which private approaches deliver fair access, indicating a need for further research and debate.

Second, the authors in this volume debate the question of how far developments in conflict management practice are strategic versus reactive in nature. This question is examined in the context of the pandemic, as well as more widely. The conclusions presented suggest that both organizational and national approaches to conflict management are determined primarily on a reactive basis. The authors in this volume further explore whether this reactive approach might actually be a strategy in and of itself—prioritizing best fit over best practice—and initiate a debate as to whether we might begin to talk about disintegrated systems of conflict management instead of integrated ones. Finally, the impact of COVID-19 on dispute resolution looms large in this volume, as you might expect of a publication planned and written during the pandemic. In the early stages of the COVID-19 era, there was a sense that the challenges and changes brought about by this startling exogenous shock might result in long-term transformative innovation in conflict management and employment relations more generally. However, the findings in this volume tend to suggest that, in reality, there has been return to the status quo as COVID-19 limitations are beginning to subside. Given the proximity of this publication to the end of the pandemic, this trend will be of interest to researchers and practitioners alike.

Chapter 2

Up for the Challenge? Alternative Dispute Resolution at a Crossroads in the United States

Ariel C. Avgar
Cornell University

J. Ryan Lamare
University of Illinois Urbana-Champaign

Katrina Nobles
Cornell University

ABSTRACT

For many decades, workplace dispute resolution in the United States had been treated as a system defined by stability. However, this perspective has recently seen a great deal of change. This chapter examines the current pressures facing the US dispute resolution system. In particular, it focuses on the increased shift to private methods of dispute resolution and the implication these methods have for individual employees, as well as the workplace as a system. Because this privatized system has shifted to a higher number of individual employment contracts as opposed to collectively bargained contracts, as new conflicts and issues arise, there are highly varied outcomes and practices associated with these conflicts. Over the course of the past five years in particular, the field of labor and employment arbitration and mediation has had to face major questions and concerns, including changing laws, environments, and mandates amid a global pandemic; the way in which parties choose neutrals and how that impacts the diversity of the neutral pool and decisions made; and whether dispute resolution approaches such as mandatory arbitration are used to effectively avoid costly, public, and possibly class-related litigation, or truly to serve justice. In addition to new issues arising, the issue of the individual versus the collective voice is evolving through the increase in worker centers and collectives, as well as social justice organizations. These examples of unrest and tension impacting the field lead directly to variations in reactive versus strategic approaches across neutrals, companies, and industries, further leading to a system in flux searching for sound footing on which to land.

THE RISE AND PROMISE OF ALTERNATIVE DISPUTE RESOLUTION OVER THE PAST 50 YEARS

Alternative dispute resolution (ADR) in nonunion workplaces represents one of the most dramatic organizational shifts in the United States over the past half century.

ADR roared into many nonunion US workplaces in the 1970s and 1980s with the promise of both addressing managerial challenges associated with conflicts and disputes and benefiting workers through enhanced opportunities for input, voice, and workplace fairness (Avgar 2021; Colvin 2003). Many ADR scholars and practitioners expressed a great deal of excitement and optimism around this significant development. Building on the long history of dispute resolution procedures in the unionized setting, ADR in nonunion firms was seen by many as a powerful alternative to litigation and/or to unchecked managerial prerogatives as the dominant means of resolving workplace conflict (Ewing 1989; Lipsky, Seeber, and Fincher 2003).

To what extent do the core assumptions regarding ADR and its expansion in the United States still hold given the profound recent changes to both the nature of work and conflict in organizations? Work and employment in the United States are at a crossroads, with fundamental long-standing premises being challenged and questioned. In this chapter, we seek to assess whether the case for ADR still holds. Have these changes affected the role that ADR can and should play within nonunion firms? In so doing, we reflect on the adequacy of ADR at this pivotal juncture.

Researchers across an array of disciplines have contributed to a robust and expansive body of research over the past half century that has examined the core assumptions and premises on which the enthusiasm for ADR was based (Avgar 2020; Colvin and Avgar 2018). Early on, this research provided a solid description of the procedural contours associated with different ADR practices, such as mediation, arbitration, and the ombuds office (Colvin, Klaas, and Mahony 2006; Roche, Teague, and Colvin 2014). Industrial relations and legal scholars, for example, pointed to the implications associated with different procedural dimensions and with the distinction between rights-based procedures that focused on who was right or wrong in a given dispute and interest-based ones that sought to assist the parties in reaching an agreement that met their underlying needs (Bendersky 2007; Colvin 2016).

Building on this early body of research, scholars in the 1980s and 1990s began exploring the antecedents to organizational use of ADR. Why had a growing proportion of organizations decided to abandon traditional managerial and court-based approaches to the resolution of conflict for internal practices and processes? What broader factors had led to this consequential shift? This literature sets forth an array of explanations for the rise of ADR that included, among other things, shifts to litigation patterns in the United States, including the legislation of a host of employment protections in the 1960s (Edelman 1990); the sharp decline in unionization (Avgar, Lamare, Lipsky, and Gupta 2013); and changes in the manner in which work was organized (Avgar 2016; Currie and Teague 2016). The portrait of ADR adoption that emerged from this research was a reactive response to a variety of pressures that resulted in the use of specific practices. As such, ADR was seen as a response to both external and internal shifts that put significant new pressures on organizations to deal with conflict with structured processes and practices and in a less public manner (Lipsky, Avgar, and Lamare 2016, 2020).

In the mid-1990s, scholars began shifting away from the study of individual ADR practices and explored the increasingly prevalent use of bundles of practices in an internally consistent manner. Conflict management systems (CMS) represented a new evolution in the transformation of nonunion organizational efforts to resolve conflict (Conbere 2001; Lipsky, Seeber, and Fincher 2003; Lynch 2001). Drawing on earlier ADR research, CMS research provided a detailed analysis of the processes and structures that made up these new bundles and the motivations driving their adoption and implementation (Bendersky 2007; Roche and Teague 2012). Here, too, a great deal of attention was given to the pressures that account for the decision some firms make to take a systems approach to the way in which they resolve conflict.

The most recent shift in the study of ADR and CMS has integrated a strategic lens. Scholars examining the workplace dispute resolution over the past decade have sought to assess this development in the context of proactive strategic orientations on the part of organizations (Avgar 2016, 2021; Lipsky and Avgar 2008; Lipsky, Avgar, and Lamare 2020). As such, this research complements earlier studies that emphasized the reactive nature of ADR adoption with a more complete accounting of the implications that different strategic considerations and motivations have for the adoption of different dispute resolution practices (Lipsky, Avgar, and Lamare 2016).

Across these stages in the development of the ADR and CMS literature over the past decades, core assumptions have been proposed that animate the continued interest in the role that these practices play. These assumptions stand at the heart of the robust scholarly and practitioner support that these practices receive, as evidenced by very active academic and professional associations that have, for the most part, been proponents for the organizational use of ADR and CMS.

A number of core assumptions around the adoption and implementation ADR and CMS in nonunion organizations stand out in particular. First and as noted above, scholars and practitioners have highlighted the mutual-gains nature of ADR, providing benefits to both employers and workers (Avgar 2021; Lewin 2001). For employers and organizations, ADR holds the promise of a more cost-effective way of dealing with workplace conflict. Furthermore, mandatory dispute resolution techniques, such as arbitration, offer organizations the opportunity to shield themselves from the scrutiny and interventions of the external court system (Avgar 2021; Colvin 2003, 2017, 2019). For workers, ADR, according to proponents, offers expanded access to more convenient ways of adjudicating or negotiating differences with the employer (Estreicher 2000). ADR growth in the United States has also been based on the notion that these practices improve relationships within organizations (Avgar 2016). Providing workers and their managers with multiple avenues to address conflict, including interest-based options such as mediation, is likely, according to this approach, to strengthen relationships across the organization (Friedman, Tidd, Currall, and Tsai 2000; Lipsky, Seeber, and Fincher 2003). Finally, recent research has suggested that firms can advance their broader organizational goals and objectives by adopting a bundle of dispute resolution practices that align with the firm's overall strategy

(Avgar 2021; Lipsky and Avgar 2008; Lipsky, Avgar, and Lamare 2020). Taken together, the continued expansion of ADR and CMS in the United States is supported by both empirical evidence and broader assumptions about the range of benefits that this transformation has offered organizations and their members.

The question motivating this chapter is the extent to which this promise, supported by volumes of research and decades of practice, is affected by the fundamental changes to the nature of work and to the manifestation of conflict within and outside organizations. Organizations are going through, arguably, one of the most dramatic periods of rapid and consequential change since the Industrial Revolution. The combination of new technologies, novel organizational forms, and dramatically different workforce preferences and expectations have led to a shift in how and where work is conducted and have upended taken-for-granted assumptions that have held for over a century. Alongside these changes, the manifestations of conflict itself have also changed dramatically with greater level of workplace polarization and value-based differences. To what extent do traditional assumptions about ADR and the role it can play hold during a period of great change inside and outside organizations?

This chapter tackles this question by reviewing some of the dominant changes that are likely to affect how conflict is managed within firms and assessing their implications for the use of ADR and CMS. We begin with a discussion of the changing nature of work. After that, we assess the extent to which the very contours of conflict are changing in today's workplace. We then explore the implications of these changes for the management of conflict within organizations and propose ways in which ADR practices may need adapt to new organizational realities. A simple argument runs through this chapter: We find ourselves at a pivotal crossroads that requires a reassessment of the role that ADR can and should play within organizations. Put differently, we seek to assess the extent to which ADR is up for the challenge it faces.

THE CHANGING NATURE OF WORK: ACCELERATED TRANSFORMATION ACROSS MULTIPLE DIMENSIONS

The scale, scope, and speed of changes taking place in the way work is organized, structured, and conducted in the United States and around the globe have surprised even experienced students of organizations. As a growing number of scholars study the *future of work*, one thing seems clear, the future is, in many respects, already here. Almost every core premise related to how and where work is done is being upended with dramatic consequences for organizational strategy, leadership, and, of course, relational dynamics, such as conflict.

To be clear, the past few decades have seen various manifestations of dramatic organizational change. The push to adopt self-managed teams in the 1980s and 1990s and the rethinking of work practices so as to increase the use of problem-solving groups and worker discretion are just a sample of the types of changes that dominated the academic and practitioner literature. These changes were characterized by a tendency toward flatter organizational structures and greater input and autonomy for workers.

And, while these changes were a dramatic departure from the traditional hierarchical and bureaucratic organizational models that dominated the 20th century, such new organizational arrangements still adhered to most of the conventional features of organizations and the work that was performed within their boundaries. Structures were flattened and hierarchy was reduced, but work was still performed mostly by employees in physical plants reporting through conventional structures.

Changes to the structure within organizations have been complemented by a number of additional factors that have dramatically altered key features of how organizations operate, including new technologies that make remote work and virtual teams commonplace and that sever the relationship between employers and employees altogether. A better understanding of what these broader changes mean for the adoption and implementation of ADR is the central focus of this chapter.

As will be highlighted below, the current wave of change has done much to challenge conventional notions of organizations. In what follows, we focus on four features of the transformation pervading a significant proportion of organizations in the United States.

Expanded Use of New Organizational Forms and Nontraditional Employment Models

As noted above, the push to revisit and redesign traditional organizational models is not new. Beginning in the 1980s, organizations facing increased international competition, among other factors, began rethinking bureaucratic structures that provided a great deal of stability and predictability at the expense of agility and flexibility (Adler, Goldoftas, and Levine 1999). Organizations seeking to respond to an accelerated pace of change began experimenting with structures that relaxed vertical and hierarchical control in favor of increased use of teams and problem-solving groups that had enhanced autonomy to make decisions without an elaborate and burdensome chain of command (Pfeffer and Baron 1988).

Much has been written about this shift and its implications for human resource management and for the rise of ADR (Appelbaum and Batt 1994; Batt, Colvin, and Keefe 2002; Colvin 2006; Colvin and Darbishire 2013). A substantial body of literature has documented significant organizational and employee benefits associated with adoption of what have been referred to as high-performance work systems (Appelbaum, Bailey, Berg, and Kalleberg 2000; Appelbaum and Batt 1994; Gittell, Seidner, and Wimbush 2010). ADR scholars have also maintained that the shift in structure has led to new conflict resolution needs, given the move away from hierarchy. Greater levels of autonomy and discretion across groups and teams increase the potential for horizontal conflict—that is, conflict between peers rather than with supervisors. ADR, according to some, offered an appropriate tool to deal with this type of conflict.

The argument we advance in this chapter is that the search for nontraditional organizational structures has accelerated and expanded over the past decade (for a discussion of the changes to organizational structures and conflict, see Riordan and Kowalski 2021). Supported by additional shifts described later in this chapter, organizations are not only enhancing flexibility through the use of flatter structures and a reliance on teams and other practices, but they are also complementing these long-standing trends with greater use of contingent work arrangements that externalize work and move away from an employment relationship (Katz and Krueger 2019). While the search for flexibility through internal structural changes appears to be consistent with the adoption of ADR and CMS, to what extent is the search for flexibility through outsourcing and contingent work consistent with this pattern? Do ADR practices address conflicts and disputes that emerge outside of traditional employment relationships? What does it mean to have dispute resolution practices designed to address conflict within the organization when a growing proportion of work is done outside the boundaries of the firm? ADR scholars must contend with these questions and the ability of dispute resolution practices to deliver on their promise in the context of greater proportions of work happening outside the boundaries of the organization and through independent contractors rather than employees.

The Rise of the Platform Economy

One of the most well-documented examples of the shift away from the traditional employment relationship is evident in the explosion of the platform economy (Cunningham-Parmeter 2016). A now-ubiquitous model, the platform economy relies on workers to perform core tasks, for the most part, as independent contractors and not as employees entitled to the legal protections associated with the employment relationship. Service-providing organizations, such as ride-sharing companies like Uber and Lyft, use technology to serve as a matchmaker between customers and workers (Maffie 2022). The range of services that make use of this app-based model has grown significantly and represents a sizable segment of certain industries, such as transportation, food delivery, and more. Proponents of this model argue that it provides workers with a great deal of flexibility and enables them to have more control over when and how to perform their work. Opponents argue that these models stripped workers of basic employment protections and created new and more sophisticated methods of control from a distance—with the appearance of flexibility (Maffie 2022).

What is clear is that platform economy models of work fundamentally shift the nature of the employment relationship (Riordan and Kowalski 2021). While contingent arrangements that rely on independent contractors rather than on employees is, of course, not new, models that mediate this relationship through technology with minimal to no actual contact between the firm and those performing core work are novel and fundamentally alter the relational dynamics between organizations and workers (Weil 2014).

Recent research focused on employment relations and conflict resolution in the platform economy has pointed to the dramatic consequences that app-based arrangements have in terms of the manifestation of conflict (Maffie 2023; Riordan and Kowalski 2021). Maffie, for example, pointed to the emergence of a much more dominant role of the customer as a stakeholder controlling and guiding the execution of work (for a similar discussion regarding the role of customers, see Riordan and Kowalski 2021). In this dominant customer role, the nature of the conflict engagement itself has also changed. Given that the exchange is primarily app driven, conflict is channeled through commenting and rating, lacking the traditional two-way exchange common in other workplace disputes (Maffie 2023). This role also means that conflict between app-based workers and customers is likely to be both more prevalent and more consequential under such arrangements. If internal restructuring of work over the past few decades has shifted the way in which conflict plays out within the organization, the rise of app-mediated work has shifted conflict around work outside of the organization altogether. Given that conflict is being shifted outside of the organization, it is also much more ad hoc in contrast to traditional long-standing employment relationships.

ADR and CMS are, by design, intended to offer organizations with more nuanced and sophisticated tools to deal with conflicts and disputes inside the firm. What are the consequences of the increase in gig economy work for the continued growth and effectiveness of ADR? Can the same practices and process that have shown promise for conflict within organizations serve these customer–worker conflicts? Furthermore, how do ADR practices address conflict between app-based workers and the companies they work for? Given the tremendous efforts app-based companies engage in to distance themselves from any responsibility for workers delivering their services, is it reasonable to expect that they will leverage ADR practices to resolve or manage conflicts that emerge with workers? If not, what does this employment pattern mean for the utility of ADR and CMS for a growing service sector domain?

New Technology and the Nature of the Employment Relationship

New technologies have influenced the nature of work well beyond the expansion of app-based delivery of services and the externalizing of the employment relationship. New information technologies and artificial intelligence capabilities have dramatically altered the manner in which work is performed and how employees interact and communicate within organizations. Knowledge sharing, transfer, and exchange, all core features of the modern organization, have been transformed through sophisticated technologies that ease teamwork, allow for robust real-time communication, and revolutionize the speed and access to insights from big data (Kellogg, Valentine, and Christin 2020). As we write this chapter, the consequences of technologies such as ChatGPT raise fascinating questions about core organizational tasks, such as writing and data analysis, that have been taken for granted throughout multiple technological advances.

As with app-based work, there are different lenses through which these changes can be assessed. For some, these technologies hold the promise of upskilling workers and enhancing the types of roles they play within an organization. Furthermore, new technologies allow, according to proponents, the facilitation of better decision making that benefits from data analysis (Molloy and Schwenk 1995). Other scholars offer a more cautious assessment regarding the role of these technologies and raise questions about the likelihood of increased control and surveillance of workers. Concerns about the role of new technology also include the potential for deskilling of workers whose decision-making and analytical contributions can more easily be replaced by these tools (De Stefano 2019).

Across many industries, new technologies are reshaping boundaries between occupations and roles and, in some cases, creating new ones. Take, for example, the healthcare industry where health information technology has fundamentally changed the manner in which patient care is delivered and the roles that physicians, nurses, and other providers play (Avgar et al. 2018). Immediate access to patient data and the ability to engage in robust communications between the care team have had profound implications for the way in which providers engage with one another and interact. Beyond information technologies, advances in robotics are also reshaping the skills and capabilities needed to perform core procedures and tasks associated with healthcare work. Other industries, such as finance, transportation, and hospitality, have all seen dramatic changes in the manner in which work gets done and in the very interactions and communication between workers (Aloisi and De Stefano 2022).

Changing the way in which organizational members interact, altering the skills and capabilities needed to perform core tasks, and affecting decision-making processes all have clear and consequential implications for the way in which conflict emerges within organizations. Redrawing the boundaries between different occupational groups, including the division of work, is also likely to contribute to the ways in which conflict plays out. The use of new communication technologies may also create fault lines across new forms of different generational groups on the basis of ease of use. Returning to our core inquiry, to what extent can ADR practices and CMS alleviate the conflict that corresponds to new technologies? Are conflict resolution tools that were developed five decades ago capable of mitigating conflicts that emerge out of 21st-century technologies and the changes they have created within organizations?

The Rise of Remote Work

One of the most recent ramifications of advances in communication technology, coupled with a push supported during the COVID-19 pandemic, is the sharp increase in telecommuting as a common work arrangement. Prior to the COVID-19 pandemic, organizations reported growing reliance on remote work arrangements (Bailey and Kurland 2002). The concepts that workers need to co-locate in order for work to be performed effectively and for organizations to manage employee performance were dispelled. During the COVID-19 pandemic, this trend became, for a considerable period, the norm. Organizations and their workers across different industries and sectors provided strong evidence for the ability of work to be dispersed in ways that surprised even scholars and proponents of remote work. The notion that effective work can take place only in the office and with in-person supervision was challenged in meaningful ways. This challenge to the default role of conventional in-person work persisted even after the COVID-19 restrictions were lifted. A sizable proportion of workers in the United States has not returned to their full-time in-person roles, with some experts suggesting that a quarter of US professional jobs have become remote as of 2022 (Robinson 2022).

It is difficult to overstate the extent to which the increase of remote work will alter key organizational dimensions, including where and how work is performed. Furthermore, remote work, like the other changes described above, significantly modifies conventional modes of communication and interaction. Discussions that were commonly conducted in person within the boundaries of organizations are now conducted remotely or using hybrid modalities.

Time will tell whether the dramatic rise in remote work that followed the COVID-19 pandemic will hold over time. It is difficult, however, to imagine that a return to pre-COVID rates of in-person work is likely. This large-scale and rapid change to a fundamental work-related norm will fuel volumes of research about a host of assumptions relating to what organizations need in order to operate effectively. Does remote work undermine levels of workplace trust? What is the role of supervision and management in a remote work reality? What is clear at this point is that remote work has the potential to change both the manifestation of conflict and the way it is resolved. As with each of the core shifts described above, the increased use of and reliance on remote work raise significant questions regarding the adequacy and capabilities of ADR and CMS to deliver on its promise.

Taken together, fundamental dimensions of how work is performed within and outside organizations have changed dramatically in a very brief period. Many of the implications of these changes have been examined carefully in scholarly and practitioner outlets. The implications that the transformation of work has for the resolution of conflict has, however, not been fully explored. Each of the trends discussed above has the potential to undermine core aspects of the role that ADR and CMS play in organizations. The study of ADR must, therefore, take into account each of these trends with an eye toward new theory and emerging practice.

THE CHANGING NATURE OF CONFLICT IN US ORGANIZATIONS: TOWARD COLLECTIVE VALUE-BASED DISPUTES

Nonunion organizations in the United States are not merely facing profound changes in how work is conducted, they are also contending with an unprecedented shift in the manner in which workplace conflict is expressed. Conflict in nonunion organizations has, for many years, been characterized by the expression of, primarily, individual disputes and grievances tied to work-related matters, whether managerial or legal. For decades, a firm distinction between conflict in union and nonunion settings held, with collective and individual disputes arising in the former and solely individual disputes in the latter (Avgar 2021). Nonunion ADR practices were set up, therefore, as a vehicle to address vertical and horizontal conflict between individual employees and their employers dealing with conflict stemming from managerial concerns or legal rights because there was no collective representation built into the system.

Over the past few years, nonunion organizations have been contending with a precipitous reconfiguration of the types of conflict that are increasingly emerging and the consequences they have for a host of outcomes. Consistent with this chapter's theme is the core question of whether traditional ADR practices and CMS that are structured to deal with a much narrower configuration of conflicts are adequately equipped to address this profound change. How does each of these new conflict dimensions affect the ADR and CMS in nonunion firms? What are the key features of this shift, and what questions do they raise regarding the adequacy of ADR and CMS?

First, the clear divide between union and nonunion settings has blurred considerably, with a dramatic increase in collective disputes surfacing in nonunion organizations or among nonunion employees in unionized settings. Examples of nonunion workers banding together to change or influence workplace policies, norms, or broader corporate behavior are abundant and cut across different states, industries, and settings. Not a day goes by without a headline highlighting a collective dispute outside of the traditional collective bargaining context. From the Google walkout over the company's use of mandatory arbitration in 2019 to the recent protests at Disney over the company's stand on LGBTQ-related legislation in Florida, workers in nonunion firms are leveraging collective action as a legitimate and effective tool to address a range of both internal and external concerns.

This increase in collective action of nonunion workers comes, of course, at a time when unionized collective action is also on the rise, be it in the form of increased organizing efforts or greater use of strike activity. What is fascinating is that there appears to be a spillover between the uptick in unionized collective action and the shift from individual to collective conflicts in nonunion workplaces. It is difficult to overstate how consequential this shift is and the range of implications it will have for how organizations address conflict and how scholars understand the distinctions between unionized and nonunion workplaces in the United States.

Is nonunion ADR equipped to deal with this aspect of the changing nature of conflict? On the one hand, ADR practices are clearly capable of facilitating the resolution of collective disputes. Decades of experience in the unionized setting have demonstrated the effectiveness of grievance systems as a tool to address both individual and collective conflict. On the other hand, ADR and CMS in nonunion firms have been, by design, set up to force conflicts and disputes into an individual framing. In contrast to the union context, individual employees making use of nonunion dispute resolution tools do not have the backing of a collective group or entity. Furthermore, conflicts are often dealt with on the basis of their statutory legal implications, which are, at their core, individual in nature. Thus, while specific ADR techniques are theoretically capable of dealing with the increase in collective disputes in nonunion organizations, the systems upon which these techniques have been implemented are very carefully and deliberately structured around individual conflicts. Any general assessment of whether ADR is suited for the challenges that organizations face will need to account for this tension.

Second, another long-standing feature of the expression of conflict inside US organizations is that it has tended to exclude external political divisions and fissures. The manifestation of these divisions has, in many organizations, been seen as inappropriate and unacceptable. Conflict in nonunion settings has, however, moved away from purely work-related or relational matters and now includes myriad broader political and societal issues and debates. Political differences, long seen as something to be kept outside the boundaries of the workplace, are now commonplace as one of many fissures surfacing within organizations. Leaving politics at the door is an apt description of the approach many organizations have taken to the potential for societal issues to create internal differences. Here too, as with the increased prevalence of collective conflicts, this seemingly impenetrable boundary has seen a considerable weakening, if not a full collapse. The increased polarization that has characterized American politics over the past decade, including the prevalence of disagreements and differing values centering on identities such as race and gender, is now replicated in much more pronounced ways within organizations.

It is important to note that this polarization within the American workplace has affected conflict in two related but distinct ways. First, anecdotal evidence suggests that a growing proportion of internal workplace conflicts stems from disagreements around political matters. Thus, for example, individual support for one political candidate or another, once seen as a private, nonwork-related matter, is increasingly the cause of internal organizational conflict (Johnson and Roberto 2018). Second and related to the above discussion regarding the rise in collective disputes, a growing proportion of organizations is facing worker expectations to take a stand on a variety of different political or value-based issues, from voting rights to Supreme Court rulings. Put differently, many organizations now experience conflicts that are infused with value-based differences rather than merely interest-based differences (for a similar argument, see Riordan and Kowalski 2021). Political dynamics outside the firm are entering the workplace in overt ways that had previously not been experienced, alongside the push for organizations to be active in external policy debates and disagreements. This is exacerbated by what Riordan and Kowalski (2021) call multiplicity, which refers to the increased number of workplace actors inside and outside the workplace who hold different goals and objectives.

To be clear, individual and collective conflicts in organizations have always been shaped by elements of identity and values. In the past, however, these were framed as primarily stemming from work-related differences, tensions, or disputes and channeled through traditional labor–management or individual rights-based mechanisms (for a similar discussion, see Riordan and Kowalski 2021). One of the distinguishing characteristics of many of the emerging collective-values and identity-based conflicts facing organizations is that they go well beyond traditional workplace issues and are related more directly to external societal developments. Workers are expecting their organizations to be proactive in addressing values-based disputes even if they do not affect the specific workplace directly.

Here, too, it is unclear to what extent ADR and CMS are capable of serving as vehicles to address and resolve these conflicts. As with collective disputes, ADR practices have traditionally been set up to address both interest and rights disputes stemming directly from and related to work and/or the employment relationship. Leveraging these systems and practices to deal with conflict over individual political differences or collective expectations about how an organization should respond to societal debates will, at the very least, require a reconfiguration and reimagining of the role of workplace dispute resolution in both union and nonunion firms.

Finally, each of these shifts in the nature of workplace conflict is happening at a time when a growing proportion of firms is engaged in important and necessary efforts to increase diversity, equity, and inclusion (DEI). As such, firms are seeing a rise of collective and value-based conflicts alongside the inclusion of workers with different backgrounds and perspectives. Successful implementation of DEI-related initiatives means that firms will expand their inclusion of workers from different racial, ethnic, religious, and gender identity backgrounds, among others. Research has documented the many benefits associated with increased diversity in the workplace (Nishii 2013; Richard 2000; Wright, Ferris, Hiller, and Kroll 1995). These benefits are delivered, in part, because of the infusion of diverse perspectives, approaches, and ways of thinking. DEI initiatives are founded on the basic notion that individuals are entitled, as a function of human dignity, to bring their complete self to work. In doing so, workers also bring the issues, values, and personal positions and priorities that animate them outside of work into the workplace context. The very notion of what is considered purely workplace related is, therefore, shifting.

One way to think about the power of diversity within organizations is that it creates the potential for healthy debates at both the strategic and tactical levels. What this means is that in pursuing DEI initiatives that hold the promise of addressing long-standing injustices and improving organizational outcomes, firms need to be aware of the inherent role that conflict will likely play. Thus, DEI efforts within organizations are likely to be supported through conflict management practices that provide the space and the tools to foster healthy disagreements that stem from the rich perspectives being integrated within the organization, as well as through systemic and organizational changes needed to support this integration. Can ADR serve in this DEI-supporting role? As with other dimensions of the changing nature of conflict, the specific ADR practices might be capable of doing so, but it will require a new approach to the use of these tools in the nonunion setting.

IMPLICATIONS FOR ADR AND CMS IN NONUNION ORGANIZATIONS AND A FUTURE RESEARCH AGENDA

What is clear from the review above is that US organizations with nonunion employees are experiencing significant changes in terms of the nature of work and conflict within their boundaries. What is also clear is that these changes have implications for the current deployment of dispute resolution systems and practices. Although ADR and

CMS are promoted as tools that are capable of addressing interest and rights disputes focused on work- and employment-related matters, a number of fundamental questions exist about whether and how ADR and CMS can serve as a means of managing conflict in this new organizational reality. Can they deliver benefits to both employers and employees as suggested in the various waves of nonunion dispute resolution research? Do core assumptions about ADR and CMS still hold? Answers to these questions require a novel examination of nonunion dispute resolution with a careful assessment of the new workplace structures and relational dynamics and the new ways in which conflict is manifested.

The dimensions of the shifts described above highlight the need for a renewed examination of the strategic underpinnings guiding the use of dispute resolution practices in nonunion settings. Much is still unknown about the relationship between changes to work and conflict and a host of ADR- and CMS-related patterns and trends. Are firms with ADR better positioned to deal with emerging forms of conflict? Are ADR practices capable of addressing collective disputes and those that involve political and value-based issues? These and many other research questions should serve as the basis for a new direction in ADR and CMS scholarship—one that builds on previous streams of research and takes into account the accelerated pace of change within organizations.

In doing so, ADR scholarship should assess the implications of these changes for a number of core and, in many cases, long-standing questions. For example, what are the implications for the due process protections offered to employees who make use of ADR? To what extent can ADR accommodate collective disputes? How does the current reality inform existing debates regarding the use of mandatory procedures and arbitration in particular? We conclude our chapter with a brief analysis of some of these questions as a way of setting the stage for a new stream of ADR and CMS research.

First, one of the most contentious debates around ADR relates to the due process protections provided to employees who make use of such practices to resolve conflict. This debate has intensified around the use of mandatory techniques, with a particular focus on mandatory arbitration. Scholars concerned about due process protections in the use of ADR worry about the imbalance of power between employers and employees. ADR, and especially mandatory arbitration, can be used as a means of buffering the organization from the external court system without offering an adequate alternative in terms of possible remedies and procedural protections. If ADR is to rise to the needs created by the changes reviewed above, it will need to expand its coverage to include a host of contingent workers and alternative organizational arrangements. Some of these arrangements exacerbate the imbalance of power between organizations and those conducting work, either as employees or independent contractors. The need for expanded and broader coverage of ADR and the pronounced imbalance of power highlights the need to re-examine the protections provided to users of ADR in the employment context. Expansion of ADR should be done in a manner that provides real alternatives to the resolution of work-related conflict rather than restricting established options such as the courts. As such, we maintain that the potential of ADR to meet the conflict needs of new organizational arrangements and structures will increase if greater attention is given to the fairness of such practices and if they are used in a voluntary and not mandatory manner.

Second and as noted above, scholars in the 1990s and 2000s began examining the use of different dispute resolution practices as a system or bundle. Researchers documented the increased use of integrated CMS in large US firms. Many organizations, according to that research, were moving away from the use of individual practices and offering multiple options with different access points within the organization for a broad range of conflict categories (Lipsky, Seeber, and Fincher 2003). As discussed, these systems primarily focus on the management and resolution of work-related conflicts. The review of the changing nature of conflict raises the question whether the current configurations of practices is capable of adequately addressing a much broader array of conflicts across a broader array of organizational arrangements. We maintain that if ADR is to be leveraged in this way, scholars and practitioners will need to rethink each of the characteristics of a CMS. Are the multiple options available to employees sufficient? Are the different access points varied enough and situated across the different organizational structures and work arrangements? And are the categories of conflicts included within the system broad enough? Our own assessment is that, across each of these dimensions, most organizations have adopted systems that are too narrow in scope and too limited in options and access points to meet the aforementioned challenges. What is needed is a new period of experimentation with different conflict management configurations that expand on the concepts of a system introduced 30 years ago.

Finally, at the heart of the current approach to ADR and CMS is the individual nature of conflict and how it is resolved. Here, too, if nonunion dispute resolution options are to meet the needs of organizations, this core assumption about conflict and how it is resolved will need to change. Conflict management practices will need to accommodate the increase in collective conflicts outside of the collective bargaining arena, both procedurally and substantively. Procedurally, organizations will need to explore ways to make use of standard techniques such as mediation and arbitration to address conflict that involves groups of workers. Questions regarding representation will become especially crucial. In the absence of a union, who speaks on behalf of a group of workers with a collective dispute or conflict? Substantively, organizations will need to accommodate a broader range of collective concerns that go beyond the historically accepted interest- and rights-based working conditions and internal organizational matters.

Taken together, we believe that the practice and study of workplace conflict management in the United States are on the precipice of significant change. As ADR researchers, we are excited by the prospect of a new generation of dispute resolution scholarship that builds on the impressive literature amassed over the past 50 years. This new research agenda should include a number of core areas of inquiry. First, there is a need for much more empirical evidence regarding the rise of collective values-based conflicts in nonunion settings. If ADR practices are to address these new forms of conflict, researchers will need to document these conflicts, their antecedents, and associated outcomes. Second, additional research is also needed about the spillover of extreme political polarization into the workplace, particularly when its connection to identity and values relates to broader conflicts beyond individual disputes. Here, too, empirical evidence related to the factors that are driving this trend and the ways in which such conflicts are resolved will serve as a foundation for the study of ADR in a polarized workplace. Finally, ushering in a new generation of ADR research and practice will require new scholarship on the use of ADR in new organizational and employment arrangements, such as app-based work.

These are turbulent times for organizations and their workers. ADR, since its rise in the 1970s, has been seen as holding the potential to serve as a mutually beneficial and stabilizing force within organizations. ADR research should now be focused on a comprehensive assessment of the extent to which nonunion dispute resolution can, in fact, deliver on this promise in the workplace of today and the future.

REFERENCES

Adler, Paul S., Barbara Goldoftas, and David I. Levine. 1999. "Flexibility Versus Efficiency? A Case Study of Model Changeovers in the Toyota Production System." *Organization Science* 10 (1): 43–68. doi: 10.1287/orsc.10.1.43

Aloisi, Antonio, and Valerio De Stefano. 2022. *Your Boss Is an Algorithm: Artificial Intelligence, Platform Work and Labour*. Gordonsville, VA: Hart Publishing.

Appelbaum, Eileen, Thomas Bailey, Peter Berg, and Arne L. Kalleberg. 2000. *Manufacturing Advantage: Why High-Performance Work Systems Pay Off*. Ithaca: Cornell University Press.

Appelbaum, Eileen, and Rosemary L. Batt. 1994. *The New American Workplace: Transforming Work Systems in the United States*. Ithaca: Cornell University Press.

Avgar, Ariel C. 2016. "Treating Conflict: The Adoption of a Conflict Management System in a Hospital Setting." In *Managing and Resolving Workplace Conflict. Advances in Industrial & Labor Relations* 22: 211–246. Somerville, MA: Emerald Group.

Avgar, Ariel. 2020. "Integrating Conflict: A Proposed Framework for the Interdisciplinary Study of Workplace Conflict and Its Management." *ILR Review* 73 (2): 281–311. doi: 10.1177/0019793919885819

Avgar, Ariel C. 2021. "Relational Exchange in Non-Union Firms: A Configurational Framework for Workplace Dispute Resolution and Voice." *ILR Review* 74 (3): 607–636. doi: 10.1177/0019793921989615

Avgar, Ariel C., J. Ryan Lamare, David B. Lipsky, and Abhishek Gupta. 2013. "Unions and ADR: The Relationship Between Labor Unions and Workplace Dispute Resolution in U.S. Corporations." *Ohio State Journal on Dispute Resolution* 28 (1): 63–106.

Avgar, Ariel, Prasanna Tambe, and Lorin M. Hitt. 2018. "Built to Learn: How Work Practices Affect Employee Learning During Healthcare Information Technology Implementation." *MIS Quarterly* 42 (2): 645–660.

Bailey, Diane E., and Nancy B. Kurland. 2002. "A Review of Telework Research: Findings, New Directions, and Lessons for the Study of Modern Work." *Journal of Organizational Behavior*:

The International Journal of Industrial, Occupational and Organizational Psychology and Behavior 23 (4): 383–400.
Batt, Rosemary, Alexander J.S. Colvin, and Jeffrey Keefe. 2002. "Employee Voice, Human Resource Practices, and Quit Rates: Evidence from the Telecommunications Industry." *ILR Review* 55 (4): 573–594. doi: 10.1177/001979390205500401
Bendersky, Corinne. 2007. "Complementarities in Organizational Dispute Resolution Systems: How System Characteristics Affect Individuals' Conflict Experiences." *ILR Review* 60 (2): 204–224. doi: 10.1177/001979390706000203
Colvin, Alexander J.S. 2003. "Institutional Pressures, Human Resource Strategies, and the Rise of Nonunion Dispute Resolution Procedures." *ILR Review* 56 (3): 375–392. doi: 10.1177/001979390305600301
Colvin, Alexander J.S. 2006. "Flexibility and Fairness in Liberal Market Economies: The Comparative Impact of the Legal Environment and High-Performance Work Systems." *British Journal of Industrial Relations* 44 (1): 73–97.
Colvin, Alexander J.S. 2016. "Conflict and Employment Relations in the Individual Rights Era." In *Managing and Resolving Workplace Conflict. Advances in Industrial & Labor Relations* 22: 1–30. Somerville, MA: Emerald Group.
Colvin, Alexander J.S. 2017 (September 27). "The Growing Use of Mandatory Arbitration." Report. Economic Policy Institute. https://files.epi.org/pdf/135056.pdf
Colvin, Alexander J. S. 2019. "The Metastasization of Mandatory Arbitration." *Chicago-Kent Law Review* 94 (1): 3–24.
Colvin, Alexander J.S., and Ariel C. Avgar. 2018. "Knowns and Unknowns in the Study of Workplace Dispute Resolution: Towards an Expanded Research Agenda." In *The Routledge Companion to Employment Relations*, edited by Adrian Wilkinson, Tony Dundon, and Alexander Colvin, Chapter 17.
Colvin, Alexander J.S., and Owen Darbishire. 2013. "Convergence in Industrial Relations Institutions: The Emerging Anglo-American Model?" *ILR Review* 66 (5): 1047–1077.
Colvin, Alexander J.S., Brian Klaas, and Douglas Mahony. 2006. "Research on Alternative Dispute Resolution Procedures." DigitalCollections@ILR. https://ecommons.cornell.edu/handle/1813/76027
Conbere, John P. 2001. "Theory Building for Conflict Management System Design." *Conflict Resolution Quarterly* 19 (2): 215–236. doi: 10.1002/crq.3890190206
Cunningham-Parmeter, Keith. 2016. "From Amazon to Uber: Defining Employment in the Modern Economy." *Boston University Law Review* 96: 1673–1728.
Currie, Denise, and Paul Teague. 2016. "Economic Citizenship and Workplace Conflict in Anglo-American Industrial Relations Systems." *British Journal of Industrial Relations* 54 (2): 358–384. doi: 10.1111/bjir.12150
De Stefano, Valerio. 2019. "Automation, Artificial Intelligence, and Labor Protection." *Comparative Labor Law & Policy Journal* 41 (1): 3–35.
Edelman, Lauren B. 1990. "Legal Environments and Organizational Governance: The Expansion of Due Process in the American Workplace." *American Journal of Sociology* 95 (6): 1401–1440.
Estreicher, Samuel. 2000. "Saturns for Rickshaws: The Stakes in the Debate over Predispute Employment Arbitration Agreements." *Ohio State Journal on Dispute Resolution* 16: 559–565.
Ewing, David W. 1989. *Justice on the Job: Resolving Grievances in the Nonunion Workplace*. Boston: Harvard Business School Press.

Friedman, Raymond A., Simon T. Tidd, Steven C. Currall, and James C. Tsai. 2000. "What Goes Around Comes Around: The Impact of Personal Conflict Style on Work Conflict and Stress." *International Journal of Conflict Management* 11 (1): 32–55. doi: 10.1108/eb022834

Gittell, Jody Hoffer, Rob Seidner, and Julian Wimbush. 2010. "A Relational Model of How High-Performance Work Systems Work." *Organization Science* 21 (2): 490–506.

Johnson, Andrew F., and Katherine J. Roberto. 2018. "Right Versus Left: How Does Political Ideology Affect the Workplace?" *Journal of Organizational Behavior* 39 (8): 1040–1043.

Katz, Lawrence F., and Alan B. Krueger. 2019. "The Rise and Nature of Alternative Work Arrangements in the United States, 1995–2015." *ILR Review* 72 (2): 382–416.

Kellogg, Katherine C., Melissa A. Valentine, and Angele Christin. 2020. "Algorithms at Work: The New Contested Terrain of Control." *Academy of Management Annals* 14 (1): 366–410.

Lewin, David. 2001. "IR and HR Perspectives on Workplace Conflict: What Can Each Learn from the Other?" *Human Resource Management Review* 11 (4): 453–485. doi: 10.1016/S1053-4822(01)00049-3

Lipsky, David B., Ariel C. Avgar, and J. Ryan Lamare. 2016. "The Evolution of Conflict Management Policies in US Corporations: From Reactive to Strategic." In *Reframing Resolution: Innovation and Change in the Management of Workplace Conflict*, edited by Richard Saundry, Paul Latreille, and Ian Ashman, 291–313. London: Palgrave Macmillan UK. doi: 10.1057/978-1-137-51560-5_14

Lipsky, David B., and Ariel C. Avgar. 2008. "Toward a Strategic Theory of Workplace Conflict Management." *Ohio State Journal on Dispute Resolution* 24 (1): 143–190.

Lipsky, David B., Ronald Leroy Seeber, and Richard D. Fincher. 2003. *Emerging Systems for Managing Workplace Conflict: Lessons from American Corporations for Managers and Dispute Resolution Professionals*. San Francisco: Jossey-Bass.

Lipsky, David B., Ariel C. Avgar, and J. Ryan Lamare. 2020. "Organizational Conflict Resolution and Strategic Choice: Evidence from a Survey of Fortune 1000 Firms." *ILR Review* 73 (2): 431–455. doi: 10.1177/0019793919870169

Lynch, Jennifer F. 2001. "Beyond ADR: A Systems Approach to Conflict Management." *Negotiation Journal* 17 (3): 206–216. doi: 10.1111/j.1571-9979.2001.tb00237.x

Maffie, Michael David. 2022. "The Perils of Laundering Control Through Customers: A Study of Control and Resistance in the Ride-Hail Industry." *ILR Review* 75 (2): 348–372.

Maffie, Michael David. 2023. "Becoming a Pirate: Independence as an Alternative to Exit in the Gig Economy." *British Journal of Industrial Relations* 61 (1): 46–67.

Molloy, Steve, and Charles R. Schwenk. 1995. "The Effects of Information Technology on Strategic Decision Making." *Journal of Management Studies* 32 (3): 283–311.

Nishii, Lisa H. 2013. "The Benefits of Climate for Inclusion for Gender-Diverse Groups." *Academy of Management Journal* 56 (6): 1754–1774.

Pfeffer, Jeffrey, and James N. Baron. 1988. "Taking the Workers Back Out: Recent Trends in the Structuring of Employment." *Research in Organizational Behavior* 10 (1988): 257–303.

Richard, Orlando C. 2000. "Racial Diversity, Business Strategy, and Firm Performance: A Resource-Based View." *Academy of Management Journal* 43 (2): 164–177.

Riordan, Christine A., and Alexander M. Kowalski. 2021. "From Bread and Roses to #MeToo: Multiplicity, Distance, and the Changing Dynamics of Conflict in IR Theory." *ILR Review* 74 (3): 580–606.

Robinson, Bryan. 2022. "Remote Work Is Here to Stay and Will Increase into 2023, Experts Say." *Forbes*. https://tinyurl.com/2hw8maxk

Roche, William, and Paul Teague. 2012. "Do Conflict Management Systems Matter?" *Human Resource Management* 51 (2): 231–258.

Roche, William K., Paul Teague, and Alexander J.S. Colvin. 2014. *The Oxford Handbook of Conflict Management in Organizations*. Oxford: Oxford University Press.

Weil, David. 2014. *The Fissured Workplace*. Cambridge: Harvard University Press.

Wright, Peter, Stephen P. Ferris, Janine S. Hiller, and Mark Kroll. 1995. "Competitiveness Through Management of Diversity: Effects on Stock Price Valuation." *Academy of Management Journal* 38 (1): 272–287.

CHAPTER 3

Do Firms Practice Conflict Management Strategically? Survey Evidence from Britain

Deborah Hann
David Nash
Cardiff University

ABSTRACT

There has been growing interest in how organizations' approaches to conflict management is related to their broader strategy. While a large body of literature has chronicled the spread of alternative dispute resolution, relatively little attention has been paid to how these practices relate to wider organizational objectives as articulated through human resource (HR) policies. Drawing on nationwide survey data, we evaluate whether there is evidence of strategic conflict management in Great Britain and ask to what degree there is an internal logic in organizations' approaches. We go on to question whether the implementation of conflict management practice matches the intended strategy articulated in written policy. Our findings suggest only weak links between organizations' approaches to conflict management and their wider HR strategy, with the exception of employee voice. In terms of the implementation of conflict management strategies, we find a marked difference between the formal written policies of organizations on the one hand and their use of dispute resolution practices on the other. We posit that this is an intentional approach to help ensure management interventions are the most appropriate given the circumstances, which is at odds with existing research that suggests consistency between policy and practice is core to employee perceptions of organizational justice. We end the chapter with a call for further research into the seemingly disintegrated approach to conflict management that is evident in Great Britain.

INTRODUCTION

Recent research suggests that the cost of organizational conflict in the United Kingdom is approaching £30 billion each year, with nearly 10 million people each year experiencing conflict in the workplace (Saundry and Urwin 2021). Within UK political dialogue, there is also an ongoing debate around the heavy reliance on public institutions for dispute resolution, such as employment tribunals, which are often seen as leading to less satisfactory outcomes. It has been claimed that the increasing focus in tribunals on who is right and who is wrong rather than reconciling underlying interests results in less effective outcomes for employers and employees (Ury, Brett, and Goldberg 1993).

The argument that the tribunal system is not the ideal way to resolve disputes has spanned multiple governments of different political persuasions over a long period and focuses on the claim that it rarely leads to justice for the parties involved (Dickens 2012). Most recently, the government consultation on "Resolving Workplace Disputes" (Department of Business, Innovation and Skills 2011) pushed to try to reduce the number of conflicts arriving at tribunal by encouraging the parties in the employment relationship to address disputes as close to their source as possible.

Despite the ubiquitous nature of organizational conflict, there is limited understanding as to how decisions are made by organizations on the approach adopted to resolving them. While Kochan, McKersie, and Cappelli (1984) note the fact that strategy is part of the conversation on a range of human resources (HR) and industrial relations (IR) issues, there has been a lack of research of the role of strategy in the area of conflict management. This gap is starting to be filled with predominantly US studies looking at the nature of strategic decision making in conflict management (Lipsky 2015; Lipsky Avgar, and Lamare 2017). The emergence of integrated conflict management systems suggests that there may be an internal logic to such systems (Lipsky 2015; Lynch 2001, 2003;). However, little is understood as to the strategy that informs the implementation of approaches to conflict management, systematic or not.

The role of HR in developing an effective organizational strategy has become an accepted part of management research (see, e.g., Ulrich, Brockbank, and Johnson 2009). Given the high costs involved, it may be considered surprising, therefore, that relatively little attention has been paid to understanding how decisions are made on the approaches taken to address organizational conflict, on how they relate to other strategies within the organization, and how they are implemented. Saundry et al. (2014) note that centering conflict management at the heart of an HR strategy is the basis for a more successful outcome rather than a piecemeal adoption—and yet there is limited evidence as to whether this is happening in practice.

This chapter looks at the role of strategy in relation to conflict management and asks to what degree there is an internal logic in organizations' approaches: does the approach taken to resolving conflict match that taken with respect to HR strategy or the pursuit of organizational objectives? It goes on to question whether the implementation of conflict management practice matches the intended strategy articulated in written policy.

We argue that there are only weak links between organizations' approaches to conflict management and their wider HR strategy, with the exception of employee voice. In examining the implementation of conflict management strategies, we also find a marked difference between the stated written policies of organizations on the one hand and the use of dispute resolution practices on the other. Our findings suggest that this is an intentional approach adopted to try to ensure that interventions taken are the most appropriate given the circumstances. However, this strategy is seemingly at odds with existing research that suggests consistency between policy and practice is core to perceptions of organizational justice (Heffernan and Dundon 2016; Purcell et al. 2009).

Traditional Versus Alternative Dispute Resolution

The "traditional" approach to addressing disputes within the workplace in the United Kingdom is based around an administratively led, managerial decision-making process with increasingly senior levels of management being involved as issues progress. In this traditional approach, the end stop for disputes is likely to be courts or a tribunal system with adjudication made by an external, independent "expert." This approach to dispute resolution allows for limited, if any, input beyond management and is often design to be adversarial and limit the role for the employee (Lipsky, Avgar, and Lamare 2017). Further, this route to resolution allows limited scope for the reparation of relationships and often leaves the parties involved continuing to feel aggrieved.

More-recent US evidence (Lipsky, Avgar, and Lamare 2017; Lipsky, Seeber, and Fincher 2003) suggests that organizations are moving away from these managerially dominated hierarchical approaches to use methods that allow for greater input by other stakeholders and that can be adapted and changed to fit the circumstances of the individual dispute. This literature suggests a notable growth in the use, and in some places dominance, of these so-called alternative approaches to dispute resolution. The notion of alternative dispute resolution (ADR) constitutes a wide range of potential approaches, and the definition of exactly which practices are included is contested. ADR techniques, including mediation, may involve independent third parties, such as state-run public dispute resolution bodies or independent contractors, or they may be explicitly designed to keep the dispute internal to the organization, between the two parties but allowing greater input from employees and other stakeholders (David 1986; Hann, Nash, and Heery 2019; Lipsky, Avgar, and Lamare 2017; Roberts and Palmer 2005). Despite the lack of an accepted definition of ADR, there is consensus among commentators that it includes mediation (Hann, Nash, and Heery 2019; Mackie, Miles, and Marsh 2000).

Existing research suggests that ADR is adopted for a wide range of reasons—from union avoidance to a greater sense of organizational justice and the generation of trust and commitment (Colvin 2004; Lipsky, Avgar, Lamare, and Gupta 2014; Roche and Teague 2012; Sander 1976). As already noted, in the United Kingdom there has been a government push to increase the use of alternative approaches to resolving disputes, with a consultation titled "Resolving Workplace Disputes" (Department of Business, Innovation and Skills 2011) identifying that where conflict is resolved as quickly and closely as possible to the source, the outcomes are not only more cost effective but also more satisfactory to the parties involved. This argument is not a new one, with Dickens (2012) highlighting that UK governments have been arguing since the early 1990s that employment tribunals do not offer the best route to achieve organizational justice. Lipsky, Seeber, and Fincher (2003) noted three key scenarios where ADR may be used: (1) in an ad hoc manner, where a speedy response is required to specific disputes, (2) when it has been agreed in advance and incorporated into contracts or policies, and (3) where it is retrospectively mandated by courts.

While there is an extensive and body of research examining the use of ADR in a US context (e.g., Lipsky, Avgar, and Lamare 2017), the understanding of its diffusion and implementation further afield is more recent and thus limited (Roche and Teague 2012; Roche, Teague, and Colvin 2014; Teague, Roche, and Hann 2012). At a seminar series in the United Kingdom in 2012, Gill Dix, then head of strategy for the Advisory, Reconciliation, and Arbitration Service (Acas), the UK's public dispute resolution body, argued that there was no wide-ranging understanding of the presence and coverage of such practices within the United Kingdom (Dix 2012). Since that time, there has been some research that suggests that while ADR is not as widespread in the United Kingdom as in the United States, it may be growing in use (Hann, Nash, and Heery 2019; Latreille and Saundry 2016). One UK study indicated that organizations within Wales do indeed use ADR to varying degrees, although the level of use depends on how narrowly ADR is defined (Hann, Nash, and Heery 2019). However, while the use of ADR practices outside of the United States is increasingly being explored and noted, the organizational decisions taken and strategies adopted in whether to use these practices need further exploration (Lipsky, Avgar, and Lamare 2017).

Are Alternative Dispute Resolution and Conflict Management Strategic?

Kochan, McKersie, and Cappelli (1984) note that the concept of strategic decision making is often applied to the broader field of IR, but this approach appears to be much less consistently applied to conflict management more specifically. A relationship between strategy and conflict management was suggested in the late 1990s (Rowe 1997), although the body of literature on ADR, as noted above, does not adequately explore the relationship between the practices in place and their strategic aims. Including conflict management within the development of a holistic HR strategy is seen as a potentially important contributor to success (Saundry et al. 2014), but there is no evidence-based understanding of whether this embedding of conflict management is happening in practice.

US research suggests that there may be a relationship between strategic approaches and the nature of practices used to resolve disputes (Lipsky, Avgar, and Lamare 2017). Beyond the United States, research suggests that conflict management is not on the radar for managers beyond those who work within HR—and even then it is often seen as an administrative process rather than a strategic issue (Latreille and Saundry 2016; Saundry et al. 2014). Existing research has tended to focus on the external strategic drivers on the choice of approach to conflict management, such as pressure from growing litigation or the desire to limit the role of unions or even competition in the market (Avgar, Lamare, Lipsky, and Gupta 2013; Lipsky, Avgar, Lamare, and Gupta 2014; Lipsky, Seeber, and Fincher 2003). More-recent studies have begun to examine how internal strategic influences might impact the approach taken to conflict management. The focus so far has been on the internal changes to management structures, such as the dismantling of the hierarchies essential to traditional methods and the development of some practices that might constitute a shift toward high-road HR practices, including a focus on employee voice and communication (Avgar 2016; Lipsky, Avgar, Lamare, and Gupta 2014; Mahony and Klaas 2014). An extension of this argument is that the nature of organizations' strategic objectives may impact the approach taken to conflict management, with mediation being a driver of both efficiency and satisfaction (Lipsky, Avgar, and Lamare 2017). However, the nature of the relationship between organizational strategy and conflict management approach is still underexplored, especially beyond the United States.

In contrast, findings from the United Kingdom and Ireland suggest that conflict management is absent from managerial discourse and is not seen as a strategic issue (Latreille and Saundry 2016; Saundry et al. 2014; Teague and Doherty 2016). In the absence of strategic, proactive, and flexible approaches to dispute resolution in the United Kingdom, there appears to be a more pragmatic orientation to the management of conflict combined with a rigid adherence to process and procedure (Saundry et al. 2014). One exception to the argument that the United Kingdom doesn't take a strategic approach is Nash and Hann's (2020) study of Welsh organizations, which found a significant relationship between organizations' HR strategy and how they approach conflict. Furthermore, this relationship appears to be an intentional one rather than simply the result of coincidence, and it is used to underpin management strategy. This notion that an organization's approach to conflict management might be informed by its HR strategy is one that would be supported by other research that finds ADR is more likely where HR specialists exist (Hann, Nash, and Heery 2019; Mahony and Klaas 2014). This chapter will further explore the relationship between conflict management and HR strategy in the United Kingdom.

The Gap Between Human Resource Policy and Practice

To better understand the intersection of organizational strategy and approach to conflict management, it is important to examine the nature of HR management in more detail, not least because of the potentially important role played by HR practitioners (Saundry et al. 2014). It has long been argued that the relationships among strategy, implementation, and outcomes within HR more generally are underexplored (Mirfakhar, Trullen, and Valverde 2018); this chapter, while focusing on conflict management, will contribute to these broader debates.

Within their longitudinal research, Gratton and Truss (2003) outline three dimensions to HR strategy articulation. First, vertical or upward integration is the relationship between an HR policy and the broader organizational strategy. Second, horizontal articulation represents the internal consistency between different HR policies. Finally, the action or implementation articulation is the degree to which practice is seen as consistent with policy. There is a mass of existing research (e.g., Huselid and Becker 1997; Ulrich 1997) examining vertical alignment—that is, between general HR strategy and overall business strategy—and there is also a well-established body of literature (Becker and Huselid 1998; Becker, Huselid, and Ulrich 2001; Ichniowski et al. 1996) around high-performance work systems (HPWS) that discusses the importance of alignment horizontally between HR practices for the pursuit of organizational objectives. The action or implementation dimension reflects the day-to-day enactment of the intended policies and focuses on the practical experiences of the employees (Gratton and Truss 2003). Research into this dimension has found that while organizations focus their strategic rhetoric on soft HR management, the reality of their day-to-day practice is often more focused on employee control, which is associated with a harder model of HR management (Gill 1999; Truss et al. 1997). The role and presence of an HR specialist is crucial here in mediating and implementing policy (Dobbin 2011) and this role is particularly notable in the area of conflict management. Saundry et al. (2014) suggest that where HR practitioners are present, organizations are more likely to develop informal dispute resolution procedures that respond to the situation at hand. In other words, the responsive nature of ADR is more evident where HR professionals exist.

The lack of research examining the relationship between HR strategy and conflict management is all the more surprising given the weight of research devoted to the internal or horizontal alignment of policy across different parts of HR (e.g., Becker, Huselid, and Ulrich 2001; Huselid and Becker 1997; Ichniowski et al. 1996). Further, organizational conflict has been found to limit the success of high-road approaches to HR, such as HPWS (Godard 2004). The majority of research in the area of progressive HR approaches tends to focus on the relationships between team working, training, and employee engagement, for example, without any clear consideration of conflict (Delery and Doty 1996; Macduffie 1995). That being said, some authors have included formal dispute resolution procedures aimed at promoting high levels of employee commitment and involvement in the workplace (Colvin 2003; Huselid 1995; Ichniowski et al. 1996), although some of this research is now dated.

There is some evidence of an implicit link between HPWS and conflict management, however. It has been suggested that elements of an effective conflict management approach, and in particular innovative approaches found in ADR, would naturally lend themselves to alignment with more high-road HR approaches. Colvin (2003) cites the exit-voice theory as a clear indication that the opportunity to voice views afforded by ADR may help retain employees at a time of dispute. Thus, the inclusion of ADR as an conduit for employee voice offers opportunity for increased productivity as well a greater work involvement and job enrichment (Mahony and Klaas 2014; Tapia, Ibsen, and Kochan 2015).

Beyond voice, there is a clear argument to develop alternative approaches to handling conflict from an organizational justice perspective. While Heffernan and Dundon (2016: 226) note that organizational justice is a "much neglected theoretical lens in much HRM [human resource management] research," the limited research there is suggests that the promotion of organizational justice through the inclusion of ADR results in more positive outcomes from HPWS (Fuchs and Edwards 2012; Wu and Chaturvedi 2009). Similarly, Colvin (2003, 2006) suggests that where ADR is present, employees may see greater levels of organizational justice, and this will in turn lead to more successful outcomes for HPWS. Heffernan and Dundon (2016) temper this by noting that it may be the enactment of organizational justice, or the successful implementation of the policy in alignment with its stated intentions, that makes a difference to outcomes as much as the high-road strategies themselves. This finding reinforces earlier arguments by Purcell et al. (2009) that for a strategy to be seen as just, it also needs to be consistently applied so that the experience of employees aligns with the written strategic intentions.

Thus, the evidence around the relationship between HR strategy and use of ADR is limited, but a growing body of research does suggest that organizations looking to implement high-performance HR strategies are more likely to establish policies that address conflict (Nash and Hann 2020). This approach is consistent with a desire to address external influences that might impact organizational efficiency (Lipsky, Avgar, and Lamare 2017; Saundry et al. 2014). One further source of potential synergy between an organization's HR strategy and approach to conflict management may be its orientation to the employment relationship. Organizations adopting innovative approaches to conflict management often display a unitarist or anti-union orientation (Colvin 2003; Nash and Hann 2020), which has also been noted within the broader HPWS approach (Zhang, Di Fan, and Zhu 2014).

Building on previous work, this chapter examines the relationship between conflict management and broader organizational strategy. Following Gratton and Truss (2003), it considers the various articulations of strategy (upward, horizontal, and implementation) to evaluate whether organizational approaches to conflict in the United Kingdom are strategic, and, if so, whether this is intentional or merely reactive in nature.

METHODS

Our analysis draws from a 2018 nationwide survey in Great Britain that was undertaken in collaboration with Acas, which examined the management of disputes within private sector organizations. The questionnaire was sent to a random sample of 5,000 organizations with over 20 employees throughout Great Britain in early 2018. The sample frame was constructed using Companies House data (official data on the characteristics of UK employing organizations) and was stratified according to organization size and economic sector to create a representative frame. Information regarding the population was drawn from the Office for National Statistics Business Population Estimates for 2017. The strata were unit proportional to the sample frame in terms of industrial sector. To increase the employee-proportional representation of the sample, the size categories were represented disproportionately to their numbers in the population, with large employers oversampled and small employers undersampled.

The target respondent was the individual most likely to hold responsibility for addressing conflict within the organization, taken to be an HR specialist where one was present. Where no such person was identified, the most appropriate second option, often a company secretary, was selected from senior management. A request was included in the letter and the cover sheet that the questionnaire be passed to the most appropriate person to comment on conflict if this were not the recipient. The unit of analysis was the organization, as opposed to the workplace, and questionnaires were, therefore, sent to the registered head-office as indicated in Companies House records.

The research instrument was adapted from earlier research by Teague, Roche, and Hann (2012) that had examined conflict management in the Republic of Ireland. The validity of the instrument was strengthened by undertaking further consultation, feedback, and reflection with both the Irish research team and Acas, Britain's public dispute resolution agency. Finally, the instrument underwent in-depth cognitive testing with HR practitioners from a range of organizations prior to the fieldwork commencing.

The survey received 400 valid responses, which equates to a response rate of approximately 8%. While the response rate was slightly lower than in other studies, we are confident in the external validity of the results. The sample achieved a 95% confidence interval, which is appropriate for surveys of this kind (Hair, Anderson, Tatham, and Black 1998). Establishment weights were applied to the data set to correct for the oversampling of large firms identified above and to make the results representative of the population of British firms. The research results presented here are based on those weighted estimates.

The survey was broad in scope; therefore, the analysis in this chapter uses a subset of variables that were chosen to address the question whether organizational responses to workplace conflict are strategic. Specifically, the analysis focuses on the following research questions:

- RQ1. What do conflict management policies look like in the United Kingdom?
- RQ2. What is the prevalence of ADR within UK organizations?
- RQ3. Is there a link between conflict management and broader HR?

Variables and Analysis

The survey asked respondents to describe the nature and incidence of conflict in their organizations before going on to outline the policies and practices that they used to manage conflict. Following the practice used in earlier research (Hann, Nash, and Heery 2019), respondents were asked to outline their approach to managing three distinct forms of conflict:

- Grievances involving individual employees in conflict with the organization (individual conflict)
- Disputes involving groups of employees in conflict with the organization (collective conflict)
- Contentious issues and disputes between employees or groups of employees (intra-employee conflict).

The incidence of individual conflict was by far the most reported in the survey, and organizations' policies were consequently the most developed in this area. For these reasons, we have, therefore, chosen to concentrate on this form of dispute in the analysis that follows.

The approach of firms to individual conflict was measured by their responses to a series of questions relating to both the policy and practice of dispute resolution. Respondents were asked to identify which of 17 possible practices were included in their formal conflict management procedures. In addition, they were asked how often they had used each of these practices in the preceding three years. This was measured on a four-point scale ranging from never to often. Details of the variables can be found in Table 1 (next page).

The use of mediation was measured by creating a dummy variable that measured whether organizations had reported using any of the mediation practices specified in the survey. These were the organization's own internal mediation service, Acas mediation, or mediation offered by another (non-Acas) external party. Other dummy variables that measured the presence of various HR specialists or HR practices were also included in the analysis. Finally, we analyzed a variable that sought to determine the competitive orientation of firms. Respondents were asked to rank the relative importance their organizations attached to competition on the basis of quality, innovation, and price. Dummy variables were created and coded 1 for the firms that assigned the highest priority to each of the three orientations.

THE NATURE OF CONFLICT MANAGEMENT AND ALTERNATIVE DISPUTE RESOLUTION IN GREAT BRITAIN

To examine the relationship between conflict management and broader HR or organizational strategy, it is first necessary to outline how British organizations actually manage workplace disputes. The survey results relating to the management of individual disputes are presented in Table 1.

The data in Table 1 show that the majority of firms still rely heavily on traditional, hierarchical approaches to dispute resolution, with rights to appeal management decisions. This is the case both in policy and in practice. This is perhaps unsurprising, not just because of the length of time that this has been the standard and expected approach to conflict, but also because this method is championed within the Acas codes of practice. These codes are influential in developing and promoting good practices within the UK employment relations system. Although they are not legally binding, they can be used by employment tribunals when deciding on relevant cases to determine whether employers have followed reasonable practice (Rahim, Brown, and Graham 2011). Both of these approaches are more commonly found in large organizations and those with HR specialists.

Beyond the traditional approach, and using the typology used by Hann, Nash, and Heery (2019), the data suggest there has been some uptake of internal forms of

Table 1
Organizational Approaches to Managing Individual Conflict

	Use of conflict management practice (% of firms)	
	In formal written policy	Used in preceding three years
Traditional		
Progressively higher levels of management resolving disputes	56.3	79.0
A right to appeal decisions made by management	59.0	72.4
Internal		
Use of organization's own internal mediation service	13.8	36.1
Use of review panels composed of managers or peers	5.2	14.8
Use of formalized open-door approach	12.8	57.3
Discussions facilitated by HR	18.3	74.0
Intensive communication regarding change with a view to avoiding disharmony	9.1	62.1
Use of conflict coaching	3.4	24.5
Informal conversations with line manager(s)	22.3	90.9
Use of personal development/improvement plan	29.7	83.7
External		
Use of Acas telephone helpline	4.9	34.4
Use of Acas website	4.9	58.1
Use of Acas conciliation to help prevent an employment tribunal claim	4.9	29.8
Use of Acas mediation	3.9	14.4
Use of professional mediation by a third-party provider (excluding Acas)	6.7	18.2
Use of lawyers	3.1	55.7
Use of an external HR expert	5.7	40.8

ADR, or what Lynch (2001) might consider "front-end" ADR (the middle group in Table 1). There is some debate as to whether these practices constitute ADR—for many, they are simply robust HR, but they don't include independent voice in the dispute resolution process. Beyond these internal, more private approaches to dispute resolution, there is extremely limited take-up of dispute resolution practices, especially when looking at policy. Public forms of ADR (Hann, Nash, and Heery 2019; Nash and Hann 2020) have much lower reported use, especially when focusing on the approaches that would be more widely agreed as ADR (conciliation, mediation, etc.). What is more noticeable is that ADR of all forms, but especially public ADR, is more widely used in practice than its presence in organizations' written policies would suggest. In short, there is clear evidence of ADR, however it is defined, within British organizations, confirming earlier findings that this is no longer solely a US phenomenon. However, the survey results also suggest that mediating factors such as organization size and the presence of an HR professional are positively associated with the adoption of alternative forms of dispute resolution, which is consistent with earlier studies (Hann, Nash, and Heery 2019).

This analysis also shows that what is included in the conflict management policies of organizations often is not an adequate reflection of practice. Organizations seemingly experiment with a variety of approaches to resolving disputes that are not included in their policies but that often adhere to the more formal approaches that focus on hierarchy over involvement and voice. This rigid use of traditional policy and more flexible use of approaches may be seen as more responsive to the situation and more fitting with a softer approach to HR and appears counter to the arguments of Truss et al. (1997), who argue that rhetoric is often soft and practice is harder.

The Link Between Alternative Dispute Resolution and Human Resource Strategy

Our analysis now moves on to consider the relationship between the use of ADR and broader organizational strategy. Existing research into this relationship has focused on the United States (Lipsky, Avgar, and Lamare 2017). Using Gratton and Truss's (2003) three-dimensional model of strategy development, we consider the horizontal articulation (i.e., with other HR strategy), followed by vertical articulation (i.e., with broader organizational strategy) and then, finally, the nature of implementation. The analysis concentrates on mediation as a proxy of ADR approaches, given the consensus around its centrality to notions of ADR. Within our definition, we include mediation internal to the organization and well as that undertaken by an external third party.

Table 2 presents an analysis that examines the relationship between ADR and broader HR strategy and specifically compares the incidence of selected HPWS practices in firms that profess to use mediation with those that do not. If there is strategic alignment between ADR and HR strategy, then we would expect to see a positive association between those practices commonly found in HPWS on the one hand and use of ADR as measured by the presence of mediation in organizations' conflict management policies on the other.

Table 2
Mediation and the Use of Selected High-Performance Work System Policies

	Firms with mediation policy (%)	
	With HR policy	No HR policy
Strategic partnership		
Presence of a dedicated HR manager	21.9	16.3
Presence of a dedicated employee relations manager	42.1***	11.6***
Most-senior HR officer sits on company board	17.0	17.4
Employee motivation and commitment/security		
Formal performance management system	21.2**	11.3**
Individual performance–related pay	18.8	17.2
Group performance–related pay	21.1	17.2
Profit sharing/share ownership	17.5	17.8
Internal career progression is formal objective for most employees	20.6	16.3
Policy of no compulsory redundancies	20.8	17.6
Employee voice		
Staff forum/consultative committee	27.9***	14.2***
Regular employee surveys	23.1**	14.8**
Formally designated team working	29.7***	14.0***
System of regular team briefings that provide employees with business information	20.9**	12.3**
Selective hiring		
Job applicants formally assessed for attitudes or personality to fit with organization	22.0*	14.8*

*Significant at 0.1, **significant at 0.05, ***significant at 0.005.

The first noteworthy finding in Table 2 is that it shows that the presence of an employment relations professional is positively associated with the use of mediation in organizational policy. This helps to corroborate the argument made by Saundry et al. (2014) that HR professionals are important champions and mediators of conflict management policy.

If we look at policies that intend to create employee motivation or develop feelings of commitment, there is limited evidence that the use of such practices is more commonly found in organizations that have a policy of mediating disputes. In five of the six policies in this grouping, we find that organizations that use mediation are more likely to adopt that HR policy, although the relationship is significant only in the case of formal performance-management schemes, which are found in twice as many organizations where there is a mediation policy compared with those where there is not.

In contrast, all four of the policies that relate to employee voice (from information to deeper forms of participation) show a significant relationship to the presence of mediation policy. Or to put it another way, organizations with a mediation policy are significantly more likely to have established HR approaches that allow employees some form of voice in their organization.

Finally, looking at the relationship between mediation and selective hiring practices to ensure that the organization has the "right" people to deliver the intended aims, we can see that organizations that have a mediation policy are significantly more likely to also have formally assessed applicants to ensure that they fit with organizational aims.

Our findings suggest that firms that have adopted a policy of mediation are also firms that have likely adopted strategic over pragmatic approaches to HR and also have implemented a HPWS approach, or at least elements of it. This finding reinforces the notion that ADR naturally aligns with an HPWS orientation (see, e.g., Colvin 2003; Huselid 1995; Tapia, Ibsen, and Kochan 2nm 015). This alignment may be partially explained by Godard's (2004) contention that conflict is seen to reduce the effectiveness of the HPWS approach.

We now turn to examine the potential link between conflict management and overall business strategy, what Gratton and Truss (2003) term "vertical alignment." An important driver of the adoption of HPWS is the link to broader organizational strategies that focus on quality and innovation (Stone, Braidford, Houston, and Bolger 2012). Therefore, given our above findings, if there is to be vertical articulation, we might expect to find increased use of ADR in organizations that adopt strategies that are quality oriented, innovation oriented, or both. The findings in Table 3 suggest that there is limited evidence of such an alignment, however. A weakly significant relationship exists between innovation and the presence of a mediation policy. However, the observed relationship suggests that mediation is negatively associated with an innovative strategy—which is at odds with a high-performance HR strategy. Beyond that, no significant relationship can be found.

Finally, the analysis now considers the relationship between conflict policy and practice, which, drawing on Gratton and Truss's (2003) typology, is the strategic dimension of implementation. The data in Table 1 clearly illustrate that although the incidence of ADR, and especially mediation, is not high in organizations' formal written conflict management policies, it is fairly well used in practice. In the case of mediation specifically, around three times as many organizations report using some form of mediation than have it in their policies. This gap between the use of ADR in practice over policy would support earlier research by Lipsky, Seeber, and Fincher (2003) that ADR may be used in an ad hoc manner, where a speedy response is required to specific disputes. However, the policy–practice gap contests their alternative suggestion that ADR is introduced because it has been agreed in advance and incorporated into contracts or policies. This finding is further reinforced by the survey

Table 3
Mediation and Organizational Strategy

	Mediation	No mediation
Price	2.16	2.22
Innovation	2.38*	2.24*
Quality	1.43	1.51

*Significant at 0.1
Mean importance (1 = most important, 3 = least important).

question that asked about organizations' overall approach to disputes, where respondents were asked to choose among various options ranging between having a formal written policy that is used consistently in all cases to the more informal option of having no written policy, with disputes dealt with on a case-by-case basis. By far the most popular response (56%) was a formal written policy but some discretion as to how it is implemented, depending on individual circumstances.

Thus, there appears to be a relationship horizontally between a high-performance approach to HR and the presence of mediation, but the links vertically and at an implementation stage are not as evident. Additionally, our findings suggest that the introduction of ADR is reactive and pragmatic rather than planned—and while it seems to fit with HR strategy—beyond that, the evidence of strategic articulation is questionable.

SUMMARY AND CONCLUSIONS

This chapter set out with the purpose of exploring the link between ADR and broader organizational strategy. Significant evidence suggests that ADR is a growing phenomenon and no longer confined to the United States. The findings presented in this chapter—that the use of ADR is fairly widespread throughout the United Kingdom—confirm previous, more-limited research on Wales (Hann, Nash, and Heery 2019). Our analysis also finds that growth in the use of ADR is apparent even if we take its narrowest definition—namely, only mediation—with significant numbers of organizations throughout Great Britain reporting having used this approach to resolving disputes.

The question around whether the adoption of these practices is intentional and/or strategic leads to important findings that develop our understanding of conflict management more generally. The findings in this chapter suggest that while there are significant relationships with HR strategy, it is not with a high-road/high-performance approach generally, as has been proposed in the past, but rather with selected aspects of this approach. The most notable HR policy area that appears to be associated with the existence of ADR is employee voice. It might be expected that organizations that have proactively attempted to design an HR system that allows for the input of other stakeholders would also move away from rigid management-led approaches to dispute resolution.

Equally, we note an association with what might be interpreted as a key element of a unitarist approach to organizations in choosing the "right" employees to fit the company approach through selective hiring. The potential relationship between ADR and a unitarist orientation is consistent with earlier research that finds some evidence that use of ADR is consistent with minimizing the role played by unions (Nash and Hann 2020). Thus, the link between ADR and employee voice may be a reflection of organizations looking at other—nonunion—ways to allow employees to participate in decision making. The findings presented here are merely indicative but suggest an important relationship between employee voice and ADR that warrants further research.

Beyond voice, the organizational justice driver within the literature is less evident. It could be argued that the lack of consistency between policy and practice is an indicator of strained organizational justice, with employees having no clear guidelines for the expected approaches and getting differing outcomes in differing circumstances. The obverse of this argument is that the ad hoc approaches taken are more adaptive and responsive compared with a one-size-fits-all tactic and prioritize pragmatism over consistency. This finding is at odds with the arguments by Purcell et al. (2009) and Heffernan and Dundon (2016) that for strategy to be seen as just, it needs to be consistent with the experience employees have, or to put it another way, the policy intention must match the policy implementation, which appears not to be the case.

We find no evidence for a strategic relationship between conflict management and top-level organizational drivers, at least in terms of vertical articulation with overall organizational strategy. However, the findings in relation to what Gratton and Truss (2003) term the "articulation of strategy" are significant. The observed gap between the implementation of ADR over its presence in organizational policy suggests that there may be an intentional strategy by HR professionals within organizations to keep written policy to a minimum and instead to use the most effective approach for the situation at hand. One interpretation of this is the strategy itself is pragmatism over dogged adherence to written documents. This approach would reflect earlier findings that suggest ADR can often be adopted in an ad hoc manner (Lipsky, Avgar, and Lamare 2017).

The acknowledgment by respondents to this survey that this is an intentional strategy represents an important additional piece of understanding. This pragmatically strategic approach sits at odds with the body of literature that talks about the growing interest, at least in the United States, in an integrated approach to conflict resolution. The fact that respondents intentionally use methods outside their written policy in a manner that suits the situation would suggest the opposite of an integrated conflict management system. This disintegrated approach to conflict management that is evident in Great Britain warrants further research to understand both its drivers and effects in terms of resolving workplace disputes.

REFERENCES

Avgar, Ariel C. 2016. "Treating Conflict: The Adoption of a Conflict Management System in a Hospital Setting." In *Managing and Resolving Workplace Conflict* 22: 211–246. *Advances in Industrial & Labor Relations*. doi: 0.1108/S0742-618620160000022009

Avgar, Ariel C., J. Ryan Lamare, David B. Lipsky, and Abhishek Gupta. 2013. "Unions and ADR: The Relationship Between Labor Unions and Workplace Dispute Resolution in U.S. Corporations." *Ohio State Journal on Dispute Resolution* 28: 63.

Becker, Brian E., and Mark A. Huselid. 1998. "Human Resources Strategies, Complementarities, and Firm Performance." Unpublished manuscript. SUNY Buffalo.

Becker, Brian E., Mark A. Huselid, and Dave Ulrich. 2001. "Making HR a Strategic Asset." *Financial Times*, November 2001.

Colvin, Alexander J.S. 2003. "Institutional Pressures, Human Resource Strategies, and the Rise of Nonunion Dispute Resolution Procedures." *ILR Review* 56 (3): 375–392. doi: 10.1177/001979390305600301

Colvin, Alexander J.S. 2004. "Adoption and Use of Dispute Resolution Procedures in the Nonunion Workplace." *Advances in Industrial & Labor Relations* 13: 69–95. doi: 10.1016/S0742-6186(04)13003-5

Colvin, Alexander J. S. 2006. "Flexibility and Fairness in Liberal Market Economies: The Comparative Impact of the Legal Environment and High-Performance Work Systems." *British Journal of Industrial Relations* 44 (1): 73–97. doi: 10.1111/j.1467-8543.2006.00488.x

David, Jennifer. 1986. "Alternative Dispute Resolution—What Is It?" In *Conference Proceedings, Australia Institute of Criminology*. Canberra.

Delery, John E., and D. Harold Doty. 1996. "Modes of Theorizing in Strategic Human Resource Management: Tests of Universalistic, Contingency, and Configurational Performance Predictions." *Academy of Management Journal* 39 (4): 802–835. doi: 10.2307/256713

Department of Business, Innovation and Skills. 2011. "Resolving Workplace Disputes: A Consultation." London: BIS.

Dickens, Linda. 2012. "Employment Tribunals and Alternative Dispute Resolution." In *Making Employment Rights Effective*, edited by Linda Dickens. Oxford: Hart Publishing.

Dix, Gill. 2012. "Dispute Resolution and Policy: Past, Present and Future." ESRC Seminar Series.

Dobbin, Frank. 2011. *Inventing Equal Opportunity*. Princeton: Princeton University Press.

Fuchs, Sebastian, and Martin R. Edwards. 2012. "Predicting Pro-Change Behaviour: The Role of Perceived Organisational Justice and Organisational Identification." *Human Resource Management Journal* 22 (1): 39–59. doi: 10.1111/j.1748-8583.2011.00167.x

Gill, Carol. 1999. "Use of Hard and Soft Models of HRM to Illustrate the Gap Between Rhetoric and Reality in Workforce Management." Citeseer.

Godard, John. 2004. "A Critical Assessment of the High-Performance Paradigm." *British Journal of Industrial Relations* 42 (2): 349–378. doi: 10.1111/j.1467-8543.2004.00318.x

Gratton, Lynda, and Catherine Truss. 2003. "The Three-Dimensional People Strategy: Putting Human Resources Policies into Action." *Academy of Management Executive* 17 (3): 74–86. https://www.jstor.org/stable/4165984

Hair, Joseph F., Ralph E. Anderson, Ronald L. Tatham, and William Black. 1998. *Multivariate Data Analysis*. Upper Saddle River: Prentice Hall.

Hann, Deborah, David Nash, and Edmund Heery. 2019. "Workplace Conflict Resolution in Wales: The Unexpected Prevalence of Alternative Dispute Resolution." *Economic and Industrial Democracy* 40 (3): 776–802. doi: 10.1177/0143831X16663013

Heffernan, Margaret, and Tony Dundon. 2016. "Cross-Level Effects of High-Performance Work Systems (HPWS) and Employee Well-Being: The Mediating Effect of Organisational Justice: High-Involvement HR, Organisational Justice and Well-Being." *Human Resource Management Journal* 26 (2): 211–231. doi: 10.1111/1748-8583.12095

Huselid, Mark A. 1995. "The Impact of Human Resource Management Practices on Turnover, Productivity, and Corporate Financial Performance." *Academy of Management Journal* 38 (3): 635–672. doi: 10.2307/256741

Huselid, Mark A., and Brian E. Becker. 1997. "The Impact of High Performance Work Systems, Implementation Effectiveness, and Alignment with Strategy on Shareholder Wealth." *Academy of Management Proceedings* 1997 (1): 144–148.

Ichniowski, Casey, Thomas A. Kochan, David Levine, Craig Olson, and George Strauss. 1996. "What Works at Work: Overview and Assessment." *Industrial Relations* 35 (3): 299–333. doi: 10.1111/j.1468-232X.1996.tb00409.x

Kochan, Thomas A., Robert B. McKersie, and Peter Cappelli. 1984. "Strategic Choice and Industrial Relations Theory." *Industrial Relations: A Journal of Economy and Society* 23 (1): 16–39.

Latreille, Paul L., and Richard Saundry. 2016. "Toward a System of Conflict Management? Cultural Change and Resistance in a Healthcare Organization." In *Advances in Industrial and Labor Relations*, edited by David B. Lipsky, Ariel C. Avgar, and J. Ryan Lamare, 22: 189–209. doi: 10.1108/S0742-618620160000022008

Lipsky, David B. 2015. "The Future of Conflict Management Systems: The Future of Conflict Resolution Systems." *Conflict Resolution Quarterly* 33 (S1): S27–S34. doi: 10.1002/crq.21133

Lipsky, David B., Ariel C. Avgar, J. Ryan Lamare. 2017. "Advancing Dispute Resolution by Unpacking the Sources of Conflict: Toward an Integrated Framework" [electronic version]. Paper presented at Conflict and Its Resolution in the Changing World of Work: A Conference and Special Issue Honoring David B. Lipsky, Ithaca, NY. http://digitalcommons.ilr.cornell.edu/lipskycrconference/8

Lipsky, David B., Ariel C. Avgar, J. Ryan Lamare, and A. Gupta. 2014. "Conflict Resolution in the United States." In *The Oxford Handbook of Conflict Management in Organizations*, edited by William K. Roche, Paul Teague, and Alexander J.S. Colvin. Oxford: Oxford University. Press, 405-424.

Lipsky, David B., Ronald Leroy Seeber, and Richard D. Fincher. 2003. *Emerging Systems for Managing Workplace Conflict: Lessons from American Corporations for Managers and Dispute Resolution Professionals*. 1st ed. San Francisco: Jossey-Bass.

Lynch, Jennifer F. 2001. "Beyond ADR: A Systems Approach to Conflict Management." *Negotiation Journal* 17 (3): 206–216.doi: 10.1111/j.1571-9979.2001.tb00237.x

Lynch, Jennifer. 2003. "Are Your Organization's Conflict Management Practices an Integrated Conflict Management System?" Mediate.com. January 27, 2003. https://tinyurl.com/bdfnkbvj

Macduffie, John Paul. 1995. "Human Resource Bundles and Manufacturing Performance: Organizational Logic and Flexible Production Systems in the World Auto Industry." *ILR Review* 48 (2): 197–221. doi: 10.1177/001979399504800201

Mackie, Karl J., David Miles, and William Marsh. 2000. *The ADR Practice Guide: Commercial Dispute Resolution*. 2nd ed. London: Butterworths.

Mahony, Douglas M. and Brian S. Klaas. 2014. "HRM and Conflict Management." In *The Oxford Handbook of Conflict Management in Organizations*, edited by William K. Roche, Paul Teague, and Alexander J.S. Colvin. Oxford: Oxford University Press.

Mirfakhar, Atieh S., Jordi Trullen, and Mireia Valverde. 2018. "Easier Said Than Done: A Review of Antecedents Influencing Effective HR Implementation." *International Journal of Human Resource Management* 29 (22): 3001–3025. doi: 10.1080/09585192.2018.1443960

Nash, David, and Deborah Hann. 2020. "Strategic Conflict Management? A Study of Workplace Dispute Resolution in Wales." *ILR Review* 73 (2): 411–430. doi: 10.1177/0019793919874031

Purcell, John, Nicholas Kinnie, Juani Swart, Bruce Rayton, and Sue Hutchinson. 2009. *People Management and Performance.* Abingdon: Routledge.

Rahim, Nilifur, Ashley Brown, and Jerry Graham. 2011. "Evaluation of the Acas Code of Practice on Disciplinary and Grievance Procedures." Acas Research Papers 06/11. https://tinyurl.com/6444md2x

Roberts, Simon, and Michael Palmer. 2005. *Dispute Processes: ADR and the Primary Forms of Decision-Making.* 2nd ed. Cambridge: Cambridge University Press. doi: 10.1017/CBO9780511805295

Roche, William K., and Paul Teague. 2012. "The Growing Importance of Workplace ADR." *International Journal of Human Resource Management* 23 (3): 447–458. doi: 10.1080/09585192.2012.641084

Roche, William K., Paul Teague, Alexander J. S. Colvin, David B. Lipsky, Ariel C. Avgar, and J. Ryan Lamare. 2014. "Conflict Resolution in the United States." In *The Oxford Handbook of Conflict Management in Organizations*, edited by William K. Roche, Paul Teague, and Alexander J. S. Colvin. Oxford: Oxford University Press. doi: 10.1093/oxfordhb/9780199653676.013.0021

Roche, William K., Paul Teague, and Alexander J.S. Colvin, eds. 2014. *The Oxford Handbook of Conflict Management in Organizations.* Oxford: Oxford University Press.

Rowe, Mary. 1997. "Dispute Resolution in the Non-Union Environment: An Evolution Toward Integrated Systems for Conflict Management?" In *Frontiers in Dispute Resolution in Labor Relations and Human Resources*, edited by Sandra Gleason, pp.79–106. East Lansing: Michigan State University Press.

Sander, Frank E.A. 1976. "Varieties of Dispute Processing." *Federal Rules Decisions* 79: 126–132.

Saundry, Richard, Paul Latreille, Linda Dickens, Charlike Irvine, Paul Teague, Peter Unwin, and Gemma Wibberly. 2014. "Reframing Resolution—Managing Conflict and Resolving Individual Employment Disputes in the Contemporary Workplace." Acas Policy Discussion Papers. https://tinyurl.com/2racaxaf

Saundry, Richard, and Peter Urwin. 2021. "Estimating the Costs of Workplace Conflict." Acas. https://tinyurl.com/mv55zcj2

Stone, Ian, Paul Braidford, Maxine Houston, and Fergus Bolger. 2012. "Promoting High Performance Working." Department for Business Innovation and Skills. https://tinyurl.com/mr32vux4

Tapia, Maite, Christian L. Ibsen, and Thomas A. Kochan. 2015. "Mapping the Frontier of Theory in Industrial Relations: The Contested Role of Worker Representation." *Socio-Economic Review* 13 (1): 157–184. doi: 10.1093/ser/mwu036

Teague, Paul, and Liam Doherty. 2016. "HRM, Organizational Citizenship Behaviour and Conflict Management: The Case of Non-Union MNC Subsidiaries in Ireland." In *Reframing Resolution: Innovation and Change in the Management of Workplace Conflict*, edited by Richard Saundry, Paul L. Latreille, and Ian Ashman. London: Palgrave Macmillan.

Teague, Paul, William Roche, and Deborah Hann. 2012. "The Diffusion of Alternative Dispute Resolution Practices in Ireland." *Economic and Industrial Democracy* 33 (4): 581–604.

Truss, Catherine, Lynda Gratton, Veronica Hope-Hailey, Patrick McGovern, and Philip Stiles. 1997. "Soft and Hard Models of Human Resource Management: A Reappraisal." *Journal of Management Studies* 34 (1): 53–73. doi: 10.1111/1467-6486.00042

Ulrich, Dave. 1997. "Measuring Human Resources: An Overview of Practice and a Prescription for Results." *Human Resource Management* 36 (3): 303–320.

Ulrich, Dave, Wayne Brockbank, and Dani Johnson. 2009. "The Role of Strategy Architect in the Strategic HR Organization." *People & Strategy* 32 (1): 24–32.

Ury, William, Jeanne M. Brett, and Stephen B. Goldberg. 1993. *Getting Disputes Resolved: Designing Systems to Cut the Costs of Conflict.* Cambridge: Harvard Law School.

Wu, Pei-Chuan, and Sankalp Chaturvedi. 2009. "The Role of Procedural Justice and Power Distance in the Relationship Between High Performance Work Systems and Employee Attitudes: A Multilevel Perspective." *Journal of Management* 35 (5): 1228–1247. doi: 10.1177/0149206308331097

Zhang, Mingqiong, David Di Fan, and Cherrie Jiuhua Zhu. 2014. "High-Performance Work Systems, Corporate Social Performance and Employee Outcomes: Exploring the Missing Links." *Journal of Business Ethics* 120 (3): 423–435. doi: 10.1007/s10551-013-1672-1628.

CHAPTER 4

Employment Relationship Problems and Workplace Conflict Management in New Zealand: Reframing Employment Dispute Resolution Policy, Processes, and Practice

GAYE GREENWOOD
Mediator; Formerly with Auckland University of Technology

ERLING RASMUSSEN
Formerly Professor with Auckland University of Technology

YASHIKA CHANDHOK
Auckland University of Technology

ABSTRACT

Historically, workplace conflict resolution in New Zealand benefited from third-party neutral intervention in labor disputes. State-funded employment institutions provided traditional and alternative dispute resolution (ADR) processes (negotiation, conciliation, arbitration, mediation, and facilitation) with litigation in the Employment Court as a last resort. New Zealand's current legislative framework aims for early, informal, low-cost resolution processes, while research has continued to focus on institutional provision of mediation, investigation, determination, litigation, and bargaining in disputes between unions/employees and employers. Research has highlighted institutional access issues in dealing with workplace conflict management, but the research is mainly silent on the extent of noninstitutional ADR interventions. This chapter argues for a fundamental shift in institutional provision of ADR services and reframes processes for early resolution of conflict. We assert the employment relationship is more complex and dynamic than the historical construct of employer–employee/union relationships. Our findings suggest escalation to formal disputes can be attributed to the influence of positional legalism on institutional and workplace interventions and to a lack of attention in the workplace context where conflict emerges. The chapter is located at the intersection of workplace conflict management and institutional provision of services for employment conflict resolution. We identify how and why complexity in the employment relationship and traditional interventions can lead to escalation of complaint to formal dispute. We reframe traditional approaches to negotiation and mediation as opportunities for early collaborative sense-making. The chapter presents literature and empirical evidence for a collaborative sense-making framework that emerged from Greenwood's (2016) research. We argue that attention to reflective collaborative sense-making is fundamental to early resolution of complex employment relationship problems.

INTRODUCTION

The chapter begins with a historical overview of the institutional provision of employment dispute resolution. New Zealand has had a comprehensive system of institutional conflict resolution for more than 100 years. Employment institutions were originally associated with the unique legislative regulation of the conciliation and arbitration system (1894–1990), but the institutional role and processes changed considerably after the introduction of the Employment Contracts Act (ECA) of 1991 (Table 1). This involved a dramatic shift from collective disputes to individualized conflicts at workplace level, with all employees being covered by employment legislation and individualized statutory employment entitlements driving significant growth in the number of cases pursued at the publicly funded employment institutions. Therefore, the focus of public debate has been on settlements delivered by employment institutions. Likewise, academic literature has detailed the processes, outcomes, and public policy issues of employment institutions (McAndrew 2010; Rasmussen and Anderson 2022).

While the aims of the current legislative framework—the Employment Relations Act (ERA) of 2000—support collectivism, the focus has remained on individual employee entitlements and rights to personal grievance, with an emphasis on mediation (Table 1). Compared with the 1990s, a rise in public funding in the new millennium aimed to enhance institutional conflict resolution and enforcement (Rasmussen and Anderson 2022). Although the numbers of dispute settlements and interventions based on legal precedent are high, there are concerns about barriers to dispute resolution for specific categories of workers (Arthur 2018; Inglis 2019). While research and debates have highlighted institutional challenges, we advocate for a more fundamental shift in the employment dispute resolution system toward collaborative processes with less institutional, positional legalism.

The chapter focuses on early, flexible employment relationship problem (ERP) resolution to meet the objectives of ERA 2000, which seeks to strengthen employment relationships by having less emphasis on contractual, legalistic approaches to resolution of ERPs than the preceding ECA 1991 (Wilson 2004, 2017). Research findings indicate ERA's objectives are yet to be fully achieved. This chapter argues that providing early, low-cost, and nonlegalistic forms of resolution, as promoted by ERA 2000, requires a focus on conflict at the intersection of workplace and institutional intervention. The chapter focuses on the complexity of relationships, processes, and practice of ERP resolution. A reflective, collaborative sense-making model for early workplace dispute resolution will need to be applied at the level of the workplace and to processes delivered by third-party neutrals.

Table 1
Employment Institutions and Their Changing Roles and Processes, 1894–2022

Legislation	Institutions	Processes
Industrial Conciliation & Arbitration Act, 1894–1973 (original act was adjusted through several amendment acts)	Changed several times but mainly: • Labour Inspectorate • Conciliation Boards (besides a judge, they included business and union representatives) • Arbitration Court: Developed legal precedent and national award settings	Conciliation Boards dealt with most collective bargaining decisions. The boards and the court were setting binding and de facto minimum wages and conditions through comprehensive awards. Limited, direct (employer–union) collective bargaining.
Industrial Relations Act, 1973–1987	• Labour Inspectorate • Industrial Mediation Service • Industrial Conciliation Service • Arbitration Court	Incorporated mediation service from 1970 amendment act. Distinction between rights and interest disputes, with rights disputes dominating workload of employment institutions.
Compulsory arbitration abolished in 1984	Kept Industrial Relations Act institutions, but limited arbitration decisions of the Arbitration Court	Removed the ability of unions to demand negotiations and agreement outcomes.
Labour Relations Act, 1987–1991	• Labour Inspectorate • Mediation Service • Arbitration Commission • Labour Court	Adjusted IRA 1973 institutional setup, with an emphasis on mediation and facilitating direct collective bargaining.
Employment Contracts Act, 1991–2000	Provision of information and advice starts in earnest: • Labour Inspectorate • Employment Tribunal • Employment Court	Tribunal had dual emphasis on mediation and adjudication (so-called med-arb approach). Employment Court cases had significant legal precedent impact, although there was often disagreement with the Court of Appeal over decisions.
Employment Relations Act, 2000–current	Expansion of provision of information and advice: • Labour Inspectorate • Mediation Service • Employment Relations Authority • Employment Court	The emphasis on low-level, low-cost, and proactive dispute resolution increased support and capabilities of information, enforcement, and mediation, with mediation prescribed as the first, default formal dispute resolution mechanism.

Source: Rasmussen and Anderson (2022). For a more detailed overview, see Rasmussen and Greenwood (2014: 450–453).

The theoretical and empirical complexity of researching ERPs has required a cross-disciplinary approach. The chapter draws on three types of research:
- A long-standing research interest in institutionalized dispute resolution by survey and investigation into access to institutionalized conflict resolution processes (Arthur 2018; Rasmussen and Greenwood 2014)
- In-depth qualitative research on workplace conflict resolution of ERPs in the education sector exploring how escalation of conflict can be avoided (Greenwood 2016; Greenwood and Rasmussen 2016)
- Insights about resolution and mediation of ERPs applied to the development of a collaborative, reflective sense-making framework, with recommendations for conflict management processes in the workplace

Beginning with a brief historical overview of institutional conflict resolution in New Zealand, the chapter highlights the dispute resolution approach of ERA 2000 and outlines the existing institutional arrangements. The second section addresses current issues associated with a rising tide of workplace ERPs and how they are dealt with both within and outside the employment institutions. The third section presents the findings from Greenwood's (2016) research recommending a focus on processes at the intersection of workplace conflict management and institutional intervention for early resolution of ERPs. Finally, we advocate for a collaborative sense-making approach to ERPs to prevent escalation of conflict to formal dispute.

HISTORICAL OVERVIEW OF INSTITUTIONAL CONFLICT RESOLUTION IN NEW ZEALAND

From 1894, the unique Industrial Conciliation and Arbitration Act and its associated conflict management system ensured that state-funded employment institutions could deal with collective employment disputes. As mentioned in Table 1, several changes occurred between 1894 and 1973, but there was the continuous presence of comprehensive institutional conflict resolution mechanisms. While the Industrial Relations Act (IRA) of 1973 continued the main hallmarks of the conciliation and arbitration system, it also introduced several features that have influenced current dispute resolution. There was a distinction between disputes of interest and disputes of rights (McAndrew, Geare, and Edgar 2017), state-funded mediation of rights disputes was introduced, and a personal grievance right dealing with wrongful dismissals became part of awards and collective agreements (Anderson 1988; Rasmussen, Bray, and Stewart 2019).

Despite the legislative intervention of the IRA 1973, collective bargaining processes became more conflictual in the 1970s and 1980s. This prompted a rise in workplace bargaining, which was accommodated by legislative changes: compulsory arbitration was abolished in 1984 and the Labour Relations Act of 1987 encouraged collective agreements and mediation (Rasmussen and Greenwood 2014). Still, the bargaining and dispute resolution system seemed unable to cope with economic and labor market pressures until ECA 1991 abolished the major features of the conciliation and arbitration system, including the award system (Harbridge 1993; Rasmussen, Lamm, and Molineaux 2022).

ECA 1991 was literally an employment relations revolution that jettisoned most of the traditional approach of the previous 100 years and moved from an exclusive focus on collective bargaining and collective employer and union "actors" to covering both individual and collective employment bargaining. It was a major hammer blow to unions and collective bargaining (Table 2), and it shifted the main bargaining locus toward workplace and individual employment agreements (Blumenfeld and Donnelly 2017). Around one-third of the workforce had previously been covered by common law; now they were covered by ECA 1991. That change released new dynamics as many of these employees—often in managerial and professional roles—vigorously pursued their employment rights. This was particularly the case with personal grievances, a right that was now extended to all employees (Anderson 2022). This prompted a more conflictual positional employee and employer mindset, also driven by many employers significantly altering their employment arrangements as a major recession pushed unemployment above 10% (Armitage and Dunbar 1993; Williamson and Rasmussen 2020).

While economic and employment relations reforms radically changed the labor market and legislative context, there was a continuation of mediation and adjudication processes now being delivered by the Employment Tribunal. However, there was a new emphasis on individual employee rights and on intervening early in disputes, along with a preference for mediation. Legal precedent became a crucial battleground

Table 2
Unions Membership and Density 1985–1999

Month	Year	Unions	Membership	Density
December	1985	259	683,006	43.5%
September	1989	112	648,825	44.7%
May	1991	80	603,118	41.5%
December	1991	66	514,325	35.4%
December	1992	58	428,160	28.8%
December	1993	67	409,112	26.8%
December	1994	82	375,906	23.4%
December	1995	82	362,200	21.7%
December	1996	83	338,967	19.9%
December	1997	80	327,800	18.8%
December	1998	83	306,687	17.7%
December	1999	82	302,405	17.0%

Source: Crawford, Harbridge, and Walsh (2000).

as new norms were developed under the nonprescriptive ECA 1991 (Anderson 1997). With a more conflictual "litigation" mindset, the employment institutions were under workload pressures from the start, and reports of long waiting times for cases at the Employment Tribunal were frequently mentioned in media and political debates (Rasmussen, Lamm, and Molineaux 2022). Employment lawyers were financial beneficiaries as the number of dispute resolution cases grew and employers sought legal advice to avoid falling afoul of shifting legal precedent and demands of procedural fairness in individual employment disputes. At the same time, low-paying sectors were experiencing increased turnover as employees sought to escape unpleasant or exploitative work situations (Anderson and Tipples 2014). A new era of market power, legalism, and labor market fragmentation was influencing the dispute resolution options of individual employers and employees, while collective disputes were relegated to secondary importance.

The Current Legislative Context: Employment Relations Act 2000

With a political transfer of power to the center-left Labour–Alliance government in 1999, there were attempts to overcome the market-oriented reforms of the 1990s, incorporate legal precedent established in the 1990s, and introduce a more collaborative and low-level resolution of ERPs (Deeks and Rasmussen 2002; Wilson 2004). These aims were embedded in ERA 2000 as well as an explicit commitment to support collectivism (McAndrew, Morton, and Geare 2004). Personal grievances remained alongside new concepts such as good faith, building "mutual trust and confidence in all aspects of the employment environment," and a preference for mediated settlements that emphasized relationships and beneficial, productive employment outcomes (Wilson 2004). There was an aim of having a "free, fast, and fair" approach in resolving ERPs, and the new concept of an ERP was defined very broadly (Greenwood 2016).

While there have been several changes to ERA 2000 (for a recent overview, see Rasmussen, Lamm, and Molineaux 2022), the main legislative architecture and legal objectives are still intact, and the legal precedent "frenzy" experienced in the 1990s has been avoided. However, the support of collectivism is not evidenced. Union density and collective bargaining coverage have languished, and union density is now below 10% in the private sector (Blumenfeld and Donnelly 2017). Under the post-2017 Labour-led governments, efforts to make union organizing and collective bargaining easier to conduct have been limited. The first serious attempt to bring back sectoral bargaining under ERA 2000 (Nielson 2022) was introduced late in 2022. It is anticipated that this Fair Pay Agreements legislation will support sectoral bargaining, lift the effectiveness and visibility of collective bargaining, and provide unions with a stronger platform. However, at the point of writing, the impact of that legislation is unclear.

The longevity of ERA 2000 has embedded institutional dispute resolution processes that have been supported by a steady rise in staffing and other resources available to the employment institutions (Rasmussen and Anderson 2022). The expansion of online information, advice, and conflict resolution has increased by necessity as a result of COVID-19 lockdowns and industry turmoil. Overall, there has been a rise in the number of mediation, ER Authority, and Employment Court cases, with nearly 10,000 mediation cases a year and another 10,000 externally agreed settlements being signed off by the Mediation Service. Despite high numbers of mediation and settlements, the long "shadow" of positional legalism during workplace negotiation and mediation can still be detected, and there exist a number of challenges in achieving the dispute resolution aspirations of mutual problem solving under ERA 2000.

There is still strong employer aversion toward institutional dispute resolution, and many employers prefer to keep negotiations and discussions of ERPs "in house" (Burton 2010; Foster, Rasmussen, and Coetzee 2013; McAndrew 2010). Employer avoidance of state-funded mediation has been viewed as a reaction to the formal, legalistic processes of institutional conflict resolution (Rasmussen, Foster, and Farr 2016). Interestingly, it appears that employers themselves have driven to a large degree the trend toward legalism and extensive use of legal advice. This is the picture established by the National Survey of Employers (NSE), where the 2012–2013, 2014–2015, and 2016–2017 survey rounds had the same questions about how employers dealt with employment relationship problems: the types of ERPs, the number/level of ERPs, the use of external involvement, and the outcomes of ERPs (Rasmussen and Anderson 2022). For example, in the 2016–2017 NSE, around 17% of all employers experienced employment relationship problems that had demanded some kind of action or intervention (Boyd, Cleland, and Hoy 2018). In dealing with ERPs, around 50% of employers used external help, with a clear preference for involving lawyers more than employer associations or the employment institutions. Furthermore, only in a minority of ERPs (27%) was there a continuation of employment because the employee resigned (35%), was being dismissed (21%), or was made redundant (9%).

A strong upsurge in new migrants and temporary visa holders prior to COVID-19 in 2020, as well as claims of worker exploitation in certain industries and jobs (Anderson and Kenner 2019), placed "access to justice" on the political agenda (Arthur 2018; Inglis 2019). Following the industry turmoil under COVID-19 in 2020–2022, the government has started to address these problems, though it remains to be seen how well government interventions—including a bill on migrant protection announced in October 2022—will ensure a significant reduction of barriers to institutional dispute resolution for exposed employee groups. There also appears to be a move to incorporate efforts of unions and community organizations in providing better access to information and advice tailored to groups experiencing barriers to engaging with institutional dispute resolution mechanisms.

Overall, current employment institutions have coped with a growing workload mainly driven by individual, workplace-based conflicts. However, embedded legalism in ERP processes and "access to justice" issues indicate that a stronger focus on solving workplace conflicts is necessary. Also, given the high percentage of ERPs resulting in the end of employment relationships, the aims of ERA 2000 for early, flexible problem solving to strengthen and support ongoing employment relationships have yet to be realized. Survey data suggest lawyers may undermine informal flexibility of process when disputes become positional, with employees losing their jobs or settlement mediation, resulting in exit negotiations. In the following section, we assert ERPs are more likely to be resolved early if attention is paid to the processes at the intersection of workplace conflict management and external provision of ADR. Thereby, early flexible problem solving could precede disciplinary action, a written complaint, or filing of a personal grievance.

At the Intersection of Conflict Management and Alternative Dispute Resolution

This section explores the nature of the employment relationship and alternatives to an adversarial legal approach when managing conflict in the workplace or implementing ADR processes and practices. As outlined in the previous section, the all-encompassing personal grievance right enhanced individualism, allowing employees to pursue their rights. With over 30% of all employees being covered for the first time by the employment relations legislative framework (Deeks and Rasmussen 2002), New Zealand mirrored the contemporary move away from collectivism to individualism (Avgar, Lamare, Lipsky, and Gupta 2013; Roche, Teague, and Colvin 2014). In the context of the shift to competitive market economies, deregulation, privatization, and new forms of employment relationships, individualized "litigation" sparked numerous problems: there were long waiting times at the employment institutions, it was the seed for employers' disdain of public dispute resolution, and, crucially, it fueled increased lawyer advocacy and legalism.

The human relational approach underpinning ERA 2000 aimed for collaborative processes of problem solving by negotiation and mediation with the goal of building "relational trust through good faith behavior" and providing institutional support to resolve relational conflict by mediation. The objective of ERA 2000 was "to build productive relationships through the promotion of mutual trust and confidence in all aspects of the employment environment and of the employment relationship" and provide a "free, fast, and fair" mediation service (Wilson 2000). The aim was self-determination whereby parties resolved employment problems early, close to the source of the conflict—in the workplace. It was a clear directive for individuals and organizations to engage in early conflict management by a problem-solving approach to negotiation and mediation, aiming to balance power between employers and employees giving voice to the issues and interests as problems arose and thereby preventing litigious escalation to dispute in employment institutions (Greenwood 2016).

While New Zealand aligned with an international rise in the interest in ADR approaches (Lipsky and Avgar 2010) in an "individual rights era" (Colvin 2012: 459), ERA 2000 indicated a rather more ambitious approach. ADR refers to processes for resolving conflict outside the traditional litigation model of adversarial judicial intervention and lawyer representation in the courts. Thus, Roche, Teague, and Colvin (2014) called for different ways of thinking about conflict management that integrates perspectives of academics, dispute resolution practitioners, organizations, unions, and employer and regulator perspectives to achieve deeper understandings of dynamic workplace conflict and its resolution. This section introduces, therefore, New Zealand's construct of ERPs and its focus on building a culture of conflict management at the workplace level preceding institutional intervention.

ERA 2000 clearly attempted to shift away from the contractual focus of the 1990s toward a more relational approach but unfortunately oversimplified the relationship as being only one between employer and employee. Greenwood (2016) found a complex web of parties involved in ERPs and complaints in the education sector, where ERPs involved stakeholders within and outside the organization. The lack of access to institutional provision of conflict resolution for complex problems left employees, subcontractors, governors, team members, and leaders, as well as organizations themselves, vulnerable to complaint, risk of escalation to legalism, and dispute. It was apparent the traditional tripartite employment relationship, in both the policy and practice of conflict management and access to institutional ADR, was oversimplified in ERA 2000. The employment relationship appeared more complex and dynamic.

Traditionally, the employment relationship was described as a series of interactions and dependencies between the three main parties: employees, employers, and the government and their various representative organizations or institutions (Rasmussen, Lamm, and Molineaux 2022). Conflict in the employment relationship was initially conceptualized as a dysfunctional negative process (Pondy 1967; Schmidt and Kochan 1972). However, in the contemporary context of interpersonal and teamwork, conflict was conceived as both constructive and destructive to the organization. Categorized as relationship and/or task related (Guetzkow and Gyr 1954; Jehn 1994), relationship conflict involved affective elements such as feelings of tension and friction, and task conflict was framed as emotionally neutral. The conceptualization of task conflict as rational and lacking affect was symptomatic of the positivist approach to survey research, with a focus on categorization by type to ascertain relationships between variables. The research was silent about the social construction of conflict through language, culture, or organizational structure, and it lacked interrogation about why and how conflict changed over time in the context of change. Likewise, diverse interpretations of conflict by culture, age, gender, ability, or context were not a feature of the research on task, relationship, process, status, and conflict management styles (Greenwood 2016).

Three meta-analyses of conflict literature by De Dreu and Weingart (2003) identify that the intensity of conflict mattered. While conflict was less likely to disrupt routine tasks—a little conflict could sometimes be beneficial in complex tasks—positive effects quickly broke down as conflict became more intense as cognitive load increased, information processing impeded, and consequently, team performance suffered. Focusing on the associations among conflict, job satisfaction, and performance, researchers sought to consider how to apply conflict management to the human resources management (HRM) function. Relationship conflict was associated with decreased satisfaction, but task conflict during complex, nonroutine tasks was found to be beneficial for creativity, innovation, learning, and development (Simons and Peterson 2000; Van de Vliert and De Dreu 1994). Jehn, Northcraft, and Neale (1999) considered that process conflict could include relational, task, and process issues, with positive and negative effects on individuals and their team's performance and satisfaction. Jehn (1995) conceptualized conflict between a group of individuals as disagreements or incompatibilities over work or nonwork-related issues.

As noted earlier, the meaning and context of ERPs and conflicts arising from ERPs have rapidly changed from being a collective conflict handled by unions to become the current dominant individual-level conflict between the employee and employer. The change in the structure of conflict and the institutional push toward a less legalistic and low-cost approach has increased the focus on ADR. As noted by Saundry, Latreille, and Ashman (2016: 346), "conflict has been traditionally resolved through collective and social processes of negotiation, accommodation and resolution; it is now generally either subject to individual manager–subordinate relations or individualized rights–based grievance and disciplinary procedures."

The international focus of ADR literature has also shifted from traditional distributive bargaining associated with union advocacy to integrative bargaining in which interest-based negotiation (IBN) is associated with behavioral change—a partnership approach to dispute resolution and early conflict management in the workplace (Cutcher-Gershenfeld and Kochan 2004; Fisher, Ury, and Patton 1991; Hunter and McKersie 1992; Kochan 1974; Ury, Brett, and Goldberg 1989; Walton and McKersie 1965; Walton, Cutcher-Gershenfeld, and McKersie 1994).

The contemporary focus on mutual interests in employment relationships when negotiating transformation of disputes (Bingham 2004; Bingham and Pitts 2002; Bush and Folger 2005; Mayer 2004; Moore 2003; Reardon 2005; Walton, Cutcher-Gershenfeld, and McKersie 2000) is threaded throughout the practitioner and academic literature on negotiation conflict management and mediation. On one hand, IBN enabled a mutual-interest, problem-solving approach; on the other hand, it was argued that an IBN approach, where employers claimed mutual alignment with employee interests, masked the natural imbalance of power in the relationship and was a barrier to access to justice.

With respect to managing issues of escalated conflict, Jehn and Mannix (2001) proposed managerial encouragement of norms for open discussion and high levels of respect among members, and they asserted that a cohesive, supportive team environment would have a positive effect on team performance. They advised that managers and leaders should conduct conflict training at the early stages of group formation. Likewise, Greenwood and Haar (2017) found supervisor support buffered the negative effect associated with intragroup conflict—such as members fighting about tasks and how work was done, along with disagreements about processes, responsibilities, and roles. Framed as both a destructive problem and an opportunity for growth, the dichotomy of conflict called on interdisciplinary research in organizational psychology, communications, negotiation, ADR, HRM, and employment relations. The importance of training in conflict management has been a recurrent theme of research on international conflict management (Amsler 2014; Roche, Teague, and Colvin 2014). Therefore, conflict management skills are important dimensions of the supervisor toolkit for early resolution of problems in complex workplace relationships.

The empirical research underpinning our discussion (Greenwood 2016) conceptualizes workplace conflict as an ongoing dynamic process of sense-making and interpretation. It calls for building a workplace culture that enables confidential, sense-making conversations preceding formal complaint filing. Greenwood (2016) drew on interviews with a range of stakeholders in employment relationships, including principals, deputy assistant or associate principals, past or present members of boards of trustees, employment relations investigators, mediators, experts in education and/or employment relations including leaders from the New Zealand Education Institute primary teachers' union, and field workers from the Board of Trustees Association. The sections below introduce the sense-making process, discuss the relevance to ERPs, and present a collaborative conflict management (CCM) model as a framework for early, informal workplace resolution.

Sense-Making, Sense-Giving, Sense-Sharing, and Collaborative Sense-Making

Weick (1995) developed sense-making as a theoretical framework of organizing. The social psychology of sense-making in organizations is theorized as a response to ambiguity, uncertainty, and change (Weick 2001, 2009). According to Festinger (1957), constructing a new sense of situations involved reframing thinking to reduce dissonance. Sense-making is, according to Weick (2009: 143), a cognitive process reliant on talk; his famous statement, "How can I know what I think until I see what I say," illustrates sense-making as a speaking–listening–thinking process applied for reflecting on self through stories or narratives.

Weick, Sutcliffe, and Obstfeld also claimed that sense-making influences identity construction. They said sense-making was a series of "micro-level actions ... but they are small actions with large consequences" (2005: 419). Sense-making is an ongoing process involving seven dimensions (Weick 1995) that "represent the situation that is present at moments of sense-making." (Weick 2010: 544). The seven dimensions of sense-making, summarized by the acronym SIRCOPE are as follows:
- **S**ocial context
- **I**dentity
- **R**etrospective

- **C**ommunication **c**ues
- **O**ngoing process
- **P**lausibility
- **E**nactive

Sense-making is a *social* phenomenon involving social context, where *identity* construction is grounded in who we are and what has shaped our lives and influenced the way we see the world. Sense-making is *retrospective* because we rely on past events to help us interpret current events, comparing and selecting the *cues* and elements that support our beliefs and interpretations. Weick (1995) argued the *ongoing* process was sequential and never ending. However, Weick's seminal work overlooked the influence of emotions and power during the sense-making process. Our research identifies how power and emotions are intertwined with Weick's seven dimensions of sense-making.

Weick's interpretation of sense-making did not provide due focus on aspects of organizational structure and power during the sense-making process or during the process of an organizational change (Helma Mills 2003). Thurlow (2007) integrated this approach by relying on the *ebbs and flows* of the sense-making of various actors as well as the discursive process. Her study depicted the role of the few people in powerful positions who can influence the sense of organizations and their perspective of a change. This called for understanding the *agency* behavior conducted by the relevant individuals or groups of power in an organization, which can also be interpreted as sense-giving (Aromaa, Eriksson, and Montonen 2020). Managers in an organization are involved in the process of sense-making to understand and construct meanings for organizational goals, strategies, and changes. Employees in an organization are involved in the sense-making process to understand each other's frames, and the alignment of these frames assisted the managers in conflict resolution (Budd, Pohler, and Huang 2022). Thus, the sense-making process influences interpretation of complex ambiguous situations and conflict between actors. In such resolution of conflicts, implementation of change requires *reframing understandings during a sense-making processes*.

While SIRCOPE acknowledges the role of identity that can influence an individual's understanding of frames to interpret conflict or any other circumstances, Greenwood (2016) critiqued the process as lacking two critical dimensions that impact sense-making: influence or power and emotion. Thus, Greenwood built on the original SIRCOPE model to develop E-SIRI-COPE as a framework for making sense of conflict and decision-making events. Overall, sense-making is the process of understanding, sense-giving is the process of sharing that understanding, and sense-breaking is the process of adopting the understanding. Greenwood has consolidated the processes of sense-making, sense-giving, and sense-breaking as a dynamic shared process of *collaborative reflective sense-making* that can be applied to day-to-day conflict management for early resolution of employment relationship problems.

It is apparent that sense-making conversations with people who are not directly involved in workplace conflict can escalate conflict. Thomas (1992) called conversations with people who are not involved with a situation "third-party sense-making." Volkema, Farquhar, and Bergman (1996) identified that third-party sense-making occurs in situations of change and that ill-structured problems such as workplace conflict involved third-party sense-making as people looking to others to help them make sense of situations. According to Miller and Jablin (1991), people engage in third-party sense-making to seek validation, clarification, and comfort in new circumstances. Olson-Buchanan and Boswell (2008) presented a sense-making model of experiencing and voicing mistreatment at work. Their findings were reinforced by our contention that the reflective nature of sense-making during responses to mistreatment is critical to early resolution. Our findings also suggested that reflective collaborative sense-making was necessary but that confidentiality should be invoked for protection from escalated workplace conflict.

Conflict management literature lacks attention to the role of an individual's sense of identity during processes of negotiation, decision making, and workplace conflict resolution. However, research by Weick (1979, 1988, 1989, 1993, 1995) and Weick, Sutcliffe, and Obstfeld (2005) highlighted that decision making was anchored in identity as people searched for meaning. A threat to identity included actions that failed to confirm self-concept. Weick et al. asserted that sense-making was influenced by efforts to maintain a positive self-concept, claiming that when people act on what seems plausible, they might forget to consider alternative possibilities, which had "large consequences" (2005: 419). Weick, Sutcliffe, and Obstfeld also introduced the concept of organized sense-making where "organization emerges through sense-making, not one in which organization precedes sense-making or one in which sense-making is produced by organization" (2005: 410). The process of sense-making starts with noticing and observing any ambiguousness, followed by a desire to label and/or categorize the same (Weick, Sutcliffe, and Obstfeld 2005). It is then followed by making presumptions based on past experiences and is completed by taking an action per the sense made. In crisis situations, Weick (2010) argued, people were engaged in ongoing sense-making by enacting decisions that both responded to and created the environment within the organization, where awareness of anomaly created struggle. We contend that collaborative sense-making following the guidelines of good faith negotiation behavior empowers parties and enables collaborative problem resolution.

Research has uncovered a gradual shift in the interpretation of sense-making from a rational cognitive process to a socially constructive process (Sandberg and Tsoukas 2015, Weick 2012). The reformed sense-making perspective emerges from the study of identity, narrative, and agency. The social constructivist perspective goes beyond "How can I know what I think until I see what I say?" (Weick 2009: 143) by focusing on the language and other nuances that surround individuals and change the aim of sense-making from creating mental maps to constructing subjectivity. Sandberg and Tsoukas (2015) conducted a critical literature review of research on the changing perspective of sense-making and summarized the most prominent situational factors that influence the sense-making process in an organization. These factors included, but were not limited to, context, language, cognitive framework, emotions, politics, and technology.

While context has always been a dimension of Weickian (1995) sense-making, Sandberg and Tsoukas (2015) expanded on context by acknowledging the *institutional context*. Institutional context relates to the cultural, ethnic, political, or economic context within which an organizational event takes place. Most of the research in the sense-making perspective focused on the social context, with few acknowledging the influence of institutional context (Nigam and Ocasio 2010; Sandberg and Tsoukas 2015; Weber and Glynn 2006). We argue in favor of a collaborative sense-making model of conflict management under the legislative directive in New Zealand, where parties to the employment relationship are required to negotiate and act in good faith during all aspects of the relationship, as evidenced by open, honest communication. Good faith communication is a legislative requirement under ERA 2000 in an attempt to build mutual trust in workplace relationships. Communication through language and ongoing discourse is threaded throughout the organization in the form of stories, narrative, and rhetoric (Cornelissen 2012). It is the linguistic approach to sense-making that influences the tone—and thus, the interpretation of text or speech (Sandberg and Tsoukas 2015). Identity relates to the character or personality of the actor or the sense-maker that can both influence the sense-making process and be developed or transformed during the sense-making. It is important for researchers to acknowledge the influence of identity on sense-making and how identity is constructed and reconstructed during the ongoing discourse in the workplace is central to conflict handling. Weick's SIRCOPE (1995) acknowledged the role identity plays during sense-making. However, the lack of attention to power and emotion during sense-making is one critique of SIRCOPE. For this reason, there is an addition to the acronyms of E (emotion) and I (influence)—and hence, the framework for analysis of conflict by conducting an early sense-making conversation becomes E-SIRI-COPE.

This section explained sense-making as a process; the next section applies sense-making to a process model for CCM of ERPs that values and enables self-determination and learning at the intersection of workplace conflict management and external intervention or provision of ADR processes.

Applying E-SIRI-COPE to Build a Collaborative Conflict Management Model

New Zealand ERP research, policy, and practice has lacked attention to establishing a bridge between conflict within organizations, complaint handling, and external institutional intervention or provision of ADR processes such as by the state-sponsored Mediation Service. Factors such as the complexity of employment relationships, the dynamic nature of ERPs, and the absence of early informal employer/employee mediation under ERA 2000, alongside the culture of complaint, have led to a propensity of exit-settlement negotiations. The association between escalation of complaint and conflict contagion highlights the need to develop processes and practices for ERP resolution early in the life cycle of a problem at workplace level.

This section presents Greenwood's (2016) four-step process model for CCM at the level of the workplace. The model draws together the function of education (learning and training) with processes for problem resolution in response to findings indicating that collaborative sense-making conversations supported trust and were associated with early resolution of workplace conflict across a range of relationships.

Developing a Code of Guidelines for Problem Management

The four-step process shown in Figure 1 is based on the finding that "collaborative, respectful dialogue builds trust" (Greenwood 2016: 220). The model aims to provide clear processes and build capacity in the conflict management capabilities of leaders to address problems early, prevent escalation, and empower all stakeholders to resolve problems themselves.

Organizations should begin this process by *collectively* designing a code for respectful dialogue specific to the organization's values and vision. Budd and Colvin (2014), Lipsky and Seeber (2003), and Lipsky and Avgar (2010) advised that strategic planning should include conflict management planning and should be consistent with the values and goals of the organization. The aim of this design should be to develop a collective mindset, supporting workplace problem resolution to ensure that all stakeholders have a voice. Generating clear expectations of conflict management processes by consultation contributes to the overall matching of expectations between various stakeholders, which can improve job satisfaction, retention, and productivity (Kotter 1973; Robinson 1996; Rousseau and Tijoriwala 1998; Tipples 1996; Wellin 2007). Organizations should also ensure that a code of guidelines is easily accessible and visible in the form of artwork or symbols so that it is embedded in the culture of the organization. The organization should also invest in building awareness and competency to clarify the processes behind proposed joint problem solving. Such clarity of process meets the policy intentions of ERA 2000 for good faith negotiations, as well as the health and safety requirements for workplaces to be free from hazards, including psychological hazards such as bullying (Rasmussen, Lamm, and Molineaux 2022).

Confidential Sense-Making Conversations

A sense-making conversation is defined as an interaction that seeks to understand a problem through storytelling and reflection. It is different from advice seeking or coaching.

Figure 1
CCM Model: A Four-Step Process for Early Resolution

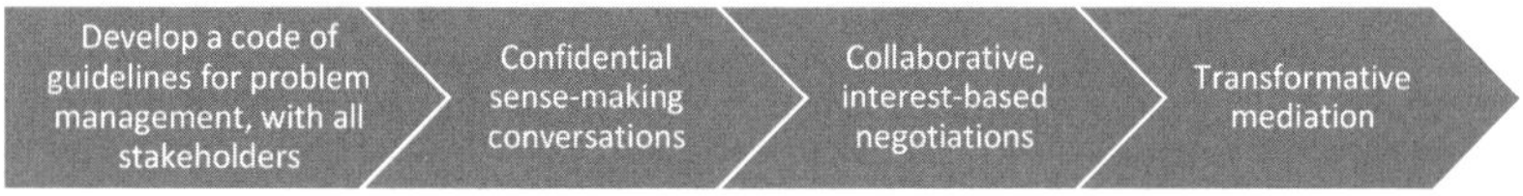

Develop a code of guidelines for problem management, with all stakeholders → Confidential sense-making conversations → Collaborative, interest-based negotiations → Transformative mediation

Source: Greenwood 2016: 220.

The process remains in the hands of the storyteller. A sense-making conversation could precede negotiation or mediation or be a process during IBN or transformative mediation. Taking an explicit sense-making approach provides a structure for conversation in situations where there is ambiguity and low trust. Building on Weickian (1995) sense-making, parties tell their conflict stories in pairs with peer confidential neutral listeners who paraphrase back in a collaborative conversation, enabling the storyteller to explore plausible explanations. The storyteller is more likely to discover meaning from reflecting on their own story or "seeing what I say," thereby enabling decision making about future actions. The process is one of collaboratively analyzing the problem by examining the aspects of the conflict in relation to the E-SIRI-COPE framework. Following application of the sense-making framework and analysis by the parties reflecting on their own sense-making of the problem story, there can be moments of discovery, examination of assumptions, and emergence of alternative views that generate new options for future negotiation/mediation and decision making. The process is framed as "learning about the problem." According to Greenwood, "reflective processes that examine mental models and perspective checking are effective for handling complaints and early resolution of ERP" (2016: 222). Conversations in which parties engage in assumption checking and open communication are explicit processes for building a culture of respectful dialogue.

Informal, collaborative, confidential sense-making conversations can build hope and trust in the process of resolution where self-efficacy and self-determination are enabled enduring agreement. Collaborative sense-making conversations can reframe the process of complaint from a process of "name, blame, and complain" to "suggestions for resolution" or "dialogic discourse" (Bakhtin 1981), or a process referred to as "mediated conversations" where peers take turns facilitating joint meetings between staff in conflict. These mindful, collaborative sense-making conversations should act as an antecedent for building trust to strengthen the psychological contract among conflicting parties and other stakeholders in employment relationships.

The idea for collaborative sense-making conversations emerged from examining the intersection between learning, sense-making IBN, and mediation of the resolution of employment relationship problems. Pedagogy provides evidence of the value of reflective learning (Gibbs 1988; Kolb 1984), assumption checking (Argyris and Schon 1974, 1978, 1996), and critical reflective practice (Brookfield 1995, 2006). Critical reflective learning overlaid with sense-making applied to Greenwood's findings suggests workplace conflict management can be a collaborative social learning process. Weick and Sutcliffe argued that when there was ambiguity, people under stress might act as individuals in crisis rather than collaboratively during decision making. They uncovered "that talk was necessary" and said, "With communication a complex system becomes more understandable (you learn some missing pieces that make sense of your experience) and more linear, predictable and controllable" (Weick and Sutcliffe 2001: 142–143).

Access to a confidential sense-making conversation is an important early aspect of the ERP resolution process because "there might be an association between managing ERP alone and being unable to make sense of, or identify, the core issues and appropriate processes to implement resolution" (Greenwood 2016: 224). Empowerment emerges from processes of collaborative sense-making over adversarial fault-finding, as well as self-determination as the parties retain decision making about process. This model allows ongoing dialogue with others to share retrospective stories, explore the problems, consider alternative ways of making sense of stories, and decide collaboratively on future actions and agreed enactments. The approach to a sense-making conversation and learning has the potential to strengthen trust in the psychological contract.

Collaborative, Interest-Based Negotiations

Embedding IBN simply means training and developing joint problem-solving IBN or integrative negotiation CCM in the workplace. Preliminary sense-making conversation with a neutral listener should precede IBN negotiation between the parties to the problem. Taking a problem-solving approach intersects with requirements for "good faith behavior in all aspects of the employment relationship" as stipulated by ERA 2000. Preparing for a negotiation after reflecting on the elements of sense-making is a process that empowers better understanding of self and others' explanations. It is a way of building negotiation skills by reflective learning and giving voice to the problems. The CCM process involves preliminary, confidential sense-making conversations with a neutral "other," followed by IBN with the parties to the problem, either with or without a support person.

Transformative Mediation

According to mediators, transforming conflict requires ongoing reflection and early engagement in recognition and acknowledgment of the conflict or problem from various points of view. Problems and complaints can be resolved early by taking a reflective learning approach and, therefore, "early coaching in recognition, acknowledgment, listening and reframing supports ERP resolution" (Greenwood 2016: 229). Likewise, Bush and Folger (1994, 2004, 2005) advocated the transformative model of mediation as an opportunity for learning by reflecting on dialogue and recognizing changes in communication and acknowledging the human capacity for reconstruction—empowering parties to change their conflict behavior themselves. This focus on empowerment and self-determination is similar to the process understood by Mezirow (1994) as "transformative learning."

The conflict management literature suggests that narrative and transformative mediation are successful approaches to resolve ERPs and retain relationships. Transformative mediation (Bush and Folger 2004, 2005) was successful in the US Postal Services' REDRESS program, where bullying was one of the issues being addressed. Amsler (2014) concluded that transformative mediation improved the disputants' "conflict management skills," suggesting that Bush and Folgers' (2004) model of transformative mediation mirrored transformative learning. Narrative mediation (Winslade and Monk 2008) encapsulates the skills of storytelling, listening, paraphrasing, mutualizing, reframing, and reflective perspective checking. Reflecting on feelings and anger and questioning assumptions suggests that an approach that encapsulates Mezirow's (1994) theory of transformative learning through disorienting dilemma could inform the processes for ERP resolution. Both transformative mediation and narrative mediation are part of facilitated, collaborative sense-making—and both require minimal intervention on the part of the mediator. If transformative mediation was provided by people who were both trained educators and mediators, it is possible that this would build the bridge needed to engage educators in early resolution if parties have been unable to negotiate satisfactory outcomes. In that respect, ERPs are not static events; they are ongoing processes of interpersonal sense-making, and the provision of transformative mediation would reinforce the concept that conflict is an opportunity for learning.

In the New Zealand context, panels of mobile mediators could be appointed and funded by the state's mediation service. The mediation process could be provided to any stakeholder relationship within an organization experiencing conflict or employment problems. Responsibility for provision would fall with state-funded providers, although organizations would be free to privately fund external private providers, with community organizations also engaging in provision. These confidential, without-prejudice transformative mediations would be considered early intervention efforts for parties to confidentially resolve problems themselves, without the intervention of lawyers or insurers. A panel of transformative mediators would help to fill the gap in ERP resolution and prevent vexatious complaints because stakeholders would have a voice early in the trajectory of an ERP.

As mentioned above, past legislatures aimed to direct employers and employees to resolve problems collaboratively, close to the workplace, in good faith, and to build mutual trust (Wilson 2000). There was an implicit message in the codification of good faith to strengthen the psychological contract by directing parties to the employment relationship to communicate openly. However, the association between good faith and ERP resolution was not immediately clear to institutional stakeholders in 2000, and, given the findings in our research, it appears that ERPs have been managed in a void, within organizations (Greenwood 2016; Rasmussen and Greenwood 2014). Attention to early resolution of ERPs through these informal, transformative processes bridges the intersection between workplace conflict resolution and institutional intervention reflecting the intentions of ERA 2000 by creating explicit processes for early conflict resolution.

CONCLUSION

This chapter presents a paradox whereby public-funded conflict resolution services have coped with a rising tide of complaints and cases, and it also highlights institutional weaknesses and how workplace conflict escalates with exit settlements dominating the outcomes. Escalation is infused with legalistic positional thinking. An adversarial approach to advocacy can be directly linked to a fundamental shift in the employment relations context toward a dominance of individualized employment relationships. The prevalence of legal approaches and "access to justice" problems falls short of the objectives of ERA 2000. While attempts to enhance access to institutional conflict resolution processes have gained movement, a legalistic, institutionalized approach still dominates state provision. Institutional conflict resolution must also deal with escalations of workplace disputes and an increase in formal disputes. This is a result of organizations failing to bridge the gap between internal complaint handling and external adversarial legal advocacy, meaning that exit settlements overshadow early resolution of ERPs.

While sense-making has been applied in organizational and communication theory and practice, the construct is yet to be explicitly applied to conflict resolution processes. Our research advocates the sense-making process and applying it to ERP management. Based on the original elements of sense-making, we suggest an enhanced E-SIRI-COPE framework that provides applied reflective learning. This reframing of ERPs as collaborative reflective learning allows us to present a CCM model at the intersection of institutional and ADR workplace conflict management.

The CCM model encourages employers and employees to engage in confidential, collaborative sense-making conversations and apply IBN and transformative mediation practices to facilitate early intervention. This early intervention is in line with the aims of ERA 2000 of building "relational trust through good faith behavior" and parties resolving employment problems early, close to the source of the conflict, in the workplace. The CCM model focuses not only on resolving the current issues but also aims to create a culture of conflict resolution that builds capacity for, and a culture of, early conflict resolution, thereby empowering stakeholders within organizations to embed collaborative sense-making conversations in day-to-day conflict interactions.

REFERENCES

Amsler, L.B. 2014. "Using Mediation to Manage Conflict at the United States Postal Service." In *The Oxford Handbook of Conflict Management in Organizations*, edited by W.K. Roche, P. Teague, and A.J.S. Colvin. Oxford: Oxford University Press, pp. 279–296. doi: 10.1093/oxfordhb/9780199653676.013.0014

Anderson, D., and R. Tipples. 2014. "Are Vulnerable Workers Really Protected in New Zealand?" *New Zealand Journal of Employment Relations* 39 (1): 52–67.

Anderson, G. 1988. "The Origins and Development of the Personal Grievance Jurisdiction in New Zealand." *New Zealand Journal of Industrial Relations* 13 (3): 257–275.

Anderson, G. 1997. "Interpreting the Employment Contracts Act: Are the Courts Undermining the Act?" *California Western International Law Journal* 28 (1): 117–143.

Anderson, G. 2022. "Employment Protection in New Zealand: 49 Years of Personal Grievance Law." *King's Law Journal* 33 (2): 278–297. doi: 10.1080/09615768.2022.2095695

Anderson, G., and L. Kenner. 2019. "Enhancing the Effectiveness of Minimum Employment Standards in New Zealand." *Economic and Labour Relations Review* 30 (3): 345–365. doi: 10.1177/1035304619862699.

Argyris, C., and D.A. Schon. 1974. *Theory in Practice: Increasing Professional Effectiveness*. San Francisco: Jossey-Bass.

Argyris, C., and D.A. Schon. 1978. *Organizational Learning: A Theory of Action Perspective*. Reading: Addison-Wesley.

Argyris, C., and D.A. Schon. 1996. *Organizational Learning II: Theory, Method and Practice*. Reading: Addison-Wesley.

Armitage, C., and R. Dunbar. 1993. "Labour Market Adjustment Under the Employment Contracts Act." *New Zealand Journal of Industrial Relations* 18 (1): 94–112. doi: 10.26686/nzjir.v18i1.3844

Aromaa, E., P. Eriksson, and T. Montonen. 2020. "Show It with Feeling: Performed Emotions in Critical Sensemaking." *International Journal of Entrepreneurship and Innovation Management* 24 (4–5): 266. doi: 10.1504/IJEIM.2020.108256

Arthur, R. 2018. "Barriers to Participation." *Law Talk* 923: 75–76.

Avgar, A.C., J.R. Lamare, D.B. Lipsky, and A. Gupta. 2013. "Unions and ADR: The Relationship Between Labor Unions and Workplace Dispute in US Corporations." *Ohio State Journal on Dispute Resolution* 28 (1): 63–106.

Bakhtin, M.M. 1981. *The Dialogical Imagination: Four Essays by M.M. Bakhtin*, edited by M. Holquist. Austin: University of Texas Press.

Bingham, L.B. 2004. "Employment Dispute Resolution: The Case for Mediation." *Conflict Resolution Quarterly* 22 (1/2): 145–174. doi: 10.1002/crq.96

Bingham, L.B., and D.W. Pitts. 2002. "Highlights of Mediation at Work: Studies of the National REDRESS Evaluation Project." *Negotiation Journal* 18 (2): 135–146.

Blumenfeld, S., and N. Donnelly. 2017. "Collective Bargaining Across Four Decades: Lessons from CLEW's Collective Agreement Database." In *Transforming Workplace Relations in New Zealand 1976–2016*, edited by G. Anderson, with A. Geare, E. Rasmussen, and M. Wilson, pp. 107–128. Wellington: Victoria University Press.

Boyd, S., A. Cleland, and A. Hoy. 2018. *National Survey of Employers 2016/17: Summary Findings*. Wellington: MBIE.

Brookfield, S.D. 1995. *Becoming a Critically Reflective Teacher*. San Francisco: Jossey-Bass.

Brookfield, S.D. 2006. "Authenticity and Power." *New Directions for Adult & Continuing Education* 11: 5–16.

Budd, J.W., and A.J.S. Colvin. 2014. "The Goals and Assumptions of Conflict Management in Organisations." In *The Oxford Handbook of Conflict Management in Organizations*, edited by W.K. Roche, P. Teague, and A.J.S. Colvin, pp. 12–30. Oxford: Oxford University Press. doi: 10.1093/oxfordhb/9780199653676.013.0001

Budd, J.W., D. Pohler, and H. Huang. 2022. "Making Sense of (Mis)matched Frames of Reference: A Dynamic Cognitive Theory of (In)stability in HR Practices." *Industrial Relations* 61 (3): 268–289.

Burton, B. 2010. "Employment Relations 2000–2008: An Employer View." In *Employment Relationships: Workers, Unions and Employers in New Zealand*, edited by E. Rasmussen, pp. 94–115. Auckland: Auckland University Press.

Bush, R.A.B., and J.P. Folger. 1994. *The Promise of Mediation: Responding to Conflict Through Empowerment and Recognition*. San Francisco: Jossey-Bass.

Bush, R.A.B., and J.P. Folger. 2004. *The Promise of Mediation: The Transformative Approach to Conflict*. San Francisco: Jossey-Bass.

Bush, R.A.B., and J.P. Folger. 2005. *The Promise of Mediation: Responding to Conflict Through Employment and Recognition*, 2nd ed. San Francisco: Jossey-Bass.

Colvin, A.J.S. 2012. "American Workplace Dispute Resolution in the Individual Rights Era." *International Journal of Human Resource Management* 23 (3): 459–475.

Corneleissen, J.P. 2012. "Sensemaking Under Pressure: The Influence of Professional Roles and Social Accountability on the Creation of Sense." *Organization Science* 23,(1: 188−137.

Crawford, A., R. Harbridge, and P. Walsh. 2000. "Unions and Union Membership in New Zealand: Annual Review for 1997." *New Zealand Journal of Industrial Relations* 25 (3): 291–302.

Cutcher-Gershenfeld, J., and T.A. Kochan. 2004. "Taking Stock: Collective Bargaining at the Turn of the Century." *Industrial and Labour Relations Review* 58 (1): 3–26.

De Dreu, C.K.W., and L.T. Weingart. 2003. "Task Versus Relationship Conflict, Team Performance, and Team Member Satisfaction: A Meta-Analysis." *Journal of Applied Psychology* 88 (4): 741–749. doi: 10.1037/0021-9010.88.4.741

Deeks, J., and E. Rasmussen. 2002. *Employment Relations in New Zealand*. Auckland: Pearson.

Festinger, L. 1957. *A Theory of Cognitive Dissonance*. Stanford: Stanford University Press.

Fisher, R., W. Ury, and B. Patton. 1991. *Getting to Yes: Negotiating an Agreement Without Giving In*, 2nd ed. London: Random House.

Foster, B., E. Rasmussen, and D. Coetzee. 2013. "Ideology Versus Reality: New Zealand Employer Attitudes to Legislative Change of Employment Relations." *New Zealand Journal of Employment Relations* 37 (3): 50–64.

Gibbs, G. 1998. *Learning by Doing*. London: Further Education Unit.

Greenwood, G. 2016. "*Transforming Employment Relationships? Making Sense of Conflict Management in the Workplace*." PhD thesis, Auckland University of Technology, Auckland.

Greenwood, G., and J.M. Haar. 2017. "Understanding the Effects of Intra-Group Conflict: A Test of Moderation and Mediation." *New Zealand Journal of Employment Relations* 43 (1): 14–35.

Greenwood, G., and E. Rasmussen. 2016. "Employment Relationship Resolution: A Gap Between Objectives and Implementation." *New Zealand Journal of Employment Relations* 41 (3): 76–90.

Guetzkow, H., and J. Gyr. 1954. "An Analysis of Conflict in Decision-Making Groups." *Human Relations* 7 (3): 367–382.

Harbridge, R., ed. 1993. *Employment Contracts: New Zealand Experiences*. Wellington: Victoria University Press.

Helms Mills, J. 2003. *Making Sense of Organizational Change*. New York: Routledge.

Hunter, L.W., and R.B. McKersie. 1992. "Can 'Mutual Gains' Training Change Labor–Management Relationships?" *Negotiation Journal* 8 (4): 319–330.

Inglis, C. 2019. "Barriers to Participation in the Employment Institutions." *Law Talk* 933: 24–25.

Jehn, K.A. 1994. "Enhancing Effectiveness: An Investigation of Advantages and Disadvantages of Value-Based Intragroup Conflict." *International Journal of Conflict Management* 5 (3): 223–238.

Jehn, K.A. 1995. "A Multimethod Examination of the Benefits and Detriments of Intragroup Conflict." *Administrative Science Quarterly* 40 (2): 256–282.

Jehn, K.A., and E.A. Mannix. 2001. "The Dynamic Nature of Conflict: A Longitudinal Study of Intragroup Conflict and Group Performance." *Academy of Management Journal* 44 (2): 238–251.

Jehn, K.A., G.B. Northcraft, and M.A. Neale. 1999. "Why Differences Make a Difference: A Field Study of Diversity, Conflict and Performance in Workgroups." *Administrative Science Quarterly* 44 (4): 741–763.

Kochan, T.A. 1974. "A Theory of Multilateral Collective Bargaining in City Governments." *Industrial & Labour Relations Review* 27 (4): 525–542.

Kolb, D. 1984. *Experimental Learning: Experience as the Source of Learning and Development*. Hoboken: Prentice Hall.

Kotter, J.P. 1973. "The Psychological Contract: Managing the Joining-Up Process." *California Management Review* 15 (3): 91–99.

Lipsky, D.B., and A.C. Avgar. 2010. "The Conflict over Conflict Management." *Dispute Resolution Journal* 65 (2/3): 11–43.

Lipsky, D.B., and R.L. Seeber 2003. "The Social Contract and Dispute Management: The Transformation of the Social Contract and Dispute Management in the US Workplace and the Emergence of New Strategies of Dispute Management." *International Employment Relations Review* 9 (2): 87–109.

Mayer, R.E. 2004. "Should There Be a Three-Strikes Rule Against Pure Discovery Learning?" *American Psychologist* 59 (1): 14–19.

McAndrew, I. 2010. "The Employment Institutions." In *Employment Relationships: Workers, Unions and Employers in New Zealand*, edited by E. Rasmussen, pp. 74–93. Auckland: Auckland University Press.

McAndrew, I., A. Geare, and F. Edgar. 2017. "The Changing Landscape of Workplace Relations." In *Transforming Workplace Relations in New Zealand 1976–2016*, edited by I.G. Anderson, pp. 23–43. Wellington: Victoria University Press.

McAndrew, I., J. Morton, and A. Geare. 2004. "The Employment Institutions." In *Employment Relationships: New Zealand's Employment Relations Act*, edited by E. Rasmussen, pp. 98–118. Auckland: Auckland University Press.

Mezirow, J. 1994. "Understanding Transformation Theory." *Adult Education Quarterly* 44 (4): 222–232.

Miller, D., and F.M. Jablin. 1991. "Information Seeking During Organizational Entry: Influences, Tactics, and a Model of the Process." *Academy of Management Review* 16 (1): 92–120.

Moore, C.M. 2003. *The Mediation Process: Practical Strategies for Resolving Conflict*, 3rd ed. San Francisco: Jossey-Bass.

Nielson, M. 2022. "Fair Pay Agreements to Become Law After Heated, Marathon Debate Marking Shift in Employment Relations." *NZ Herald*, October 26: A1.

Nigam, A., and W. Ocasio. 2010. "Event Attention, Environmental Sensemaking, and Change in Institutional Logics: An Inductive Analysis of the Effects of Public Attention to Clinton's Health Care Reform Initiative." *Organization Science* 21 (4): 823–841.

Olson-Buchanan, J., and W.R. Boswell. 2008. "Organizational Dispute Resolution Systems." In *The Psychology of Conflict and Conflict Management in Organizations*, edited by C.K.W. De Dreu and M.J. Gelfand, pp. 321–352. New York: Erlbaum.

Pondy, L.R. 1967. "Organizational Conflict: Concepts and Models." *Administrative Science Quarterly* 12 (2): 296–320.

Rasmussen, E., and D. Anderson. 2022. "The Changing Face of Public Dispute Resolution in New Zealand." Report. Auckland University of Technology.

Rasmussen, E., M. Bray, and A. Stewart. 2019. "What Is Distinctive About New Zealand's Employment Relations Act 2000?" *Labour & Industry* 29 (1): 52–73.

Rasmussen, E., B. Foster, and D. Farr. 2016. "The Battle Over Employer-Determined Flexibility: Attitudes Amongst New Zealand Employers." *Employee Relations* 38 (6): 1–23.

Rasmussen, E., and G. Greenwood. 2014. "Conflict and Dispute Resolution in New Zealand." In *Oxford Handbook of Conflict Management*, edited by W.K. Roche, P. Teague, and A.J.S. Colvin, pp. 449–474. Oxford: Oxford University Press.

Rasmussen, E., F. Lamm, and J. Molineaux. 2022. *Employment Relations in Aotearoa New Zealand: An Introduction*. Auckland: ER Publishing.

Reardon, K. 2005. *Becoming a Skilled Negotiator*. Hoboken: John Wiley & Sons.

Robinson, S.L. 1996. "Trust and Breach of the Psychological Contract." *Administrative Science Quarterly* 41 (4): 574–599.

Roche, W.K., P. Teague, and A.J.S. Colvin, eds. 2014. *Oxford Handbook of Conflict Management.* Oxford: Oxford University Press.
Rousseau, D.M., and S. Tijoriwala. 1998. "Assessing Psychological Contracts: Issues, Alternatives and Measures." *Journal of Organizational Behavior* 19 (10): 679–696.
Sandberg, J., and H. Tsoukas. 2015. "Making Sense of the Sensemaking Perspective: Its Constituents, Limitations, and Opportunities for Further Development." *Journal of Organizational Behavior* 36 (1): 6–32.
Saundry, R., P. Latreille, and I. Ashman. 2016. *Reframing Resolution: Innovation and Change in the Management of Workplace Conflict.* Basingstoke: Palgrave Macmillan.
Schmidt, S.M., and T.A. Kochan. 1972. "Conflict: Toward Conceptual Clarity." *Administrative Science Quarterly* 17 (3): 359–370.
Simons, T.L., and R.S. Peterson. 2000. "Task Conflict and Relationship Conflict in Top Management Teams: The Pivotal Role of Intragroup Trust." *Journal of Applied Psychology* 85 (1): 102–111.
Thurlow, C. 2007. "Fabricating Youth: New-Media Discourse and the Technologization of Young People." In *Language in the Media: Representations, Identities, Ideologies*, edited by S. Johnson and A. Ensslin, pp. 213–233. London: Bloomsbury Academic.
Tipples, R. 1996. "Contracting: The Key to Employment Relations." *International Employment Relations Review* 2 (2): 19–41.
Thomas, K.W. 1992. "Conflict and Conflict Management: Reflections and Update." *Journal of Organizational Behavior* 13 (3): 265–274.
Ury, W., J. Brett, and S. Goldberg. 1989. *Getting Disputes Resolved: Designing Systems to Cut the Cost of Conflict.* San Francisco: Jossey-Bass.
Van de Vliert, E., and C.K.W. De Dreu. 1994. "Optimizing Performance by Conflict Stimulation." *International Journal of Conflict Management* 5 (3): 211–222.
Volkema, R.J., K. Farquhar, and T.J. Bergman. 1996. "Third-Party Sensemaking in Interpersonal Conflicts at Work: A Theoretical Framework." *Human Relations* 49 (11): 1437–1454.
Walton, R.E., J.E. Cutcher-Gershenfeld, and R.B. McKersie. 1994. *Strategic Negotiations: A Theory of Change in Labor–Management Relations.* Boston: Harvard Business Review Press.
Walton, R.E., J.E. Cutcher-Gershenfeld, and R.B. McKersie. 2000. *Strategic Negotiations: A Theory of Change in Labor–Management Relations*, 2nd ed. Ithaca: Cornell University Press.
Walton, R.E., and R.B. McKersie. 1965. *A Behavioral Theory of Labor Negotiations.* New York: McGraw Hill.
Weber, K., and M.A. Glynn. 2006. "Making Sense with Institutions: Context, Thought and Action in Karl Weick's Theory." *Organization Studies* 27 (11): 1639–1660.
Weick, K.E. 1979. *The Social Psychology of Organizing*, 2nd ed. New York: McGraw Hill.
Weick, K.E. 1988. "Enacted Sensemaking in Crisis Situations." *Journal of Management Studies* 25 (4): 305–317.
Weick, K.E. 1989. "Theory Construction as Disciplined Imagination." *Academy of Management Review* 14 (4): 516–531.
Weick, K.E. 1993. "The Collapse of Sensemaking in Organizations: The Mann Gulch Disaster." *Administrative Science Quarterly* 38 (4): 628–652.
Weick, K.E. 1995. *Sensemaking in Organizations.* Thousand Oaks: Sage.
Weick, K.E. 2001. *Making Sense of the Organization.* New York: Blackwell.
Weick, K.E. 2009. *Making Sense of the Organization (Volume 2): The Impermanent Organization.* New York: John Wiley & Sons.
Weick, K.E 2010. "Reflections on Enacted Sensemaking in the Bhopal Disaster." *Journal of Management Studies* 47 (3): 537–550.

Weick, K.E. 2012. "Organized Sensemaking: A Commentary on Processes of Interpretive Work." *Human Relations* 65 (1): 141–153.

Weick, K.E., and K.M. Sutcliffe. 2001. *Managing the Unexpected, Volume 9*. San Francisco: Jossey-Bass.

Weick, K.E., K.M. Sutcliffe, and D. Obstfeld. 2005. "Organising and the Process of Sensemaking." *Organization Science* 16 (4): 409–421.

Wellin, M. 2007. *Managing the Psychological Contract: Using the Personal Deal to Increase Business Performance*. London: Routledge.

Williamson, D., and E. Rasmussen. 2020. "The Big Bang: The Birth of Human Resource Management in the New Zealand Hotel Sector." *Journal of Management History* 16 (1): 99–115.

Wilson, M. 2000. Speech in Parliament on the Third Reading of the Employment Relations Act, August 15, 586 NZPD 940.

Wilson, M. 2004. "The Employment Relations Act: A Framework for a Fairer Way." In *Employment Relationships: New Zealand's Employment Relations Act*, edited by E. Rasmussen, pp. 9–20. Auckland: Auckland University Press.

Wilson, M. 2017. "The Politics of Workplace Reform: 40 Years of Change." In *Transforming Workplace Relations in New Zealand 1976–2016*, edited by G. Anderson, pp. 44–59. Wellington: Victoria University Press.

Wilson, M. 2021. *Activism, Feminism, Politics and Parliament*. Wellington: Bridget Williams Books.

Winslade, J., and G. Monk. 2008. *Practicing Narrative Mediation: Loosening the Grip of Conflict*. San Francisco: Jossey-Bass.

CHAPTER 5

Understanding Workplace Conflict and Its Management in the Context of COVID-19

Julian Teicher
Central Queensland University

Bernadine Van Gramberg
Federation University

Greg J. Bamber
Monash University

ABSTRACT

Arguably, the COVID-19 pandemic was responsible for accelerating and bringing to the fore a range of emerging (largely individual) disputes between workers and their employers over issues such as remote working, electronic surveillance, blurring of work/family boundaries, worker resignations, and health and safety. This has been a global phenomenon that has been accompanied by an unusual intrusion into workplaces by governments seeking public health solutions to curb the pandemic but at the same time regulating employment arrangements. The pandemic thus offers a rare opportunity to explore conflict through the viewpoints of those most affected by the changes. We examine the changing pattern of workplace conflict and its management since the onset of COVID-19 in a contextually sensitive manner by adopting neopluralism as an overarching frame of reference, supplemented by using unitarism and pluralism as lenses through which to consider conflict and its management. We use the concepts of agonism and antagonism to provide insights into phenomena such as the Great Resignation. In considering the changing contours of workplace conflict, we posit that the way in which conflict is perceived is an important prerequisite to understanding how it is manifested and how it is likely to be managed. This is especially important for employers and workers and their representatives as we consider the post-pandemic future of work in an age of remote working and health issues (along with pervasive use of artificial intelligence).

COVID, WORK, AND CONFLICT: INTERNATIONAL PERSPECTIVES

In spite of some media commentary, we argue that COVID-19 did not cause novel changes in the nature of work and work practices but has accelerated existing trends and also facilitated work intensification among some categories of workers (e.g., Aloisi and De Stefano 2022). Consequently, some recent conflicts are best characterized as a "straw that broke the camel's back" by adding to underlying currents of discontent in workplaces in many countries. There was, however, a novel element to COVID-19 disputes because government decisions or the manner of their implementation by employers often precipitated these conflicts. Various forms of remote working—especially working from home (WFH) are examples that were enabled by developments in information and communications technology and were initiated by governments in many countries mandating vaccinations, social distancing, and mask wearing, along with who could or must or could not work onsite.

Compared with in Europe, remote working in the United States was relatively rare before the pandemic, but survey evidence consistently demonstrates increasing demand for WFH, particularly among those who had not had this option previously. According to Parker, Horowitz, and Minkin (2020):

> Now, 71% of those workers are doing their job from home all or most of the time. And more than half say, given a choice, they would want to keep working from home even after the pandemic.

While WFH has been welcomed by many, there were challenges, including the following:
- Blurring of work–home boundaries, with the potential to give rise to a range of conflicts (Chan et al. 2023)
- Increased surveillance arising from employers' "perceived lack of control of those employees who were out of sight" (Kniffin et al. 2022: 8)
- Virtual team-working, which lacks communication richness and can lead to misunderstandings, conflict, and coordination problems
- Workplace health and safety challenges when working remotely

Discussion of the pandemic emphasizes the "Great Resignation," but that covert and unorganized response is only one of the categories of conflicts arising from the responses of employees, employers, and governments to COVID-19. Somewhat neglected are the consequences for the numerous vulnerable workers who have been unable to work from home.

The dichotomy between WFH workers and those required to attend workplaces (sometimes called essential or key workers) obscures another division, between behind-the-scenes and frontline workers "who were required to continue working in person, facing overwhelming complexities and putting their lives in danger" (Aloisi and De Stefano 2022: 292). Typically, this was a distinction drawn between those serving the public in situations as diverse as retail, education, and healthcare, compared with workers who were only indirectly involved in service delivery.

For workers who were required to attend their workplaces, the challenges were diverse. The literature pays considerable attention to the rise of workplace bullying and violence inflicted on health workers. Workplace bullying of nurses increased dramatically around the world during the pandemic (Somani et al. 2022: 48). But bullying has been rampant in a range of other customer-facing roles, including education, public transport, and retail.

The health risks from exposure to COVID-19 and the associated conflicts have received less attention in the literature than other risks. One illustration that risk and management responses have led to conflicts was a walkout of 4,800 nonunionized poultry workers led by Arkansas-based Venceremos (Paschal and Sanchez-Smith 2020). The strike was precipitated by management changing shift times, effectively preventing social distancing as workers passed each other in narrow hallways. The action was preceded by "speed ups" on the line and management failures in relation to minimizing the spread of COVID-19. Amazon, a company with a history of opposing unions, faced unprecedented demand resulting from the pandemic. This led to 400 Amazon tech workers across the United States staging an informal strike by calling in sick in protest against their treatment, including the termination of six workers who called for better safety precautions (Douglas 2020; Dzieza 2020). Similarly, health workers in Hong Kong organized and called a strike in protest of poor protections at work (Taylor and Chan 2022). In these examples, the distinguishing feature seems to be the presence or absence of a union in shaping the conflict manifestation.

This dichotomy between WFH and essential workers in countries as diverse as Italy, Spain, the United States, the United Kingdom, and Australia highlights stratification between income levels and occupations. The "place dependent" groups of workers include disproportionately large numbers of women, disadvantaged minorities, less-educated people, migrants, and minorities who operate on the fringes of labor markets (Aloisi and De Stefano 2022: 292). Many of those required to attend usual workplaces whatever the circumstances also face precarious work—for example, ride share and food delivery drivers.

In the United States, sectors most affected by social distancing protocols were bars, travel and transport, entertainment, personal services, and some retail and manufacturing (Kantamneni 2020). Such places disproportionately employ workers who are women, less-educated, migrants, and minorities (US Bureau of Labor Statistics 2020). Consequently, such people were more likely to suffer reduced hours or layoffs and unemployment as a result of social distancing requirements and lockdowns. Typically, they are also frontline workers, who are among the lowest paid and may not have adequate safety equipment, thereby exposing them to the "stress and anxiety of going to work, resulting in some workers staying home or quitting work" (Kantamneni 2020: 2).

Less attention has been given to another set of changes associated with the pandemic: the unemployment and rising inequality that affected millions worldwide. We particularly emphasize the growth of insecure work in various forms and not confined to the growth of the so-called platform economy. While this experience might not lead to immediate conflicts, it is likely that workers who were displaced but return to work have changed attitudes as a result of their experience with loss of income or employment (Kniffin et al. 2022).

The circumstances of precariously employed workers is even starker in developing economies and among former Eastern-bloc European countries. In India, there are at least five million domestic workers; in the early stages of the pandemic, they were subjected to greater restrictions on their freedom than normal (Saluja 2022), and there was a dramatic rise in the numbers of people who moved into self-employment (Abraham, Basole, and Kesar 2020). In Poland, it has been argued that government policies created opportunities for employers to intensify exploitation and increase the size of the precariat through wage and job cuts and moving employees to less-secure employment under threat of dismissal (Żuk and Żuk 2022). In addition, laws that restricted movement (among other things) limited the capacity for unionization or other forms of collective organization. There is also mounting evidence that some employers responded opportunistically to the situation created by COVID—for example, by dismissing workers they did not like or saw as redundant—by fostering work intensification and undermining worker rights. For two contrasting examples, see Myles-Baltzly et al. (2021) on the plight of female academics and Huang (2022) on the precarity and risks faced by Chinese food delivery drivers. Many of these conflicts may go largely unnoticed as a result of their individualized manifestations or remote locations. Such examples highlight that the pandemic provided an opportunity for some employers to intensify the exploitation of already disadvantaged workers.

As observed above, much attention has been given to conflicts arising from employer demands for workers to return to their usual workplaces as COVID-19 became more normalized or regulatory controls of onsite work were relaxed. In the United States, the "Great Resignation" saw many employees prioritizing job quality or leaving their jobs to enjoy more flexibility and other benefits of WFH:

> It's interesting to reflect on why there is more conflict between staff and organization. Many people's attitude [toward] work has shifted over the pandemic. For some, the pandemic has led to a change in priorities, putting their own needs or dreams first. For others, the way they perceive they've been treated during the pandemic has affected their view of their employer. Whether staff want to take a different career path or fight for hybrid working, some now feel in a stronger position to stand up for what they want, or they'll walk, prompting some economists to forecast the "great resignation." (Shields 2021)

However, the option of resigning is confined to a relatively privileged strata of workers, even in developed nations, where those workers have been able to take advantage of tight labor markets. According to Parker, Horowitz, and Minkin (2020), the opportunity for remote work in the United States varies by income level, with 76% of surveyed low-income workers being unable to work remotely and 61% being concerned about the risk of exposure to COVID-19 at work. For many workers, the requirement to attend work is not one that they can change directly unless they are willing to resign. It is unclear how many workers would have access to informal or formal dispute resolution procedures and would utilize these as an alternative to resigning when directed to return to their workplaces.

Work pressures for essential workers, particularly in healthcare, have given rise to conflicts at work—but whether and how they are resolved is rarely addressed in the literature. For example, in an Australian study of nearly 6,776 healthcare workers across a range of occupations, the focus was on "challenges," including increased workloads and work–life imbalances; following orders or caring for patients; unpredictability, disruption, and inconsistency at work; and the right to be safe at work. Characterizing this as "extreme work," the authors argue that this was a system already under stress before the pandemic "due to pressures for efficiency and performance." They continued:

> There are ... parallels between the experience of these frontline workers and those previously reported in other "essential services" such as food services where risk is high and control over the work environment is low (Willis et al. 2021: 10178).

There is also evidence of a new class of conflicts emerging in the wake of employer efforts to mandate a return to their usual work premises. These include issues of work–family balance and risks to health. Returning workers back to pre-pandemic workplaces should be done with care, given the variety of worker concerns. According to Shields (2021),

> [We] have seen an increase in team mediations. Some have been driven by specific pandemic-related issues, such as colleagues not respecting social distancing or safety protocols. Others are indirectly related, such as team behaviors on video calls.

Further illustrating how the pandemic has accelerated trends, there is abundant evidence that WFH employees are making extensive use of Web-based communication (WBC) tools to keep in touch with co-workers:

> For many who are working from home, online communication tools have become a vital part of the workday.... Roughly eight in ten adults who are working from home all or most of the time ... say they use video calling or online conferencing services like Zoom or WebEx to keep in touch with co-workers, with 59% saying they often use these types of services. Some 57% say they use instant messaging platforms such as Slack or Google Chat at least sometimes (43% use these often). (Mitchell 2022: 14)

Use of online communication and Web-based tools seems to be inversely related to age and positively associated with education level (Choi and DiNitto 2013). Less widely commented on is the growing use of online communication for workers to organize, to share their grievances, and, in some cases, to express them in physical spaces. Again, we see that COVID-19 has led to an acceleration of existing trends—in this case online collaboration and expression of conflict—but these trends do not necessarily find an organized or physical expression.

In cases of conflicts such as those arising from COVID-19, WBC enables "distributed discourse" and "accelerated pluralism." Distributed discourse refers to the way in which social medial may distribute the tools of discourse framing and accelerated pluralism to the way in which social media may lead to "mobilising a plurality of grievances into separate and/or consolidated social movements (Upchurch and Grassman 2016: 640). Social media conversation has also translated into participation in public protests (Gilbert 2021; Schermann and Rivera 2021) and also as a medium of protest. Workers in the United States have used Instagram and other platforms to try to hold employers accountable (Liu 2020). An international study found a continuing global upsurge in platform-based protests in 2020 "despite the restrictions in place in many countries to combat the coronavirus disease" and perhaps because of the increased demand for platform-based services in many countries (Bessa et al. 2022).

As explained above, the pandemic led to a wide range of overt and covert conflicts. Some of them arose from employers seeking a mandatory return to the office (Thorbecke 2021), with some journalists at Hearst filing unfair labor practice charges with the National Labor Relations Board. They alleged a failure to negotiate in good faith about return-to-office protocols. Some of these conflicts also arose from employer opportunism, as demonstrated by Australia's largest airline, Qantas, which used the guise of financial exigency to outsource its ground handling at ten airports and fire nearly 2,000 employees. Their union successfully challenged Qantas's decision, with Australia's Federal Court finding that the outsourcing was partly designed to remove the workers' collective bargaining rights (Khadem 2022).

In some cases, protests by workers over issues including lockdowns, payment of workers who were unable to work, workplace closures, and vaccine and mask mandates for workers became conflated with the activism of far-right groups, which seized the opportunity to recruit members. In Australia, there were widespread street protests including workers and others (MC 2021). Protesters against governments perceived erosion of their rights, and protests against employer vaccine and mask mandates also erupted across Europe, the United States, and Canada (BBC News 2021; Faiola 2021).

FRAMES OF REFERENCE RECONSIDERED

Fox's (1974) influential analysis of frames of reference provides concepts for examining employment relationships. Originating as a research paper for the UK Donovan Commission on Industrial Relations, Fox (1966) drew on the work of Thelen and Withall (1949: 159) in describing a frame of reference as when each person perceives and interprets events by means of a conceptual structure of generalizations or contexts, postulates about what is essential, assumptions as to what is valuable, attitudes about what is possible, and ideas about what will work effectively.

The frames of reference provide a set of interpretive assumptions about those who adopt a particular belief that is discerned by observation. For present purposes, the belief systems and their assumptions influence the emergence of workplace disputes and shape their subsequent trajectory. These beliefs can also influence the way in which the state regulates workplace conflict. In the US context, the state's role has been implicitly to create an enabling environment for enterprises to improve their performance (Budd and Bhave 2019). Others have noted that political parties actively engage with employer or employee organizations and their lobby groups because, in doing so, they may receive political support once in government (Swenson 1997).

Unitarism

Fox (1966, 1971, 1973, 1974) developed the distinction between unitarism and pluralism in organizations as a reflection of the reality of British industrial relations in the post-1945 period. The defining feature of the unitarist frame is the assumption that, in workplaces, managers and employees have the same goals and that those goals are aligned with corporate objectives. Fox analyzed the unitarist frame of reference as portraying an employing organization as having "one source of authority and one focus of loyalty" (1966: 3).

The hierarchy of the management structure in employing organizations symbolizes the power of managers to make decisions and set goals for the enterprise, which should be followed by those at lower levels in the hierarchy. Managers and government policy makers are drawn to a unitarist frame of reference partly because it serves to legitimize management decision-making power and helps them to achieve corporate goals. This focus on senior executives who determine the agenda and strategy for an organization is managerialist in orientation (Clark, Mabey, and Skinner 1998). The predisposition of employers toward unitarism reflects and reinforces management authority (Wright 1995).

The increasingly widespread adoption of the unitarist frame in human resource management (HRM) has been linked to the increasing prevalence of individualistic ideologies associated with neoliberalism (Ackers 2002; Noon 1992). By implication, there are only limited roles for unions and the state in such a setting. Unitarism does not contemplate an explicit role for the state beyond providing an enabling environment for "law and order" (Sycholt and Klerck 2000). There is no role for an intervening state to interfere with the employment relationship or its balance of power. Ironically, there is research that describes the ways in which governments internationally have intervened specifically to benefit unitarist employers (Cooper and Ellem 2008). This is best exemplified by industrial action that prompts legislative or judicial intervention either to restore or preserve the status quo. With the onset of COVID-19, the rapidity and extent of state interventions, even in societies that are characterized as neoliberal, highlight the need for a reconsideration of the unitarist frame of reference. While unitarism may aptly describe the lens employed by many managers, the nature and extent of state intervention in many cases negate the scope for unitarism.

Under unitarism, managers see unions as a source of conflict because they divide employee loyalty (Fox 1974) and as diverging from otherwise "good" management practice (Forster and Browne 1996). Managers generally see "political behavior" or overt conflict led by employees in work organizations as unacceptable resistance, which can threaten employer interests and should be eradicated (Badham and Buchanan 1996). Conflict therefore reflects a breakdown of authority relationships and organizational stability (Velasquez 1988). Given an assumption of the desirability of worker cooperation with management, the unitarist management literature, unsurprisingly, tends to downplay the realities of organizational power and politics.

In striving to achieve shared organizational goals, there is an assumption that harmony and cooperation will prevail between employees and their managers (Fox 1974; Thompson and McHugh 1995). It is assumed that manifestations of conflict in such a system would be abnormal and, consequently, that transgressors are considered aberrant. Fox (1966: 13) describes managers' view of transgressors as being illogical or even having a pathological social condition. This is not only because transgressors fail to obey management rules and decisions but also because, despite knowing the goals of an employing organization, they continue their transgressions.

Pluralism

The development of the pluralist frame of reference and the systems model of industrial relations (Dunlop 1958) reflected World War II and New Deal politics in the United States. Rather than envisaging enterprises as unitary structures, Fox saw pluralism as more realistic than the unitarist frame of reference. Pluralism recognizes that workplace actors form coalitions of individuals and groups who may have divergent interests. These coalitions collaborate in ways that enable each to pursue their different (individual and sectional) goals, while also working toward the goals of the employing organization. Thus, conflicting and shared interests coexist within organizations, and this is seen as part of the normal functioning of a democratic society.

Strikes (or lockouts) are the most visible mechanisms used by parties to impose costs on each other in attempts to secure desired outcomes. A collective form of action, a strikes may also require the participation and leadership of unions, in which case it is categorized as organized conflict. The outcome can variously be a return to work, negotiations and agreement, or one of a range of third-party forms of assisted dispute resolution. Scholars have sometimes used individualism and collectivism interchangeably with "unitarism" and "pluralism," therefore suggesting that "collectivism comes to be equated with trade unionism and individualism with non-unionism" (Storey and Bacon 1993: 670). Strikes have been so closely associated with collectivism that some see the study of industrial relations itself as *inextricably* linked to industrial conflict (Guest 1987).

Pluralism also challenged the unfettered terrain of managerial prerogative envisaged in the unitarist frame of reference by presenting managers as decision makers—but within a set of constraints, including those imposed by the views of various stakeholders such as employees, consumers, suppliers, governments, and regulatory agencies. Decisions made within a pluralist frame therefore reflect compromises—forged in a competitive environment in which enterprises had to be "managed" so that the complex web of tensions and conflicts did not threaten the viability of the collaborative arrangements.

From a pluralist perspective, conflict is portrayed as a normal and inevitable part of life. Pluralist accounts of organizational life acknowledge the pursuit of conflicting interests, the development of political behavior, the reality and ramifications of the imbalance of power (Pfeffer 1992), and the struggles about scarce resources (Kochan and Katz 1988). Pluralism and the associated rule-making procedures are designed to accommodate conflicting interests and resolve disputes between the parties (Poole 1981).

Importantly, pluralism assumes a neutral and mediating state, which provides and supports the mechanisms and institutions for collective dispute resolution. The state can act as the arbiter of disputes that cannot be resolved at the workplace, or state agencies (more often) act as the facilitator of a continual series of compromises between the parties (Clegg 1975). Because of their role in representing employees, Fox argued that unions play an important role in readjusting or balancing power in workplaces and providing a voice for employees. Provis (1996) suggests that unions also play a role in providing a group identity and creating social cohesion among their members, which allows them to argue more effectively with one voice.

Neopluralism

We observed earlier that unitarism and pluralism have been criticized for many reasons but particularly because they provide an account of the relations of management and workers in two distinct historical periods and also because of they neglect human agency. The development of the neopluralist frame was advanced as in part "retooling" the pluralist frame "for a very different employment world" (Ackers and Wilkinson 2008: 3). Ackers and Wilkinson argued that pluralism focuses on unions and collective bargaining institutions as the liberal-democratic "voice" alternative to both pro-business unitarism and anti-capitalist radicalism.

Also, in the 1960s, it was argued that strikes were seen as symptomatic of the wider problem of order in society, but in the third decade of the 21st century, there are fewer strikes and less unionism, and the problem of order has shifted to the linkage between employment and society. Hence, Ackers argued that neopluralism carries forward the "institutional spirit" of pluralism "to explore the empirical complexity of contemporary employment relationships around the world" (2021: 264). It is also about a fundamental shift in the English-speaking world from an industrial economy focused on full-time employment of white male manual workers to a post-industrial employment model that is more diverse in relation to gender, ethnicity, working hours, and employment types. It is also an era, at least until the onset of the pandemic, of increased global competition. Neopluralism, then, provides an opportunity to examine questions of power, conflict, and collective behavior in the "political socioeconomic context" (Ackers and Wilkinson 2008).

Another feature of neopluralism sets it apart: recognition that work and employment are inseparable from society (Ackers 2021), and it has been argued (Van Buren, Greenwood, Donaghey, and Reinecke 2021) that this feature gains increased salience in an era when *consumption* rather than *work* is central to the lives of many people. We thus view neopluralism as providing a framework for examining employment relations that is not limited to a specific historical period. In applying this frame, however, there is a need to consider the lenses employed by individual actors. It is in this context that unitarism and pluralism can provide insights into the attitudes, behaviors, and actions of workplace actors in and beyond the workplace. As observed above, unitarism guides much of the practice of HRM and, while unions may be in decline, pluralism can accurately characterize the interactions of employers and employees in many, typically larger, workplaces. The persistence of unitarist and pluralist lenses at work is evidenced by the vast and growing literature on employee voice (for a review, see Della Torre, Gritti, and Wilkinson 2022).

One of the troublesome issues in understanding workplace conflict and its expression in the third decade of the 21st century is that, while strike incidence has declined dramatically in most countries, new and diverse manifestations of conflict are appearing. And, especially among some younger workers, concerns about unacceptable management recourse to unitarist approaches are being met with withdrawal from the workplace (Liu-Lastres, Wen, and Huang 2023; Vyas 2022). Understanding this phenomenon may help explain the Great Resignation or perhaps even the widespread demands from workers to continue to work from home. Accordingly, we consider Budd and Bhave's (2019) reformulation of frames of reference in terms of neoliberal-egoist, unitarist, pluralist, and critical.

In the neoliberal-egoist frame, employers and employees are seen as rational individual agents pursuing goals based on self-interest. This explanation may be an oversimplification of an individual's desire to resign from their job or request WFH on a regular basis. Self-interest is one motivator but must be seen in a wider social and family-related context where individuals act according to motivators based on values, ethics, and loyalty. Additionally, workplaces themselves rely on a level of cooperation and shared interests between workers and managers. As Bray, Budd, and Macneil write, a "central tension within co-operation is the duality between mutuality and self-interest" (2020: 116). The concept of agonism, described by Mouffe (2013), depicts the ongoing struggle between protagonists, who have a core of shared interests but from time to time express divergent interests, creating conflict. She contrasts this with "antagonists," who share no common ground and can be considered mutual enemies.

Agonism has been applied to workplace relations, where such conflicts illuminate a more nuanced view of pluralism. Van Buren, Greenwood, Donaghey, and Reinecke say that "pluralism and agonism have implications for an organisation's willingness and capability to move beyond adversarial, antagonistic employment relations" (2021: 195). Also absent from Budd's notion of egoism is a recognition of the significant role of the state, an omission that looms larger in the wake of the large-scale state intervention in the pandemic, even in the United States.

MANAGING CONFLICT AND THE COVID-19 PANDEMIC

COVID-19 affected most employment sectors around the world, leading to a range of workplace conflicts and disputes, some of which overflowed into public protests as exemplified above. It is relevant to consider the nature of these conflicts and how they were resolved given the changes to employment and the economy since Fox (1974) outlined his frames of reference. Neopluralism (Ackers 2002) provided an analytical frame to examine work and employment in an era when neither a unitarist or pluralist frame was adequate to address the connections between work and society. It is associated with a stage in history marked by the implementation of neoliberal policies, decline in unionization, rise of the "gig" economy and its associated prevalence of precarious employment, outsourcing, offshoring, expansion of global supply chains, new technologies, and generally less-secure employment.

With the onset of COVID-19, there has been an upsurge of conflict, though much of it not of the traditional organized type. Many of the issues in dispute were novel—for example, arising from work–life conflict—and complex. During the pandemic, many employers tried to apply unitarist solutions, whether by work intensification or recourse to electronic surveillance of WFH (see, for example, Ball 2021). However, the pandemic demonstrated the limitations of unitarism and managerial control. This observation is underpinned by four features of the post-2019 world of work that have been at the root of a range of conflicts:

- Government-enforced lockdowns, curfews, and travel restrictions in many countries during the peak of the pandemic, which represented key interventions into labor markets, forcing some enterprises to close and others to introduce remote work and social distancing measures (Webster, Khorana, and Pastore 2022)
- The inability of employers to order their workers back to their workplaces (even after the lockdowns) as more workers prefer to work from home (Liu et al. 2020; Suder and Siibak 2022)
- The Great Resignation, as increasing numbers of workers re-evaluated their working lives (Serenko 2022)
- Labor shortages in areas most exposed to COVID-19, such as health and related services, aviation, education, tourism, and construction—where employers found it difficult to recruit and retain people (Veenema et al. 2022)

Despite the potential categories of workplace conflicts to be shared by workers across different industries and workplaces, often voiced through social media (Bessa et al. 2022), many of these conflicts were seen as private and individual. With low unionization rates, it could be argued that the unitarist frame of reference might be best used to envisage conflict resolution. According to a study of an application of the unitarist framework for analyzing conflict in a US enterprise (Kochan 1982), the management of conflict was concerned about winning employee conformity with organizational goals and decisions or by firing the transgressors. Managers would try to do this through a combination of ("hard") authoritarian repression and a resort to contractualism; or through the ("soft") engagement of employees' emotional commitment by promoting team and family metaphors (Legge 1995). Such managers might assume that these measures would induce a belief that, in a properly ordered world, managerial prerogatives could always be enforced against the few malcontents, by means of coercive power if necessary (Fox 1974: 249–250). As noted above, the unitarist view of conflict resolution (with its emphasis on communication and managerial prerogative) was significantly impeded in the pandemic, first by government interventions and second by mass resignations.

The pluralist frame of reference predicts that conflicts would be resolved by negotiations to reconcile differing interests with access to a formal, independent hearing if settlement cannot be achieved, leading to an overarching precedent (Hyman 1989). However, such avenues are not generally available to nonunion employees, who account for a majority of the workforce. The transition from collective to individual disputes, along with the implication that these conflicts will be categorized as private matters based on individual preferences (rather than on workplace norms, rules, or rights), is no doubt shaping how these conflicts are resolved.

In responding to these private conflicts, it is appropriate to consider what insights might arise from applying a neopluralist frame. Neopluralism, with its recognition of multiple interests and values, suggests a negotiation-based approach with the aim of achieving a mutually acceptable solution. Conceivably, this would involve an informal conversation focusing on the needs of the employee and the enterprise. Depending on individual cases, along with individuals' own abilities to put their case to an employer, outcomes will differ among employees, even those in similar circumstances. Whether this is seen as affording flexibility or unfairness will be a legacy of conflict resolution during the pandemic.

We can extend the neopluralist frame by considering how agonism (and, indeed, antagonism) might assist our understanding of how private conflicts are resolved. In agonism, like pluralism, there is a platform of shared values and goals underpinning the view of workplaces that tells us that the parties are motivated to remain in a working relationship and will strive to gain common ground in reaching a settlement. But agonism does not imply consensus. Rather, Mouffe (2013) explains that such settlements are typified by dissensus and that there will always be some level of disagreement between parties. This means that settlement is not final and not permanent. Instead, the parties agree to a level of (sometimes uncomfortable) acceptance of a particular outcome, which in time will lead to another conflict and another resolution. In this way, it can be seen that there are changing patterns of work, whether it be an agreement to work remotely for a greater number of days per week or something else.

CONCLUSIONS

Rather than discussing the Great Resignation, might it be more appropriate to refer to the "Great Adaptation"? The COVID-19 pandemic brought profound changes in the way we live, work, and interact with each other. Some have described it as the future of work, with greater numbers of workers performing their duties remotely and greater use of communication technologies (Bessa et al. 2022; International Labour Organization 2021). Although many describe other employment relations issues as international, to a much greater extent than with other issues, COVID-19 has had global implications, both in its manifestation and in its consequences. Its impact on conflict, however, has been twofold. First, the actions of governments and employers in responding to the pandemic have led to a variety of disputes. Second, changes in location and the nature of work (an acceleration of existing trends) have fostered other disputes—for example, in relation to work intensification or surveillance and in calls for an increase of employee voice in matters of where and when work should be done to better suit individual needs.

While COVID-19 has led to a proliferation of disputes, these have largely been individualized in their expression, with resignations being an obvious example. But resorting to social media to express grievances had become increasingly common; typically, this takes the form of shared individual conflicts rather than organized conflict. In this regard, at least initially, COVID-19 led to an acceleration of the trend to increased protest by platform-economy workers, sometimes in the form of demonstrations (Bessa et al. 2022).

A novel aspect of conflicts induced by COVID-19 has been public protests against government interventions or employer interpretations of those interventions; for example, seeking an end to mask or vaccination mandates. While those protests often had a collective element, many people participated individually as workers or as citizens expressing a political view. In some cases, right-wing groups led or infiltrated public protests to pursue wider agendas (Das and Ahmed 2022). Addressing these conflicts is beyond the scope of conventional dispute resolution systems. This indirectly highlights the relevance of the neopluralist frame. With time, these protests have dwindled—but employers are still left with the challenge of managing in changed workplaces and work arrangements.

In considering the issues raised above, neopluralism enables a fruitful consideration of the complex causes and consequences of the conflicts that have emerged. Mouffe's (2013) social science–derived concepts of agonism and antagonism help to provide further insights into the motivating factors for phenomena such as the Great

Resignation and the greater use of employee voice in social media. The pandemic has given the work–life interface an unprecedented prominence in employment relations, rather than it being regarded as a side issue. While some of the issues arising, such as risks of infection, can be partly addressed by individual employers, public policy has a major role in achieving enduring resolution—including by regulating flexible working arrangements.

Finally, the pandemic has thrown up a major puzzle for dispute resolution. With a proliferation of shared, individual disputes, what processes, if any, are being used for resolution and are those processes both efficient and just—or are similar disputes being determined on different terms and are the solutions enduring? Employers have a crucial role to play in answering such questions. They need to sustain complex and difficult dialogues with employees, particularly younger ones, who have shown that they can, and will, make decisions based on their own priorities and needs. It will be a dialogue in which the building of shared values and goals will be central to workplace stability as we move toward the future of work. For unions, COVID-19 created opportunities to demonstrate their value to workers and other sections of society, but it is unclear whether this will lead to increased membership. This uncertainty points to the important role of governments in ensuring that all employees have access to effective forms of employee voice, such as works councils and joint consultation, without which disputes cannot be resolved either fairly or efficiently (Van Gramberg, Teicher, Bamber, and Cooper 2020).

ACKNOWLEDGMENTS

We thank Brian Cooper, Peggy Currid, Ryan Lamare, Penny Sara, and LERA. We discussed this chapter at an Association of Industrial Relations Academics in Australia and New Zealand Conference; we are grateful to conference participants for their comments. We also acknowledge the Australian Research Council, which awarded us a grant (DP120103054). We would welcome any discussion: julian.teicher@gmail.com, bernadine.vangramberg@gmail.com, gregbamber@gmail.com.

REFERENCES

Abraham, Rosa, Amit Basole, and Surbhi Kesar. 2020. "Pandemic Effect: 9 Months On, More Younger Workers Remain Jobless." *India Spend*, Centre for Sustainable Employment.
Ackers, Peter. 2002. "Reframing Employment Relations: The Case for Neo-Pluralism." *Industrial Relations Journal* 33 (1): 2–19. doi: 10.1111/1468-2338.00216
Ackers, Peter. 2014. "Rethinking the Employment Relationship: A Neo-Pluralist Critique of British Industrial Relations Orthodoxy." *International Journal of Human Resources Management* 25 (18): 2608–2625. doi: 10.1080/09585192.2012.667429
Ackers, Peter. 2019. "Neo-Pluralism as a Research Approach in Contemporary Employment Relations and HRM: Complexity and Dialogue." In *Elgar Introduction to Theories of Human Resources and Employment Relations*, edited by Keith Townsend, Kenneth Caffekey, Aoife M. McDermott, and Tony Dundon, 34–52. Cheltenham: Edward Elgar.

Ackers, Peter. 2021. "Pluralisms? Social Philosophy, Social Science and Public Policy in Employment Relations and Human Resource Management." *Journal of Industrial Relations* 63 (2): 263–279.

Ackers, Peter, and Adrian Wilkinson. 2008. "Industrial Relations and the Social Sciences." In *The Sage Handbook of Industrial Relations*, edited by Paul Blyton, Jack Fiorito, Nicolas A. Bacon, and Edmund Heery, 89–109. London: Sage.

Aloisi, Antonio, and Valerio De Stefano. 2022. "Essential Jobs, Remote Work and Digital Surveillance: Addressing the COVID-19 Pandemic Panopticon." *International Labour Review* 161 (2): 289–314. doi: 10.1111/ilr.12219

Badham, Richard, and David Buchanan. 1996. "Power-Assisted Steering and the Micropolitics of Organizational Change: A Research Agenda." Paper presented at the Australian and New Zealand Academy of Management Conference, Wollongong, December.

Ball, Kirstie. 2021. "Electronic Monitoring and Surveillance in the Workplace." European Commission Joint Research Centre. https://tinyurl.com/2pjf7na8

Bamber, Greg. J., Fang Lee Cooke, Virginia Doellgast, and Chris F. Wright, eds. 2021. *International & Comparative Employment Relations: Global Crises & Institutional Responses*. 7th ed. London: Sage.

BBC News. 2021. "Covid: Huge Protests Across Europe over New Restrictions." https://tinyurl.com/yptyak2e

Bessa, Ioulia, Simon Joyce, Denis Neumann, Mark Stuart, Vera Trappmann, and Charles Umney. 2022. "A Global Analysis of Worker Protest in Digital Labour Platforms." ILO Working Paper 70. https://tinyurl.com/3hwwsufe

Bray, Mark, John W. Budd, and Johanna Macneil. 2020. "The Many Meanings of Co-operation in the Employment Relationship and Their Implications." *British Journal of Industrial Relations* 58 (1): 114–141. doi: 10.1111/bjir.12473

Budd, John W., and Devasheesh P. Bhave. 2019. "The Employment Relationship: Key Elements, Alternative Frames of Reference, and Implications for HRM." In *Sage Handbook of Human Resource Management*, 2nd ed., edited by Adrian Wilkinson, Nicolas Bacon, Scott Snell, and David Lepak, 41–64. London: Sage.

Budd, John W., Dionne Pohler, and Wei Huang. 2022. "Making Sense of (Mis)Matched Frames of Reference: A Dynamic Cognitive Theory of (In)Stability in HR Practices." *Industrial Relations: A Journal of Economy and Society* 61 (3): 268–289. doi: 10.1111/irel.12275

Chan, Xi Wen, Sudong Shang, Paula Brough, Adrian Wilkinson, and Chang-qin Lu. 2023. "Work, Life and COVID-19: A Rapid Review and Practical Recommendations for the Post-Pandemic Workplace." *Asia Pacific Journal of Human Resources* [early view]. doi: 10.1111/1744-7941.12355

Choi, Namkee G., and Diana M DiNitto. 2013. "The Digital Divide Among Low-Income Homebound Older Adults: Internet Use Patterns, eHealth Literacy, and Attitudes Toward Computer/Internet Use." *Journal of Medical Internet Research* 15 (5): e93. doi: 10.2196/jmir.2645

Clark, Timothy, Christopher Mabey, and Denise Skinner. 1998. "Experiencing HRM: The Importance of the Inside Story." In *Experiencing Human Resource Management*, edited by Christopher Mabey, Denise Skinner, and Timothy Clark. London: Sage. doi: 10.4135/9781446280263

Clegg, Hugh A. 1975. "Pluralism in Industrial Relations." *British Journal of Industrial Relations* 13 (3): 309–316. doi: 10.1111/j.1467-8543.1975.tb00613.x

Cooper, Rae, and Bradon Ellem. 2008. "The Neoliberal State, Trade Unions and Collective Bargaining in Australia." *British Journal of Industrial Relations* 46 (3): 532–554. doi: 10.1111/j.1467-8543.2008.00694.x

Das, Ronnie, and Wasim Ahmed. 2022. "Rethinking Fake News: Disinformation and Ideology During the Time of COVID-19 Global Pandemic." *IIM Kozhikode Society & Management Review* 11 (1): 146–159. doi: 10.1177/22779752211027382

Della Torre, Edoardo, Alessia Gritti, and Adrian Wilkinson. 2022. "Employee Voice: Meanings, Approaches, and Research Directions." In *Oxford Research Encyclopedia of Business and Management*, edited by Edoardo Della Torre, Alessia Gritti, and Adrian Wilkinson: Oxford University Press. doi: 10.1093/acrefore/9780190224851.013.326

Douglas, D. 2020. "Amazon's Mobile Workforce and Its Protest Movement in the United States During the COVID-19 Pandemic." MoLab Inventory of Mobilities and Socioeconomic Changes, Department of Anthropology of Economic Experimentation. Halle/Saale: Max Planck Institute for Social Anthropology.

Dzieza, Josh. 2020. "Amazon Tech Workers Are Calling Out Sick to Protest COVID-19 Response." The Verge. https://tinyurl.com/5n8hxedz

Dunlop, John T. 1958. *Industrial Relations Systems*. New York: Holt, Reinhart and Winston.

Faiola, Anthony. 2021. "Squeezed by Mandates and Restrictions, Europe's Anti-Vaxxers Rebel." *Washington Post,* November 22, 2021. https://tinyurl.com/e2nje7j4

Forster, John, and Michael Browne. 1996. *Principles of Strategic Management*. Melbourne: Macmillan.

Fox, Alan. 1966. "Industrial Sociology and Industrial Relations." Royal (Donovan) Commission on Trade Unions and Employers' Associations, Research Paper 3. London: HMSO.

Fox, Alan. 1971. *A Sociology of Work in Industry*. London: Collier-Macmillan.

Fox, Alan. 1973. "A Social Critique of Pluralist Ideology." In *Man and Organisation*, edited by John Child. London: Allen and Unwin.

Fox, Alan. 1974. *Beyond Contract: Work, Power and Trust Relations*. London: Faber.

Gilbert, E. 2021. "The Role of Social Media in Protests: Mobilising or Polarising?" 89 Initiative. https://tinyurl.com/5yyu9wzk

Guest, David E. 1987. "Human Resource Management and Industrial Relations." *Journal of Management Studies* 24 (5): 503–521. doi: 10.1111/j.1467-6486.1987.tb00460.x

Huang, Hui. 2022. "Riders on the Storm: Amplified Platform Precarity and the Impact of COVID-19 on Online Food-Delivery Drivers in China." *Journal of Contemporary China* 31 (135): 351–365. doi: 10.1080/10670564.2021.1966895

Hyman, Richard. 1989. *The Political Economy of Industrial Relations Theory and Practice in a Cold Climate*. London: Macmillan.

International Labour Organization. 2021. "How the COVID-19 Pandemic Is Changing Business: A Literature Review." Geneva: International Labour Organization. https://tinyurl.com/4yycx5kc

Kantamneni, Neeta. 2020. "The Impact of the COVID-19 Pandemic on Marginalized Populations in the United States: A Research Agenda." *Journal of Vocational Behavior* 119 (June): 103439. doi: 10.1016/j.jvb.2020.103439

Khadem, Nassim. 2022. "Court Rules Qantas Acted Illegally When It Outsourced Ground Crew During the Pandemic." ABC News. May 4. https://tinyurl.com/22xps8ku

Kniffin, Kevin M., Jayanth Narayanan, Frederik Anseel, John Antonakis, Susan P. Ashford, Arnold B. Bakker, Peter Bamberger, et al. 2021. "COVID-19 and the Workplace: Implications, Issues, and Insights for Future Research and Action." *American Psychologist* 76 (1): 63–77. doi: 10.1037/amp0000716

Kochan, Thomas, A. 1982. "A Review Symposium: A Reply by Professor Kochan." *Industrial Relations* 21 (1):115–122.
Kochan, Thomas, A., and Harry C. Katz. C. 1988. *Collective Bargaining and Industrial Relations*. Homewood: Irwin.
Legge, Karen. 1995 *Human Resource Management: Rhetorics and Realities*. Basingstoke: Macmillan.
Liu, Jennifer. 2020. "Glossier and the Rise of Workers Using Social Media to Hold Employers Accountable." CNBC. October 14, 2020. https://tinyurl.com/2zhzvwmx
Liu, Zihan, Drake Van Egdom, Rhona Flin, Christiane Spitzmueller, Omolola Adepoju, and Ramanan Krishnamoorti. 2020. "I Don't Want to Go Back: Examining the Return to Physical Workspaces During COVID-19." *Journal of Occupational & Environmental Medicine* 62 (11): 953–958. doi: 10.1097/JOM.0000000000002012
Liu-Lastres, Bingjie, Han Wen, and Wei-Jue Huang. 2023. "A Reflection on the Great Resignation in the Hospitality and Tourism Industry." *International Journal of Contemporary Hospitality Management* 35 (1): 235–249. doi: 10.1108/IJCHM-05-2022-0551
MC, Ali. 2021. "Australia's Far Right Gets COVID Anti-Lockdown Protest Booster." Al Jazeera. https://tinyurl.com/45zsk4n4
Mouffe, C. 2013. *Agonistics: Thinking the World Politically*. Chicago: Verso.
Myles-Baltzly, Colleen C., Helen K. Ho, Ivanna Richardson, Jennifer Greene-Rooks, Katharina A. Azim, Kathryn E. Frazier, Maggie Campbell-Obaid, Meike Eilert, and Stacey R. Lim. 2021. "Transformative Collaborations: How a Motherscholar Research Collective Survived and Thrived During COVID-19." *International Perspectives in Psychology* 10 (4): 225–242. doi: 10.1027/2157-3891/a000029
Noon, Michael. 1992. "HRM: A Map, Model or Theory?" In *Reassessing Human Resource Management*, edited by Paul Blyton and Peter Turnbull, 16-32. London: Sage
Parker, Kim, Juliana M. Horowitz, and Rachel Minkin. 2020. "How the Coronavirus Outbreak Has and Hasn't Changed the Way Americans Work." Pew Research Center. https://tinyurl.com/33k3e4c8
Paschal, Olivia, and Rachell Sanchez-Smith. 2020. "George's Poultry Workers Walk Out in Arkansas to Protest COVID-19 Conditions." Facing South. https://tinyurl.com/2566drve
Mitchell, Travis. 2022. "COVID-19 Pandemic Continues to Reshape Work in America." Pew Research Center's Social & Demographic Trends Project (blog). February 16, 2022. https://tinyurl.com/yckrs3rj
Pfeffer, Jeffrey. 1992. *Managing with Power: Politics and Influence in Organizations*. Boston: Harvard Business School Press.
Poole, Michael. 1981. *Theories of Trade Unionism*. London: Routledge & Kegan Paul.
Provis, Chris. 1996. "Unitarism, Pluralism, Interests and Values." *British Journal of Industrial Relations* 34 (4): 473–495. doi: 10.1111/j.1467-8543.1996.tb00486.x
Saluja, Romita. 2022. "How COVID-19 Worsened Hardships of India's Domestic Workers." The Wire. https://tinyurl.com/pembcjya
Scherman, Andrés, and Sebastian Rivera. 2021. "Social Media Use and Pathways to Protest Participation: Evidence from the 2019 Chilean Social Outburst." *Social Media + Society* 7 (4). doi: 10.1177/20563051211059704
Serenko, Alexander. 2022. "The Great Resignation: The Great Knowledge Exodus or the Onset of the Great Knowledge Revolution?" *Journal of Knowledge Management*, June. doi: 10.1108/JKM-12-2021-0920

Shields, Anna. 2021. "The Impact of Covid on Workplace Conflict." *Forbes,* July 28. https://tinyurl.com/fzwn2asr

Somani, Rozina, Carles Muntaner, Peter Smith, Edith M. Hillan, and Alisa J. Velonis. 2022. "Increased Workplace Bullying Against Nurses During COVID-19: A Health and Safety Issue." *Journal of Nursing Education and Practice* 12 (9): 47. doi: 10.5430/jnep.v12n9p47

Storey, John, and Nicolas Bacon. 1993. "Individualism and Collectivism: Into the 1990s." *The International Journal of Human Resource Management* 4 (3): 665–684. doi: 10.1080/09585199300000042

Suder, Seili, and Andra Siibak. 2022. "Proportionate Response to the COVID-19 Threat? Use of Apps and Other Technologies for Monitoring Employees Under the European Union's Data Protection Framework." *International Labour Review* 161 (2): 315–335. doi: 10.1111/ilr.12331

Swenson, Peter. 1997. "Arranged Alliance: Business Interests in the New Deal." *Politics & Society* 25 (1): 66–116. doi: 10.1177/0032329297025001004

Sycholt, Martin, and Gilton Klerck. 2000. "The State and Labour Relations: Walking the Tightrope Between Corporatism and Neo-Liberalism." In *State, Society and Democracy: A Reader in Namibian Politics*, edited by Christiaan Keulder. Windhoek: Gamsberg Macmillan.

Taylor, Bill W.K., and Ming Yui Issac Chan. 2022. "A Strike in the Time of COVID-19 Pandemic: The 2020 Health Workers' Dispute in Hong Kong." *Journal of Industrial Relations* 64 (5): 711–733. doi: 10.1177/00221856221114449

Thelen, Herbert A., and John Withall. 1949. "Three Frames of Reference: The Description of Climate." *Human Relations* 2 (2): 159–176. doi: 10.1177/001872674900200206

Thompson, Paul, and David McHugh. 1995. "Studying Organisations: An Introduction." In *Work Organisations*, edited by Paul Thompson and David McHugh, 3–22. London: Macmillan Education UK. doi: 10.1007/978-1-349-24223-8_1

Thorbecke, Catherine. 2021. "Hearst's Magazine Workers Protest Mandatory Return-to-Office Through the National Labor Relations Board." ABC News. https://tinyurl.com/2a38ay5x

Upchurch, Martin, and Rickard Grassman. 2016. "Striking with Social Media: The Contested (Online) Terrain of Workplace Conflict." *Organization* 23 (5): 639–656. doi: 10.1177/1350508415598248

US Bureau of Labor Statistics. 2019. "Labor Force Characteristics by Race and Ethnicity, 2018: BLS Reports: U.S. Bureau of Labor Statistics." https://tinyurl.com/3c3czdhd

Van Buren, Harry J., Michelle Greenwood, Jimmy Donaghey, and Juliane Reinecke. 2021. "Agonising over Industrial Relations: Bringing Agonism and Dissensus to the Pluralist Frames of Reference." *Journal of Industrial Relations* 63 (2): 177–203. doi: 10.1177/0022185620962536

Van Gramberg, Bernadine, Julian Teicher, Greg J. Bamber, and Brian Cooper. 2020. "Employee Voice, Intention to Quit, and Conflict Resolution: Evidence from Australia." *ILR Review* 73 (2): 393–410. doi: 10.1177/0019793919876643

Markets." *Policy and Society* 41 (1): 155–167. doi: 10.1093/polsoc/puab011

Veenema, Tener Goodwin, Diane Meyer, Cynda Hylton Rushton, Richard Bruns, Matthew Watson, Sarah Schneider-Firestone, and Rebecca Wiseman. 2022. "The COVID-19 Nursing Workforce Crisis: Implications for National Health Security." *Health Security* 20 (3): 264–269. doi: 10.1089/hs.2022.0022

Velasquez, M. 1988. *Business Ethics*. Englewood Cliffs: Prentice Hall.

Vyas, Lina. 2022. "'New Normal' at Work in a Post-COVID World: Work–Life Balance and Labor

Webster, Allan, Sangeeta Khorana, and Francesco Pastore. 2022. "The Labour Market Impact of COVID-19: Early Evidence for a Sample of Enterprises from Southern Europe." *International Journal of Manpower* 43 (4): 1054–1082. doi: 10.1108/IJM-04-2021-0222

Willis, Karen, Paulina Ezer, Sophie Lewis, Marie Bismark, and Natasha Smallwood. 2021. "'Covid Just Amplified the Cracks of the System': Working as a Frontline Health Worker During the COVID-19 Pandemic." *International Journal of Environmental Research and Public Health* 18 (19): 10178. doi: 10.3390/ijerph181910178

Wright, Christopher, A. 1995. *The Management of Labour: A History of Australian Employers*. Melbourne: Oxford University Press.

Żuk, Paweł, and Piotr Żuk. 2022. "The Precariat Pandemic: Exploitation Overshadowed by COVID-19 and Workers' Strategies in Poland." *The Economic and Labour Relations Review* 33 (1): 200–223. doi: 10.1177/10353046211067255

Chapter 6

Establishment-Level Conflict Management in the Time of the COVID-19 Pandemic: The Case of Germany

Martin Behrens
Institute for Economic and Social Research (WSI) / Hans Böckler Foundation

ABSTRACT

This chapter highlights the role of works councils (WCs) as a conflict resolution mechanism. Drawing on a large-scale study of German WCs, the author empirically investigated whether and how works councils contribute to resolving work-related conflict under the severe conditions caused by the pandemic. Because the COVID-19 pandemic caused labor market disruptions at an unprecedented scale, this chapter treats the event as akin to a stress test for interest representation at the establishment level. Two broad perspectives were tested with evidence. The first, so-called crisis corporatism, is informed by earlier experiences during the global financial crisis and assumes that, at times of severe economic pressures, key actors tend to avoid conflict in an effort to guarantee the economic survival of a firm. In contrast, a second perspective is that it is mostly employers who have strategically used the COVID-19 crisis as a window of opportunity to transform employment relations in their favor. It is assumed that such a strategy might be associated with increased establishment-level conflict. The chapter provides evidence examining both perspectives in Germany, giving an interesting, country-specific case.

INTRODUCTION

Works councils (WCs) are at the center of what is known as the German dual system of labor relations. While collective bargaining is conducted mostly at the industry level in negotiations between unions and powerful employer associations, the regulation of basic standards of work such as the distribution of working time, health and safety at the workplace, further training, and work organization is submitted to negotiations between plant management and WCs, whereby distributional conflict is mostly removed from the establishment. Given that the COVID-19 pandemic has caused labor market disruptions on an unprecedented scale, it is akin to a stress test for interest representation at the establishment level.

On the basis of a large-scale (n = 2,924) study of German WCs, I discuss in this chapter an empirical investigation into whether and how WCs contribute to resolving work-related conflict under the severe conditions caused by the pandemic. Two broad perspectives were tested with evidence. A first perspective, "crisis corporatism," is informed by earlier experiences during the world financial crisis and assumes that, at times of severe economic pressures, key actors tend to cooperate in an effort to guarantee the economic survival of a firm. Intensified cooperation is associated with comparatively low levels of conflict. In contrast, a second perspective argues that it is mostly employers who strategically use the COVID-19 crisis as a window of opportunity to transform employment relations in their favor. It can be assumed that such a strategy could be associated with increased levels of establishment-level conflict.

In the following section, I first outline key features of the German system of conflict management before moving to a discussion of the relationship between societal disruptions in a situation of crisis and conflict within the company. I then present this relationship in greater depth on the basis of a multivariate statistical analysis of data provided by the representative WSI Works Council Survey. The results of this analysis are discussed in the final section.

SYSTEM OF CONFLICT MANAGEMENT IN GERMAN INDUSTRIAL RELATIONS[1]

One key concept in structuring conflict management in German labor relations is the so-called dual system of interest representation (Keller and Kirsch 2021; Markovits and Allen 1984; Müller-Jentsch 1979; Thelen 1991). According to this system, worker interests are represented at the plant level through establishment-level WCs, while issues of pay and the length of the workweek are addressed within the system of collective bargaining, conducted between trade unions and employer associations above the company level. WCs can be (but do not have to be) formed in establishments with more than five employees and are elected by the entire workforce. The legal rights of WCs are determined by the Works Constitution Act (WCA) and involve, among other aspects, participation in the area of hiring, transfers, dismissals, company restructuring, discipline, working time regulation, and overtime work, as well as health and safety at the workplace—an area which gained particular emphasis during the COVID-19 pandemic.

Yet the WCA also imposes limits on the scope of WC activities because they are not allowed to bargain collectively (Section 77(3)) or call a strike (Section 74(2)). In 2020, 40% of all west German employees in establishments with more than five employees (excluding the public sector and employees of the church, who have different representation bodies) were represented by a WC. In east Germany, only 36% of all employees were covered (Ellguth and Kohaut 2021: 311).

Collective bargaining is the responsibility of unions and employer associations. Agreements are negotiated mostly for an entire industry within a certain region, but there are also some national-level agreements—for example, in banking and the public sector. The German Collective Bargaining Act (*Tarifvertragsgesetz*), however, also allows for company-level agreements to be negotiated between a union and a company's management. Today, most multi-employer agreements are negotiated between one of the approximately 700 employer associations, most of them directly or indirectly associated with the Confederation of German Employers' Associations (the *Bundesvereinigung der Deutschen Arbeitgeberverbände*; BDA) and one of the eight affiliates of the German Trade Union Confederation (*Deutscher Gewerkschaftsbund*; DGB). In 2020, 26% of all establishments—both industry and plant levels—in Germany were covered by a collective agreement (Ellguth and Kohaut 2021: 308). Collective bargaining coverage increases along with company size, which has led to 51% of all German employees being covered by a collective agreement (Ellguth and Kohaut 2021: 308).

Both pillars of the dual system—establishment-level codetermination through WCs, and company and multi-employer collective bargaining—are based on a number of distinct core principles. While the WCA prohibits WCs from negotiating collective agreements, Section 2 of the Collective Bargaining Act assigns the sole responsibility for concluding agreements on wages, hours, and working conditions to unions, employers, and employer associations.

Because responsibility for matters such as wages, hours, and working conditions is mostly removed from the establishment level and assigned to collective bargaining parties, responsibility for conflicts on distributive issues has largely been removed from the plant level. Being relieved of the task of having to negotiate over wages (at least to some degree), plant-level management and WCs are free to address other issues and problems. Despite conflict on pay usually being removed from the establishment level, there still remains plenty of scope for diverging interests. Take, for example, the issue of working time: while the length of the working week is to be regulated by collective bargaining, the distribution of the hours over the working week, rules determining the beginning and end of the working day, overtime work, the introduction of working time accounts (whereby hours can be banked to use as time off later), and procedures for the measurement and documentation of working time are all the responsibility of the WCs.

Although the law separates key actors, responsibilities, and conflict into different spheres, unions have consistently sought connections between each sphere. Besides establishing shop steward bodies, which were, however, set up in only a limited share of plants, unions make some effort to organize WC members into their organizations. Based on this cross membership, a mutual dependency has been established whereby unions provide WCs with training seminars and support when major conflict erupts involving plant-level management, while, in turn, works councilors significantly assist in the recruitment of new members into the union (Behrens 2009; Müller-Jentsch 1997: 276).

Although the two key institutions that constitute the dual system (i.e., multi-employer collective bargaining and establishment-level participation through WCs) provide for a separation of tasks and responsibilities, they also use differing patterns of conflict management. At the level of participation through WCs, the dominant form is arbitration panels. Such panels can be set up at the establishment level and are primarily used to resolve collective-level conflict between WCs and management. For workplace conflict concerning "difference of opinion," an arbitration panel is required by the WCA to produce a legally binding decision (Section 76(1)).

In general, the WCA grants three types of participation rights. The weakest rights are pure "information rights" that require the employer to provide the WC with sufficient information in a timely manner. "Consultation rights" are more substantial: in addition to information rights (which are included in consultation rights), an employer must provide the WC with the opportunity to voice its view on the matter and to listen to any suggestions it may put forward. Stronger still are "codetermination rights," which require an employer to obtain the consent of the WC before acting on a particular matter. The employer cannot act unilaterally. Codetermination rights exist in areas such as the distribution and extension of working time, principles of workers taking vacation time, occupational health and safety, general principles of pay (performance-based pay), surveillance, company facilities (such as cafeterias), training, and group work. As part of a reform package that was passed during the COVID-19 pandemic, the codetermination rights of WCs in the field of remote work/home office were strengthened.

In conflicts that involve matters where WCs enjoy statutory codetermination rights (not just information and consultation rights), the arbitration procedure can be activated by either the WC or the employer. Although both parties have the right to initiate arbitration, it is the WC that does so in a majority of cases (Oechsler and Schönfeld 1989: 35). Panels are composed of equal numbers of WC and employer representatives, as well as a neutral chair. In practice, the chair is usually a professional judge from the local labor court. The decision taken by the arbitration panel has the character of a work agreement, which is an enforceable contract-like document. Because the panel decides according to a simple majority, the neutral chair has the casting vote.

Empirical research has established that the use of arbitration panels at German workplaces has been relatively stable over time (Behrens 2007; Knuth, Büttner, and Schank 1984; Oechsler and Schönfeld 1989), with about one out of ten WCs having used the procedure in the previous two years.

Conflict in the field of collective bargaining, the second pillar of the dual system, is mostly expressed in the form of strikes and lockouts. While there is no elaborated strike law in Germany, there is still a general legal framework for the regulation of strikes. On the basis of Section 9(3) of the German constitution, which guarantees the freedom to build unions and employer associations, the federal labor court (*Bundesarbeitsgericht*) and federal constitutional court (*Bundesverfassungsgericht*) developed basic standards for strikes and lockouts. In essence, strikes must be authorized by a union (which needs to be independent of the employer and sufficiently strong to sustain a strike), aim at regulating issues that can be subject to collective bargaining, and cannot be conducted at times when a peace obligation is in force. Peace obligations apply, for example, when a collective agreement regulating a certain issue is still active or when a valid mediation agreement provides for a cooling-off period after negotiations have stalled. While still disputed, German courts have decided to exclude lifetime public servants in the public sector as well as church employees from the right to strike (Dribbusch and Birke 2019: 8). To be legal, strikes must be about issues subject to collective bargaining; therefore, strikes over political issues are prohibited.

Because the right to strike is not an individual right under the German constitution, unions and employer associations are key for regulating the specific conditions under which collective disputes are to be conducted. In their by-laws, unions provide for membership ballots that must be conducted before a strike can be called. To guarantee sufficient support for a strike, most unions require membership support of at least 75% among the members who would be called to take part in the strike. Both unions and employer associations maintain special funds to support their members during a strike (Kittner 2005: 644–646).

With a decline beginning about 30 years ago, lockouts by employers have almost disappeared—a total of only 83 days have been lost as a result of lockouts in the period between 2000 and 2009 (Schroeder and Silvia 2014: 357). Union strike activity, in contrast, has remained comparatively stable, with the total number of strikes per year fluctuating between 152 (2010) and 221 (2021) but with substantial variation in terms of working days lost from strikes, depending on the sectors involved in a particular strike (Frindert, Dribbusch, and Schulten 2022). Comparing ten-year averages (2011–2020), this puts Germany in a middle position, with 18 working days lost per year for every 1,000 employees, trailing more strike-prone countries such as Spain, France, Belgium, and Norway, but leaving behind countries with less strike activity such as Austria, Sweden, Portugal, and the United States (Frindert, Dribbusch, and Schulten 2022: 14).

Although the dual structure of German labor relations is still in place, scholars have identified different challenges to the stability and functioning of the system. Part of this debate has focused on various forms of decentralization, which have challenged the balance within the system. Decentralization takes two forms: wildcat decentralization includes works councils making unauthorized concessions at the local level to collectively agreed standards at the industry level (Bispinck and Schulten 1999; Traxler 1995); in a controlled variety, decentralization is based on so-called opening clauses, whereby the parties to a collective agreement empower plant management and WCs to adjust standards to the specific needs of their companies (Ellguth and Kohaut 2014; Whittall and Trinczek 2019). On the basis of both perspectives, decentralization has the potential to blur the distribution of specific responsibilities within the dual system because WCs are increasingly pulled into collective bargaining.

A second strand in the debate on the dual system assumes that WCs have lost power to new competitors in workplace representation, such as semi-autonomous teams in high-performance work systems (Keller 2008; Schumann 2003) or so-called other representative bodies such as spokespersons or committees (Hertwig 2011). Finally, as discussed in the debate on the erosion or liberalization of German labor relations (Hassel 1999; Schulten 2019), scholars have observed declining coverage by both the key institutions: WCs and multi-employer collective bargaining that leads to a constantly declining share of the German workforce that is covered by both institutions.

This declining market share of the dual system, as well as challenges to its functioning, raises the question of whether the system is still capable of channeling or managing conflict within the employment relationship. Given that the COVID-19 crisis has put new pressures on labor relations, in the following sections I discuss to what degree those challenges have affected labor–management cooperation at the establishment level.

CONFLICT IN TIMES OF CRISIS

It is a cornerstone of industrial relations theory that the potential for conflict is inherent in the employment relationship (Behrens, Colvin, Dorigatti, and Pekarek 2020: 312). Correspondingly, a substantial body of research focuses on institutions and practices of conflict management at the workplace (Behrens, Colvin, Dorigatti, and Pekarek 2020; Heiden 2014). There is, however, little research on how specific systems of conflict management function under the condition of extraordinary pressures exposed by a severe crisis. Within the past two decades, two truly global crises have tested industrial relations systems as well as mechanisms for dispute resolution at the workplace. While the world financial crisis of 2007–2008 caused substantial economic disruptions around the world, the COVID-19 pandemic is an unprecedented public health crisis, resulting in the deaths of 6.9 million people to date globally (World Health Organization 2023). Beyond the devastating effects on public health, the COVID-19 pandemic has also caused tremendous disruptions to the world of work: lockdowns affecting single production facilities as well as entire industries, more extensive use of short-time work, and expanded opportunities to working from home, to name just a few (Behrens and Pekarek 2023).

While both crises differ in several respects, they have created tremendous pressures on employment relations in general and conflict levels at the plant level in particular. In examining the experiences of the world financial crisis more than ten years ago, researchers have found that, even under severe shocks, the dual system of interest representation maintained much of its capacity to keep conflict within bounds (Behrens 2014; Detje, Menz, Nies, and Sauer 2011). Applied to the current situation of the COVID-19 crisis, this finding would lead us to expect that key actors of German labor relations have a tendency to switch to a mode of cooperative crisis management. Because WCs as well as employers are concerned about the company's survival, they work together for the purpose of stabilizing production and employment (Detje and Sauer 2021; Urban 2022). This does not mean, however, that conflict disappears altogether—it is, at least for the moment, suspended.

A second perspective would lead us to expect that employers use the health crisis as a window of opportunity to change the balance of power at the establishment level in their favor. As Herman, Rubery, and Hebson (2021) put it in their analysis of labor relations in the United Kingdom in the time of COVID-19, employers seek to "never let a good crisis go to waste." In this sense, employers use the distractions caused by the dominating focus of fighting the health crisis to push for a different agenda. In the shadow of the pandemic, employers implement programs for job cuts or company restructuring. As a consequence, one would expect conflict at the establishment level to increase and, correspondingly, labor–management cooperation to suffer.

Identifying which of these two perspectives finds more support is the subject of empirical analysis to which I now turn in the next section.

EMPLOYER AND WORKS COUNCIL RELATIONSHIPS DURING THE PANDEMIC

The analysis to follow is based on data provided by the WSI Works and Staff Council Survey. This panel survey was established in 2015 and first included WCs only. In 2021, during the fifth survey, the panel was extended to include staff councils, which is the special form of establishment-level interest representation in the public sector.

I analyzed only the responses of WCs from the private sector and referred to the most recent survey, conducted in the fall of 2021. In the case of the longitudinal analysis, I also referred to a balanced panel, which included the surveys in 2018 and 2021.

The survey included establishments with more than 20 employees and was drawn as a disproportional random sample from the establishment file of the Federal Employment Agency. The survey was conducted by the polling institute *uzbonn* as a computer-aided telephone interview. In most cases, interviews were conducted with the chair of a WC, who was asked to provide answers on behalf of the entire representative body. In the case of WCs, the 2021 survey drew 2,924 valid responses. The balanced panel, based on the 2018 and 2021 surveys, was based on 1,263 cases.

The WSI works council panel included a number of questions that referred to the estimated relationship between the WC and other key actors within the establishment. Figure 1 displays the estimates of WCs on their relationship vis-à-vis the employer and compares their answers from 2018 (two years before the world was hit by the COVID-19 pandemic) and compares these data with responses from the peak of the

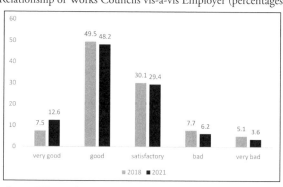

Figure 1
Relationship of Works Councils vis-à-vis Employer (percentages)

Source: WSI Works Council Panel 2018–2021.

pandemic (interviews were conducted between May and December 2021). While in both years—2018 and 2021—only a small minority of works councilors considered the relationship to the employers to be bad or very bad (about 13% in 2018 and 10% in 2021), the data also indicate that this relationship had somewhat improved up to the time of the pandemic: 12.6 % of respondents considered the relationship to be very good in 2021, while this share was only 7.5% in 2018.

As Figure 2 indicates, this relationship is probably not simply the result of a generally improved workplace climate because, when asked how they perceive the WC relationship vis-à-vis the workforce, respondents indicated almost constant levels.

I could not control whether the survey was completed by the same person in both years (2018 and 2021), nor could I be sure when respondents provided an estimate of the WC's relationship vis-à-vis the employer that it was an expression of the personal expectations rather than of the relationship. Even when respondents belonged to the same WC's body, their estimates might be biased if they had a special personal relationship to the individual representing the employers' side or had differing personal expectations regarding what the WC–employer relationship should be about. That is why, in the following, I use data from the 2021 survey only, where respondents indicated whether and in which direction cooperation between the WC and the employer has changed.

As shown in Figure 3, more than two-thirds of respondents (69.5%) indicated that, since the beginning of the COVID-19 crisis, cooperation has not changed much at all, while 18.3% of works councilors reported improved cooperation. Those reporting that cooperation had become worse than before the spread of the virus around the world amounted to only 12.1%. At a first glance, these findings better support the crisis-corporatism view than the perspective of employers taking advantage of bad times.

In the following, I track the root causes that drive the perception that works councilors have of their relationship to the employers. I discuss the channels through which a general crisis situation is associated with establishment-level labor–management

Figure 2
Relationship of Works Councils vis-à-vis Workforce (percentages)

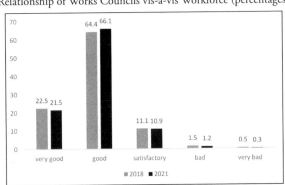

Source: WSI Works Council Panel 2018–2201.

Figure 3
Development of Cooperation Between Works Council and Employer:
2021 Compared with Before the COVID-19 Crisis

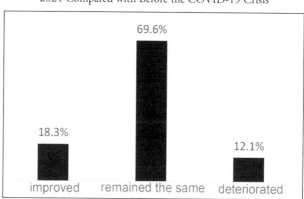

Source: 2021 WSI Works Council Survey.

cooperation. To do so, I employed multivariate binary logistic regression analysis and used the two different directions in which levels of cooperation between WCs and employers have changed during the pandemic. I provide for two estimates to allow different combinations of factors to be identified that might be associated with differing directions of change.

The first model used the deterioration of the cooperative relationship with the employer as a dependent variable, which takes the value of 1 when respondents indicated that the relationship deteriorated during the COVID-19 pandemic and 0 when it either improved or remained the same. A second model used cases of the improved relationship as the dependent. That variable was given the value of 0 when respondents indicated that cooperation with the employer has either deteriorated or remained the same when compared to the time prior to the pandemic. Descriptive statistics for both models are shown in Table 1.

Both models included different factors with the potential to mediate the impact of the crisis in labor–management cooperation. A first set of variables considered ways through which the COVID-19 crisis might affect the business model of a firm. I first included a variable for cases when the establishment, or significant parts of it, had to be closed during the crisis (1 = yes). Although lockdowns most severely affected industries such as entertainment, hotels and restaurants, and important segments of retail, I also identified a limited number of industries that benefited from the pandemic, including grocery stores and essential health services but also online shops and some sections of transportation. Thus, the second independent variable identified those cases. The third variable (cut investments) identified establishments that had to cut planned investments in staff or machinery as a consequence of the COVID-19 crisis.

Table 1
Descriptive Statistics for the Cooperation Model (weighted data)

	Sample mean or proportion	Cooperation deteriorated (%)	Cooperation improved (%)	Variable range
Dependent variables				
Cooperation deteriorated	12.1%	—	—	0 or 1
Cooperation improved	18.2%	—	—	0 or 1
Independent variables				
Business mostly closed during pandemic	19.3%	24.1%	23.5%	0 or 1
Firm benefited from crisis	23.9%	28.0%	27.1%	0 or 1
Cutbacks in investment	30.7%	36.1%	32.1%	0 or 1
Firm took advantage of short-time work	48.8%	48.3%	54.3%	0 or 1
Share of workforce working from home (1 = not offered, 5 = more than 75%)	2.27	2.20	2.31	1–5
(1) Home office not used at all	23.3%	23.5%	24.2%	0 or 1
(2) Up to 25% in home office	46.0%	48.1%	40.0%	0 or 1
(3) Up to 50% in home office	16.7%	17.9%	21.2%	0 or 1
(4) Up to 75% in home office	8.3%	6.0%	10.2%	0 or 1
(5) More than 75% in home office	5.6%	4.6%	4.4%	0 or 1
WC work more stressful during COVID-19 crisis (1 = yes)	58.0%	74.4%	65.4%	0 or 1
Regular working hours sufficient to do WC work (0 = not at all, 10 = absolutely)	7.83	6.93	7.95	0–10
Strike activity during the preceding 24 months	12.4%	18.2%	9.8%	0 or 1
WC had a say when deciding on measures to fight the virus (1 = not at all, 4 = comprehensively)	3.27	2.81	3.55	1–4
Multi-employer collective agreement (1 = yes)	53.9%	51.8%	49.2%	0 or 1
General works council (GBR) at company level (1 = yes)	41.3%	43.7%	42.0%	0 or 1

Table 1 (cont.)
Descriptive Statistics for the Cooperation Model (weighted data)

	Sample mean or proportion	Cooperation deteriorated (%)	Cooperation improved (%)	Variable range
Establishment run by the owner (1 = yes)	13.7%	16.1%	10.9%	0 or 1
Change in top-level management during the preceding 24 months (1 = yes)	39.3%	43.2%	45.9%	0 or 1
Job cuts during the preceding 24 months (1 = yes)	31.2%	37.8%	28.1%	0 or 1
Negotiations on measures to protect employment during the preceding 24 months (1 = yes)	45.8%	38.9%	57.4%	0 or 1
Company restructuring during the preceding 24 months (1 = yes)	48.0%	57.3%	42.5%	0 or 1
Number of employees (log)	5.24	5.25	5.39	2.08–9.96
Industry: Manufacturing (investment goods)	16.9%	21.4%	13.7%	0 or 1
Industry: Manufacturing (other), mining	16.1%	15.1%	14.7%	0 or 1
Industry: Insurance, banking	3.9%	1.4%	3.5%	0 or 1
Industry: Other industries	2.4%	1.8%	2.1%	0 or 1
Industry: Public services	18.8%	22.5%	22.3%	0 or 1
Industry: Retail	15.4%	16.5%	17.0%	0 or 1
Industry: Services for manufacturing firms	12.7%	10.9%	15.1%	0 or 1
Industry: Transportation, logistics, and hotels and restaurants	6.5%	5.6%	5.8%	0 or 1
Industry: Information/communication	2.8%	1.4%	3.7%	0 or 1
Industry: Construction	4.0%	3.2%	1.6%	0 or 1
Industry: Administration	0.5%	0.4%	0.5%	0 or 1

Source: Author's calculations based on the 2021 WSI Works Council Survey.

Another set of variables included factors that helped firms deal with the consequences of the pandemic. Short-time work (*Kurzarbeit*) is a compensation scheme provided by the Federal Employment Agency that enables companies to keep workers employed in times of economic downturn (Pusch and Seifert 2020). I assumed that WCs find it easier to cooperate with management when the threat of workers losing their jobs is reduced by way of taking advantage of short-time work. I also included another variable that considers the degree to which establishments use home office arrangements (1 = not used at all, 2 = up to 25%, 3 = up to 50%, 4 = up to 75%, and 5 = more than 75%). By enabling employees to work from home, employers not only reduce the risk of infection from crowded workspaces or from commutes via public transportation (Gabler, Raabe, Röhrl, and von Gaudecker 2021; Neumann et al. 2020), they also help balance work and family life demands (Ahlers, Mierich, and Zucco 2021; Lott, Ahlers, Wenckebach, and Zucco 2021) and consequently reduce potential conflict with their WC as a result of unhealthy working conditions. As far as the descriptive statistics are concerned, there is some support for this assumption. When respondents indicated that provisions for mobile work were not available in their company, 12% considered cooperation with the employer to have deteriorated. Moving to the opposite end of the distribution: when more than 75% of all employees within the establishment worked from home, the chances were high that WCs feel that cooperation with the employer remained stable or even improved, while only 10% report cooperation to have worsened.

Two variables identified whether labor–management cooperation in the workplace could be driven simply by an excessively high workload on the site of the WC because works councilors conduct WC duties in addition to their regular work. Although the WCA makes provision for WC work to be done during regular working hours (in establishments with more than 200 employees, WCs have the right to free one member from regular work duties entirely), the position of a WC member can be highly demanding, either because WC members continue their representative work during their leisure time or because they are involved in making emotionally stressful decisions. One variable considered the absolute workload of WC members. Respondents were asked to identify whether their regular working hours were sufficient to do WC work (0 = not at all, 10 = absolutely). In addition, respondents were asked how they assessed their workload during times of COVID-19 when comparing it with their representative duties prior to the pandemic (more stressful than before the pandemic = 1, less stressful or about the same = 0). As shown in Table 1, 58% of WC members considered their job to be more stressful when compared to the time prior to the COVID-19 crisis.

The estimates also considered specific situations that had the potential to affect cooperative relations at the establishment level. One situation was closely linked to the pandemic: respondents were asked whether they had a say in deciding on measures to fight the pandemic (1 = not at all, 4 = entirely). Because deciding how to deal with the pandemic was crucial for the well-being of the entire workforce, I assumed that a WC's perception of being ignored would be an obstacle to labor–management cooperation. To account for conflict, which is imposed on the establishment from the industry level, my model also controlled for strike activities. The variable takes the value of 1 when the workforce or parts of it had taken part in strike activities (at least once) during the preceding two years. As discussed above, the German dual system of industrial relations seeks to separate different spheres of conflict, and it prohibits WCs from calling a strike. Thus, the variable controlled for whether strike activity spilled over into the WC–employer relationship. Among respondents, 12.4% reported strike activity during the preceding 24 months (Table 1).

Other variables controlled for the impact of two other important industrial relations institutions: whether the establishment was covered by a multi-employer collective agreement (1 = yes) or whether the WC was part of a larger representative structure within the company.

In investigating establishment-level labor–management cooperation, my estimates also controlled for important features characterizing the management side. As identified in earlier research, it makes a difference whether the establishment is run by management or by the owner (Jirjahn and Mohrenweiser 2015), and there is also evidence that incidences of employer resistance to the election of WCs were more likely to occur when the establishment was run by the owner (Behrens and Dribbusch 2020). Considering that, when it comes to cooperation, personal relationships between people might be important, I also included a variable identifying whether during the preceding 24 months any changes occurred at the level of top management or the owner (1 = yes).

Both models also statistically controlled for job cuts (previous 24 months), plant-level alliances for jobs, and log number of employees and industry (11 industry clusters with manufacturing of investment goods served as the reference category).

As shown in Table 2 (Model 1, but see multinomial regression model in the appendix to this chapter), the closure of the establishment was associated with labor–management cooperation becoming worse, while the impact of of cutbacks in investment failed to reach conventional levels of significance. This was also true for the two variables identifying establishment-level strategies to buffer the harmful effects of the pandemic (short-time work and working from home), which turned out to be not significant.

In the examples of associations showing both variables of a WC's workload (both significant at the 1% level), the impact of the crisis on workplace cooperation with the employer seems to be moderated by the works council representatives' stress level. When respondents indicated that their regular working hours were sufficient to handle their WC duties, chances were low that they considered labor–management cooperation to have deteriorated during the pandemic. Cooperative relations with the employer became worse when representatives felt that their work had become more stressful in the time of the COVID-19 pandemic.

Also, cooperation with the employer suffered when respondents indicated that they were not sufficiently involved when deciding on specific measures to fight the virus ($p < 0.1$). Clearly, when employers acted without involving the WC, it substantially harmed the basis for cooperation. I also found a significant association with the strike variable ($p < 0.1$). While only 12% of respondents indicated that their establishment

Table 2
Binary Logistic Regression: Development of Cooperation Between WC and Employer

Independent variables	Dependent variable: Cooperation with management deteriorated (1 = yes, 0 = remained the same or improved)	Dependent variable: Cooperation with management improved (1 = yes, 0 = remained the same or deteriorated)
Business mostly closed during pandemic	0.359** (0.167)	0.202 (0.140)
Firm did benefit from crisis	0.263* (0.160)	0.233* (0.135)
Cutbacks in investment	0.025 (0.145)	0.067 (0.121)
Firm took advantage of short-time work	0.052 (0.161)	0.112 (0.130)
Share of workforce working from home (0 = not used, 5 = more than 75%)	−0.010 (0.070)	0.039 (.056)
WC work more stressful during COVID-19 crisis (1 = yes)	0.749*** (0.148)	0.252** (0.115)
Regular working hours sufficient to do WC work (0 = not at all, 10 = absolutely)	−0.165*** (0.030)	0.035 (0.028)
Strike activity during the last 24 months	0.586*** (0.175)	−0.408** (0.180)
WC had a say when deciding on measures to fight the virus (1= not at all, 4 = comprehensively)	−0.566*** (0.069)	0.421*** (0.072)
Multi-employer collective agreement (1 = yes)	−0.057 (0.139)	−0.096 (0.114)
General works council (GBR) at company level (1 = yes)	−0.030 (0.140)	0.200* (0.115)
Establishment run by the owner (1 = yes)	0.301 (0.205)	−0.207 (0.187)
Change in top-level management during the last 24 months	0.033 (0.137)	−0.430*** (0.112)
Job cuts during the last 24 months (1 = yes)	0.098 (0.148)	−0.168 (0.128)
Negotiations on measures to protect employment during last 24 months (1 = yes)	−0.336** (0.144)	0.360*** (0.117)
Company restructuring during the last 24 months (1 = yes)	0.373*** (0.142)	−0.371*** (0.118)
Number of employees (log)	−0.003 (0.060)	0.074 (0.050)
Industry: Manufacturing (investment goods)	Reference	Reference
Industry: Manufacturing (other), mining	−0.163 (0.227)	−0.039 (0.197)
Industry: Insurance, banking	−1.034** (0.469)	0.294 (0.295)
Industry: Other industries	−0.301 (0.326)	−0.159 (0.275)
Industry: Public services	−0.145 (0.222)	0.408** (0.192)
Industry: Retail	−0.188 (0.242)	0.122 (0.209)
Industry: Services for manufacturing firms	−0.297 (0.261)	0.274 (0.211)
Industry: Transportation, logistics, hotels, and restaurants	−0.056 (0.313)	−0.214 (0.290)
Industry: Information/communication	−0.565 (0.445)	0.319 (0.295)
Industry: Construction	−0.259 (0.428)	−0.311 (0.390)
Industry: Administration	0.177 (0.537)	0.493 (0.460)
Constant	0.386 (0.464)	−4.496*** (0.498)
Valid cases/R^2 (Nagelkaerke)	2,477, 0.150	2,477, 0.085

Statistical significance: ***1% level; **5% level; *10% level.

Source: Author's calculations based on the 2021 WSI Works Council Survey.

was involved in strike activities during the previous 24 months, if strikes did occur, they were associated with deteriorating levels of labor–management cooperation. This finding points to important spillover effects: although under the provisions of the WCA, WCs cannot call a strike on their own, in their function as union members or even members of a union's collective bargaining commission, they are directly involved in strike activities and thus become part of the bargaining conflict.

Two sets of variables on important industrial relations institutions failed to reach conventional levels of significance (multi-employer bargaining and general WCs); the same applies to employer characteristics (ownership and changes in top management). While, somewhat surprisingly, collective bargaining at the industry level is not associated with (a weakening) cooperation at the establishment level, there was a significant ($p < 0.1$) association with local bargaining on measures to protect worker health. At the time of the COVID-19 pandemic and even when controlling for job cuts (variable not significant), local job protection schemes kept labor–management cooperation from becoming worse, as the negative sign of the coefficient indicates. Incidents of company restructuring, however, pointed in the opposite direction: they were associated ($p < 0/1$) with weakening levels of cooperation.

Finally, no significant associations could be found between establishment size (log of employees) and most of the industry dummies (with the exception of the insurance and banking industries). This is remarkable because, for many other aspects of establishment-level industrial relations (WC and collective bargaining coverage, trade union density, and number of work agreements, to name just a few examples), size and industry turn out to be among the strongest predictors. As the first model indicated, when explaining aspects that are strongly based on social interaction (such as cooperation), influences other than the formal structure of institutions seem to be more important.

Turning to the second model, which used cases of improving labor–management cooperation as the dependent variable, I found a number of associations that to some degree mirror the results of the first model in that coefficients were significant and the indication, when compared to the first model, pointed in the opposite direction, which is good for improving cooperation correlates negatively with the dependent variable, indicating the weakening of labor–management cooperation. As displayed in Table 2, this applied to strike activity and company restructuring (negatively associated with improved cooperation in Model 2 and driving the weakening of cooperative relations in Model 1) and also to the negotiation of measures to protect employment and of giving WCs a say when deciding on measures to protect the workforce from infection (supporting improved cooperation in Model 2 but slowing down the rate of weakening in cooperative relations in Model 1).

There are, however, some remarkable departures from this mirror-image pattern, with the variables indicating how the COVID-19 crisis affected the business model of a firm but also the variables indicating the workload and stress levels of a WC pointing in opposite directions when indicating labor–management cooperation at the establishment level. As already indicated by the descriptive statistics (see Table 1), the degree to which an establishment is exposed to the COVID-19 crisis was positively associated with improving and deteriorating cooperation at the same time (in the multivariate model, this was significant only in the case of firms benefiting from the crisis). The same is true for the increased workload of WCs during the pandemic, which was positively associated with improved and deteriorating cooperation (significant at the 1% level in Model 1 and 5% level in Model 2). Apparently, and independent of the direction of change in cooperative labor–management relations, the exposure of an establishment to the crisis, as well as the workload of a WC tended to challenge the status quo and open a window of opportunity for revising established labor–management relations on the shop floor.

This leads us to another departure from the mirror-image pattern: the correlation between changes in top management and cooperation within the establishment. While this association was not significant in Model 1, it appeared to be highly significant in the second model ($p < 0.1$). When respondents indicated that changes in top-level management had occurred over the preceding 24 months, it exposed a somewhat chilling effect on the improvement of cooperative relations (albeit not being associated with worsening cooperation). As these findings suggest, in order to improve the relationship with the boss, WCs benefit from an established social relationship. Because trust identifies a state whereby people have reason to believe that the other person will treat them in a favorable way (Kerkhof, Annemieke, Winder, and Klandermans 2003), some informed knowledge on how another person has acted in previous years certainly helps when cooperative relations need to be established.

DISCUSSION AND CONCLUSIONS

As Rainer Dulger, the president of the German employers' association (BDA) argued in a recent interview: "We've always been good at dealing with a crisis!" ("*Krise haben wir noch immer gekonnt!*") (*Süddeutsche Zeitung* 2022: 19). At least when it comes to labor relations within the firm, however, "dealing with" does not automatically include a joint effort to address a global health crisis of a magnitude such as the COVID-19 pandemic. Thus, I suggested two different perspectives on how WCs and employers reacted to the challenges of the pandemic: *cooperative* crisis management in an effort to save the firm or *unilateral* crisis management by employers who use the opportunity to change the balance of power at the establishment level in their favor.

At a first glance, the results of the analysis seem to support the perspective of cooperative crisis management. A majority of works councilors felt that labor–management cooperation remained stable or even improved compared with the time before the pandemic. Only a minority of respondents reported deteriorating labor–management cooperation.

As my more detailed analysis revealed, the economic challenges accompanying the pandemic called into question the status quo but—somewhat surprisingly—they did not provide a specific direction of change in labor–management relations. Thus, major expressions of the crisis, such as cutbacks in investment or the closure of a business, but also when firms benefited economically from the pandemic, were associated with both deteriorating and improving relations.

Four factors turned out to be more important in terms of establishment-level conflict and the direction of cooperation: when employers were willing to negotiate on job protection schemes as well as rules for addressing the pandemic, cooperation was improved (and, correspondingly, the deterioration of labor–management cooperation was avoided). In contrast, labor–management cooperation was in danger when employers pursued company restructuring and were involved in strike activity.

APPENDIX

Table A.1
Multinomial Regression

Variable	Cooperation with management deteriorated; coefficient B (standard error)	Cooperation with management improved; coefficient B (standard error)
Business mostly closed during pandemic	0.412** (0.170)	0.263* (0.142)
Firm benefited from crisis	0.318* (0.162)	0.277** (0.137)
Cutbacks in investment	0.036 (0.147)	0.073 (0.123)
Firm took advantage of short-time work	0.077 (0.163)	0.117 (0.132)
Share of workforce working from home (0 = not offered, 5 = more than 75%)	−0.002 (0.071)	0.039 (0.056)
WC work more stressful during COVID-19 crisis (1 = yes)	0.807*** (0.149)	0.341*** (0.116)
Regular working hours sufficient to do WC work (0 = not at all, 10 = absolutely)	−0.162*** (0.031)	0.011 (0.029)
Strike activity during the preceding 24 months	0.529*** (0.178)	−0.319* (0.183)
WC had a say when deciding on measures to fight the virus (1 = not at all, 4 = comprehensively)	−0.506*** (0.070)	0.341*** (0.073)
Multi-employer collective agreement (1 = yes)	−0.079 (0.141)	−0.106 (0.115)
General works council (GBR) at company level (1 = yes)	−0.011 (0.141)	−0.204* (0.117)
Establishment run by the owner (1 = yes)	0.267 (0.208)	−0.171 (0.190)
Change in top-level management during the preceding 24 months (1 = yes)	0.052 (0.139)	0.437*** (0.114)
Job cuts during the preceding 24 months (1 = yes)	0.066 (0.150)	−0.160 (0.130)
Negotiations on measures to protect employment during the preceding 24 months (1 = yes)	−0.273* (0.146)	0.327*** (0.119)
Company restructuring during the preceding 24 months (1 = yes)	0.312** (0.144)	−0.328*** (0.119)
Number of employees (log)	0.010 (0.060)	0.075 (0.050)

		Reference
Industry: Manufacturing (investment goods)	Reference	
Industry: Manufacturing (other), mining	−0.170 (0.229)	−0.063 (0.200)
Industry: Insurance, banking	−0.998** (0.472)	0.201 (0.297)
Industry: Other industries	−0.335 (0.329)	−0.200 (0.277)
Industry: Public services	−0.062 (0.226)	0.404** (0.195)
Industry: Retail	−0.167 (0.245)	0.103 (0.212)
Industry: Services for manufacturing firms	−0.251 (0.266)	0.241 (0.214)
Industry: Transportation, logistics, and hotels and restaurants	−0.092 (0.316)	−0.227 (0.293)
Industry: Information-communication	−0.506 (0.450)	0.257 (0.298)
Industry: Construction	−0.294 (0.430)	−0.335 (0.392)
Industry: Administration	0.282 (0.547)	0.533 (0.469)
Constant	0.238 (0.471)	−3.560*** (0.452)
Valid cases/R^2 (Nagelkaerke)	2,477, 0.149	

Reference group: Cooperation with management has not changed.

Statistical significance: ***1% level; **5% level; *10% level.

Source: Author's calculations based on the 2021 WSI Works Council Survey.

ENDNOTES

1. Parts of this section are based on Behrens (2014).

REFERENCES

Ahlers, E., S. Mierich, and A. Zucco. 2021. "Home Office. Was wir aus der Pandemie für die zukünftige Gestaltung von Homeoffice lernen können." Wirtschafts- und Sozialwissenschaftliches Institut der Hans-Böckler-Stiftung, Report No. 65, Düsseldorf.
Behrens, M. 2007. "Conflict, Arbitration, and Dispute Resolution in the German Workplace." *International Journal of Conflict Management* 18 (2): 175–192. doi: 10.1108/10444060710759363
Behrens, M. 2009. "Still Married After All These Years? Union Organizing and the Role of Works Councils in German Industrial Relations." *ILR Review* 63 (3): 275–293.
Behrens, M. 2014. "Conflict Resolution in Germany." In *The Oxford Handbook of Conflict Management in Organizations*, edited by W.K. Roche, P. Teague, and A.J.S. Colvin, pp. 363–384. Oxford: Oxford University Press.
Behrens, M., and W. Brehmer. 2022. "Betriebs- und Personalratsarbeit in Zeiten der COVID-Pandemie." Wirtschafts- und Sozialwissenschaftliches Institut der Hans-Böckler-Stiftung, Report No. 75, Düsseldorf.
Behrens, M., and H. Dribbusch. 2020. "Employer Resistance to Works Councils: Evidence from Surveys Amongst Trade Unions." *German Politics* 29 (3): 422–440. doi: 10.1080/09644008.2018.1543410
Behrens, M., and A. Pekarek. 2023. "Delivering the Goods? German Industrial Relations Institutions During the COVID-19 Crisis." *Industrial Relations: A Journal of Economy and Society* 62 (2): 126–144. doi: 10.1111/irel.12319
Behrens, M., A.J.S. Colvin, L. Dorigatti, and A. Pekarek. 2020. "Systems for Conflict Resolution in Comparative Perspective." *ILR Review* 73 (2): 312–344.
Bispinck, R., and T. Schulten. 1999. "Flächentarifvertrag und betriebliche Interessenvertretung." In *Konfliktpartnerschaft. Akteure und Institutionen der Industriellen Beziehungen*, 3rd ed., edited by W. Müller-Jentsch, pp. 185–212. Munich/Mehring: Rainer Hampp Verlag.
Detje, R., and D. Sauer. 2021. *Corona-Krise im Betrieb. Empirische Erfahrungen aus Industrie und Dienstleistungen.* Hamburg: VSA.
Detje, R., W. Menz, S. Nies, and D. Sauer. 2011. *Krise ohne Konflikt? Interessen- und Handlungsorientierungen im Betrieb—Die Sicht der Betroffenen.* Hamburg: VSA.
Dribbusch, H., and P. Birke. 2019. *Gewerkschaften in Deutschland. Herausforderungen in Zeiten des Umbruchs.* Berlin: Friedrich-Ebert-Stiftung.
Ellguth, P., and S. Kohaut. 2014. "Öffnungsklauseln—Instrumente zur Krisenbewältigung oder Steigerung der Wettbewerbsfähigkeit?" *WSI-Mitteilungen* 67 (6): 439–449.
Ellguth, P., and S. Kohaut. 2021. "Tarifbindung und Betriebliche Interessenvertretung: Ergebnisse aus dem IAB-Betriebspanel 2020." *WSI-Mitteilungen* 74 (4): 306–314.
Frindert, J., H. Dribbusch, and T. Schulten. 2022. "WSI Arbeitskampfbilanz 2021: Normalisierung des Arbeitskampfgeschehens im Zweiten Jahr der Corona-Pandemie." Wirtschafts- und Sozialwissenschaftliches Institut der Hans-Böckler-Stiftung, Report No. 74, Düsseldorf.
Gabler, J., T. Raabe, K. Röhrl, and H.-M. von Gaudecker. 2021. "Der Effekt der Heimarbeit auf die Entwicklung der Covid-19-Pandemie in Deutschland." IZA Standpunkte No. 100, Bonn.
Hassel, A. 1999. "The Erosion of the German System of Industrial Relations." *British Journal of Industrial Relations* 37 (3): 483–505. doi: 10.1111/1467-8543.00138

Heiden, M. 2014. *Arbeitskonflikte. Verborgene Auseinandersetzungen um Arbeit, Überlastung und Prekarität.* Berlin: Edition Sigma.

Herman, E., J. Rubery, and G. Hebson. 2021. "A Case of Employers Never Letting a Good Crisis Go to Waste? An Investigation of How Work Becomes Even More Precarious for Hourly Paid Workers Under Covid." *Industrial Relations Journal* 52 (5): 442–457. doi: 10.1111/irj.12344

Hertwig, M. 2011. *Die Praxis "anderer Vertretungsorgane": Formen, Funktionen und Wirksamkeit.* Berlin: Edition Sigma.

Jirjahn, U., and J. Mohrenweiser. 2016. "Owner–Managers and the Failure of Newly Adopted Works Councils." *British Journal of Industrial Relations* 54 (4): 815–485. doi: 10.1111/bjir.12148

Keller, B. 2008. *Einführung in die Arbeitspolitik. Arbeitsbeziehungen und Arbeitsmarkt in Sozialwissenschaftlicher Perspektive,* 7th ed. Munich: Oldenbourg.

Keller, B., and A. Kirsch. 2021. "Employment Relations in Germany." In *International and Comparative Employment Relations: Global Crises and Institutional Responses,* 7th ed., edited by G.J. Bamber, F.L. Cooke, V. Doellgast, and C.F. Wright, 183–212. London: Sage.

Kerkhof, P., A.B. Winder, and B. Klandermans. 2003. "Instrumental and Relational Determinants of Trust in Management Among Members of Works Councils." *Personnel Review* 32 (5): 623–637. doi: 10.1108/00483480310488379

Kittner, M. 2005. *Arbeitskampf. Geschichte, Recht, Gegenwart.* Munich: C.H. Beck.

Knuth, M., R. Büttner, and G. Schank. 1984. *Zustandekommen und Analyse von Betriebsvereinbarungen und Praktische Erfahrungen mit Einigungsstellen.* Bonn: Institut für Sozialforschung und Sozialwirtschaft.

Lott, Y., E. Ahlers, J. Wenckebach, and A. Zucco. 2021. "Recht auf Mobile Arbeit—Warum Wir Es brauchen, Was Es Regeln Muss." Wirtschafts- und Sozialwissenschaftliches Institut der Hans-Böckler-Stiftung, Policy Brief No. 55, Düsseldorf.

Markovits, A.S., and C.S. Allen. 1984. "Trade Unions and the Economic Crisis: The West German Case." In *Unions and Economic Crisis: Britain, West Germany, and Sweden,* edited by P. Gourevitch, A. Martin, G. Ross, C. Allen, S. Bornstein, and A. Markovits, 89–188. London: George Allen & Unwin.

Müller-Jentsch, W. 1979. "Neue Konfliktpotentiale und Institutionelle Stabilität." In *Sozialer Wandel in Westeuropa. Verhandlungen des 19. Deutschen Soziologentages in Berlin 1979,* edited by J. Matthes, 185–205. Frankfurt: Campus.

Müller-Jentsch, W. 1997. *Soziologie der Industriellen Beziehungen. Eine Einführung,* 2nd ed. Frankfurt: Campus.

Neumann, J., L. Lindert, L. Seinsche, S. Zeike, and H. Pfaff. 2020. *Homeoffice- und Präsenzkultur im Öffentlichen Dienst in Zeiten der Covid-19-Pandemie. Ergebnisbericht August 2020.* Cologne: Institut für Medizinsoziologie, Versorgungsforschung und Rehabilitationswissenschaft.

Nienhüser, W. 2020. "Works Councils." In *Handbook of Research on Employee Voice,* edited by A. Wilkinson, J. Donaghey, T. Dundon, and R.B. Freeman, 259–276. Cheltenham: Edward Elgar.

Oechsler, W., and T. Schönfeld. 1989. *Die Einigungsstelle als Konfliktlösungsmechanismus. Eine Analyse der Wirkungsweise und Funktionsfähigkeit.* Schriften zur Personalwirtschaft Band 15. Neuwied/Frankfurt: Kommentator-Verlag.

Pusch, T., and H. Seifert. 2020. "Kurzarbeit in der Corona-Krise mit Neuen Schwerpunkten." Wirtschafts- und Sozialwissenschaftliches Institut der Hans-Böckler-Stiftung, Policy Brief No. 47, Düsseldorf.

Schroeder, W., and S.J. Silvia. 2014. "Gewerkschaften und Arbeitgeberverbände." In *Handbuch Gewerkschaften in Deutschland*, 2nd ed., edited by W. Schroeder, pp. 337–365, Wiesbaden: Springer VS.

Schulten, T. 2019. "German Collective Bargaining—From Erosion to Revitalization?" In *Industrial Relations in Germany. Dynamics and Perspectives*, edited by M. Behrens and H. Dribbusch, pp. 11–30. Baden-Baden: Edition Sigma.

Schumann, M. 2003. *Metamorphosen von Industriearbeit und Arbeiterbewusstsein*. Hamburg: VSA.

Süddeutsche Zeitung. 2022. "Wir Stehen vor der Größten Krise, die das Land je Hatte." Interview with Rainer Dulger, July 14.

Thelen, K. 1991. *Union of Parts: Labor Politics in Postwar Germany*. Ithaca: Cornell University Press.

Traxler, F. 1995. "Farewell to Labour Market Associations? Organized Versus Disorganized Decentralization as a Map for Industrial Relations?" In *Organized Industrial Relations in Europe: What Future?*, edited by C. Crouch and F. Traxler, pp. 3–19. Aldershot: Avebury.

Urban, H.-J. 2022. "Zwischen Notfall-Pragmatismus und Pfadwechsel. Erfahrungen aus der Corona-Pandemie und Blick auf die neue Normalität." In *Arbeitspolitik nach Corona. Probleme, Konflikte, Perspektiven. Jahrbuch Gute Arbeit 2022*, edited by H.-J. Urban and C. Schmitz, pp. 29–47. Frankfurt: Bund-Verlag.

Whittall, M., and R. Trinczek. 2019. "Plant-Level Employee Representation in Germany: Is the German Works Council a Management Stooge or the Representative Voice of the Workforce?" In *International Comparative Employee Relations: The Role of Culture and Language*, edited by K. Koch and P. Manzella, pp. 119–138. Cheltenham: Edward Elgar.

World Health Organization. 2023. "WHO Coronavirus Disease (COVID-19) Dashboard." https://covid19.who.int

CHAPTER 7

COVID-19 and the Resolution of Workplace Conflict: The Case of Ireland

Paul Teague
Queen's University Belfast

William Roche
University College Dublin

Denise Currie
Queen's University Belfast

ABSTRACT

This chapter offers a unique exploration of how the Workplace Relations Commission (WRC) adapted its work when the pandemic happened and examines how and to what degree this dispute resolution body was able to deliver its important services under unanticipated circumstances. COVID-19 happened five years after the creation of the WRC, at a time when a lot of the initial "teething" issues had already been addressed. The chapter explores the challenges faced by a dispute resolution agency in delivering important services during a period of disruptive organizational change and examines the degree to which some of these changes may be longer term. The question of whether there was a shift in the nature and volume of conflict as the world of work changed overnight as a result of COVID-19 is also addressed. The authors draw on interviews with key stakeholders inside the WRC as well as within a major private provider to consider the extent to which some of these changes are longer term. The authors find some important evidence of disruptive change in the response to the constraints put in place by lockdowns and social distancing—and that those changes are not long-term revolutions in the way dispute resolution and conflict management are addressed, but rather they are simple responses to the environment. In that vein, the chapter contributes not just to our understanding of the way conflict can be addressed but also importantly to current industrial relations debates about the degree to which the potential for disruptive organizational change was caused by COVID-19.

INTRODUCTION

The COVID-19 pandemic has had a profound impact on economic and social life almost everywhere. Debates continue about the long-term consequences of the pandemic on macroeconomic management, on the well-being of young people, and so on. One interesting line of argument that gained traction during the crisis was that businesses would use the pandemic as an opportunity to adopt radical, highly disruptive organizational strategies. By and large, this argument had two subparts. One was that the emergency shift to remote working that occurred in most countries in response to the virus is likely to mutate into a permanent feature of working life because the experience of most businesses with remote working has been better than expected. The other is that an unintended consequence of the pandemic has been the adoption of automation-forcing innovation strategies by businesses with far-reaching implications for work and employment. In this view, either to facilitate remote working or reduce the demand for labor, organizations have made substantial sunk investments in physical and human capital that most will be reluctant to write off. If we add to the mix the apparent growing acceptability, relative to pre-pandemic times, of remote working and a reluctance by many employees to return to pre-pandemic ways of working, then the assumption is that COVID-19 will pave the way for a far-reaching reordering of working life.

Within the sphere of employment relations alone, there are many ways to test the plausibility of this interesting and influential view. The starting point of this chapter is that much can be learned about the argument by looking at how the pandemic affected the work of a national public dispute resolution agency for workplace conflict—in this case, the Workplace Relations Commission (WRC) in Ireland. An examination of this type provides insight into the extent to which the WRC was obliged to introduce new forms of work as a result of COVID-19 and assess whether those adjustments are likely to be permanent. It also permits an analysis of the extent to which the WRC invested in new technologies and digital capabilities to address the challenges introduced by the pandemic—in other words, did COVID-19 have an "automation-forcing" effect on the work of the public dispute resolution service? For example, did the crisis accelerate the implementation of technologies that digitally enabled the delivery of services such as online mediation, conciliation, or adjudication and, if so, are those innovations likely to be permanent?

Finally, the chapter assesses the degree to which COVID-19 affected the nature and scale of employment disputes. On paper, the potential for a significant increase in employment disputes appeared high. Large-scale redundancies, the freezing (if not reduction) of pay and bonuses, and the rush to introduce new flexible work practices unilaterally—all fertile ground for workplace conflict—emerged very quickly as real possibilities at the start of the pandemic. Thus, it is useful to gain some sense of whether the WRC experienced a spike in disputes arising from employers finding themselves unable (or unwilling) to comply with existing employment contracts, employment standards, or collective agreements as a result of COVID-19.

The chapter is organized as follows. The first section provides important contextual information by outlining the main characteristics of the WRC before the pandemic. Then an overview is set out of the impact of COVID-19 on employment and work patterns in Ireland. After this assessment, a thorough examination is made of how the pandemic affected the work of the WRC not only as an organization overall but also in the three critical areas of adjudication, conciliation, and enforcement of employment rights. After that, the chapter addresses the question of whether the pandemic gave rise to new or peculiar forms of workplace conflict. The penultimate section provides insight into patterns of private forms of workplace conflict resolution to ascertain whether any patterns emerged that were at odds with the WRC experience. The conclusions brings together the argument of the chapter.

THE WRC AND THE EMERGENCE OF COVID-19

The WRC was set up in 2015 to end what was seen as a highly fragmented public dispute resolution regime. Previously, five separate bodies had been making decisions on employment matters—spanning workplace conflict, dismissals, discrimination, and an array of expanding employment rights. With the creation of the WRC, all those activities were brought together within a single integrated agency. The objective was to deliver a higher-quality service and faster outcomes for parties involved in employment disputes. Figure 1 sets out the organizational architecture of the WRC. It shows that the new agency had four constituent parts: inspection and enforcement, adjudication, voluntary conciliation (and facilitation) of collective employment disputes, and information and customer services. These separate functional activities are supported by a shared, centralized corporate and legal team. Combining these diverse functional activities within one organization was certainly innovative and challenging. Traditionally, across the Anglo-

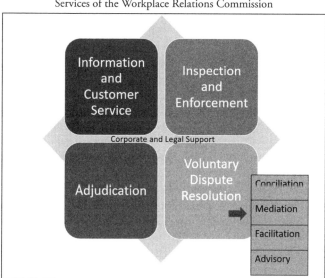

Figure 1
Services of the Workplace Relations Commission

Source: Workplace Relations Commission.

American world, some of these functional activities have been kept separate from one another—adjudication and enforcement, for example.

In its early years, the senior management team of WRC was understandably preoccupied with developing an effective organizational infrastructure and work program that fostered a set of internal values and modes of behavior to secure staff buy-in and deliver its core mission. For the most part, the team was successful in these endeavors. Perhaps the development of a corporate strategy that simultaneously promoted organizational integration and differentiation was key to this success. With the creation of a single agency, the temptation must have been very strong to devise a strategy that produced a fully integrated, homogeneous organization. But such an approach would have caused enormous tension because different skill sets and methods of working are required to accomplish the wide-ranging dispute resolution services the WRC is charged with delivering. As a result, from very early on, the core services of the WRC—inspection and enforcement, adjudication, and collective dispute resolution—were set up to operate fairly autonomously. At the same time, recognizing that differentiation needed to be a core organizational design feature of the organization posed the danger of the WRC operating like a holding company, consisting of largely independent divisions with minimal overarching integration.

Senior management made sustained efforts to avoid this outcome. First, the devolution of decision making to the core divisions was constrained: whether it is conciliation, labor enforcement, or adjudication, key strategic and operational decisions are made by the senior management team collectively. Second, a series of measures was taken to tie the separate functional areas to the new organization as a whole. The central corporate support team was charged with sustaining organizational coordination and coherence by, among other things, continually monitoring the progress each division was making toward reaching its goals and targets. Essentially, the role of the corporate team was to maintain an internal organizational web that connects separate functional areas of the WRC with each other. Third, a communications strategy was developed for the organization that simultaneously sought to transmit a set of core values for the WRC yet allow promotional and informational activity to be tailored to the needs of users of each functional area of the organization. Last, a battery of initiatives was implemented to integrate people working for the organization. The key purpose was to encourage people working in all parts of the organization to internalize the new overarching WRC culture that was being fostered by senior managers. Thus, through cultivating a distinct organization design that pursued alignment, if not complementarity, between organization diversity and unity, the WRC sought to be a "world-class provider" of multiple employment-related services.

The WRC entered the 2020s confident that the organizational foundations had been laid for a new type of public dispute resolution agency to address workplace conflict. There was certainly recognition that more fine tuning would be required in forthcoming years, but there was general satisfaction that an organizational structure had been established permitting differentiated service delivery in the context of overall organizational coherence. This internal self-confidence was to be massively tested with the outbreak of COVID-19, which, like everywhere else, had a huge impact on the Irish economy. The Irish government did not hesitate in its response to COVID-19, imposing one of the most restrictive lockdown regimes in the European Union. On March 12, 2020, Taoiseach (Prime Minister) Leo Varadkar announced that schools, colleges, cultural institutions, and childcare facilities would close. Restrictions were imposed on indoor and outdoor mass gatherings. People were advised to work from home when possible. Working times and break times were to be staggered. Shops, public transport, and hospitality continued to operate. Restrictions were further tightened later in the year, loosened in the run-up to Christmas but soon thereafter reimposed when a wave of infections caused by the alpha variant of the virus developed. For much of 2021, tight restrictions remained in force. They were relaxed again in summer 2022. Some restrictions were reimposed later in the year as the omicron variant threatened public health.

COVID-19 and Work Patterns

The measures implemented to counter COVID-19 had a major impact on the labor market, collective bargaining, and work patterns. Unemployment climbed to 25% in January 2021. The government introduced a series of measures to support businesses and people who had lost their jobs from the pandemic. An employment wage-subsidy scheme was introduced to support the retention of staff in firms where turnover or orders had declined by 30% or more as a result of the effects of the pandemic. By early 2021, more than half a million workers had received wage supports. Overall growth in the economy continued to be strong. A 3.4% GDP growth rate in 2020 and projected growth of 14.6% for 2021 were buoyed by the strong performance of multinational firms in the trading sectors of the economy. When restrictions were eased in summer 2021, the economy and employment rebounded quickly and strongly: unemployment declined to 6.9% in November 2021.

The effects of the pandemic restrictions on collective bargaining were significant but uneven. In sectors heavily impacted, such as transport, nonessential retailing, and hospitality, retrenchment programs and concession bargaining returned. In other areas of the economy and, in particular, the multinational sector, collective bargaining continued to focus on improvements in pay and conditions. However, the incidence of newly negotiated collective agreements declined significantly compared with the years preceding the advent of COVID-19. The median of basic pay increases in 2020 was 2.5%—on par with the pattern for 2019. Some existing agreements were renegotiated, and some agreed pay raises were deferred. During the first nine months of 2021, the incidence of pay settlements increased, and pay raises averaged between 2% and 2.5% (*Industrial Relations News,* October 21, 2010).

The pandemic restrictions also had a significant effect on work patterns. A survey in April–May 2020 found that 69% of firms had implemented remote working (Central Statistics Office 2020a). A Chartered Institute of Personnel and Development

(CIPD) survey in June indicated that 52% of employers had more than 75% of their employees working remotely, and 70% of employers said that they would facilitate more employees to work remotely when the COVID-19 crisis ended (Chartered Institute of Personnel and Development 2020). A July–August survey by the Central Statistics Office found that 23% of firms planned to make remote working a permanent part of their operations (Central Statistics Office 2020b). An October 2020 survey by the employer organization, the Irish Business and Employers' Confederation (IBEC), found that remote and hybrid working were "high priorities" for 45% to 51% of member firms (Irish Business and Employers' Confederation 2020).

Surveys of employees also revealed a consistent picture of significant change in work practices and priorities. A large online survey found that 68% of employees were working remotely in October 2020. More than nine of out ten respondents said they wanted to work remotely some or all of the time when the COVID-19 crisis ended, and most expressed a preference for hybrid working (National University Galway and Western Development Commission 2020). Another large national online survey conducted by the Central Statistics Office in November 2021 found similar results showing that of those who could work remotely, 88% said they would like to work that way all or some of the time when all pandemic restrictions were lifted (Central Statistics Office 2021a).

A survey of members of Ireland's largest public service union, Fórsa, found that 86% were interested in working remotely in the future and most preferred a hybrid model (Fórsa Trade Union 2020). In autumn 2021, as COVID-19 restrictions were relaxed, employers and the government began a phased and staggered return to workplaces. A survey of IBEC members in spring 2021, examining the intentions of employers about requiring employees to return to the workplace, showed that just over eight out of ten employers expected some form of hybrid working in their organizations post COVID-19 (Irish Business and Employers' Confederation 2021a). A subsequent IBEC survey of member priorities for 2022 showed that 62% expected that some or all employers would operate a hybrid working week (Irish Business and Employers' Confederation 2021b). A survey by the Institute of Directors in 2022, however, suggested that businesses may have rowed back on earlier positive assessments of remote working. Opinion was split between those who viewed it too soon to judge the success (or otherwise) of hybrid working in their organizations, with 36% of directors and CEOs agreeing and 26% disagreeing; most of the remainder stated that the issue was "under review" (Institute of Directors 2022).

The extent to which work patterns and preferences evident following the advent of the pandemic may continue post-pandemic will be influenced by public policy, legislation, and collective agreements. The government launched a National Remote Work Strategy in 2021, announcing legislation to provide a "right to request remote work" from employers (Government of Ireland 2021). A Right to Request Remote Work Bill of 2021 was subsequently published and entered the legislative process. The bill envisages a right by employees to request remote working. Employers may refuse such requests on "business grounds." Ten such grounds (not intended as exhaustive) are included in the bill. The bill attracted heavy criticism from the Irish Congress of Trade Unions, which views the proposed arrangements as "fatally flawed" and tantamount to a charter for employers to refuse employee requests for remote work. The bill provides for the referral of grievances for adjudication by the WRC and Labour Court, but only on procedural grounds—for example, where employers fail to respond to employee requests within the period stipulated. IBEC viewed the establishment of the proposed right as premature (Dáil Eireann 2022).

The National Remote Work Strategy contained a pledge by government to facilitate remote working for 20% of public servants by the end of 2021. A "right to disconnect" was also provided for, guided by a code of practice developed by the WRC (Workplace Relations Commission 2021). The code envisages unresolved grievances being referred to the WRC for resolution or adjudication.

Fórsa announced its intention to negotiate a collective agreement on remote and hybrid working across the public service. In July 2021, the government, unions, and employers developed a COVID-19 Return to Work Safely Protocol, which assigned a role to the WRC in conjunction with other agencies in carrying out workplace inspections to provide guidance for employers regarding their obligations under the protocol (Department of Enterprise, Trade and Employment 2021).

The Effects of COVID-19 on the Delivery of Dispute Resolution Services

The scale of the restrictive countrywide lockdown announced in March 2020 was not fully anticipated by the senior management team of the WRC. But they quickly realized that the impact on the WRC's work would be far reaching. A crisis-management mode of working kicked in almost instantaneously. At a hastily convened staff meeting, senior management announced to staff that everyone would be working from home with immediate effect, apart from a few exceptions where office attendance was considered essential. All face-to-face adjudication hearings and conciliation conferences, as well as other planned meetings, were suspended. Staff were told that they would be provided with laptops, mobile phones, and other technical equipment so that they could work from home effectively.

Maintaining the WRC website and the telephone service that provided information, advice, and guidance on employment rights (among other things) was identified as a priority for the organization. Because it was likely that, in the context of the lockdown, large numbers of employers and employees would be reaching out for advice on multiple employment-rights matters, keeping those services in operation was considered important, particularly as none, on paper at least, required any, or only minimal, face-to-face contact. However, the ability of the WRC to deliver those information services digitally by staff working from home presented one big problem—it did not possess the necessary phones and supporting equipment. In the words of one senior official of the organization, "a mad scramble" ensued to source the appropriate devices and technology. After several days of near round-the-clock efforts, an old telephony system was secured from the WRC's sister organization in Northern Ireland, the Labour Relations Agency. Within a week, the WRC was in a position to reboot its full information and advice service via employees working from home.

This episode encapsulates the focused, problem-solving approach that the WRC adopted throughout the COVID-19 crisis. Some important, long-planned-for organization changes such as the opening of regional offices were mothballed so that the emphasis could be squarely placed on identifying the immediate pandemic-related challenges faced by the organization and then designing feasible solutions. Thus, after the move to working remotely was secured, attention switched to determining how the organization could best function and remain coherent in the absence of face-to-face interactions among staff. To this end, each division was asked to develop procedures and safeguards to ensure that orderly and comprehensive filing systems were maintained during the period of working from home. Each division was also asked to explore alternative ways of delivering services for which it was responsible. Senior management recognized that any type of virtual or digital delivery of services would require a comprehensive training program to make staff proficient in the use of the enabling technology. No effort was spared on this front. Those who operated the information service from home were trained in the telephony machinery that had been acquired. When the adjudication division started to offer virtual hearings, all relevant staff were trained to use the digital platform (WebX) that the WRC adopted to deliver those meetings.

Faced with staff working remotely, the senior team also considered it important to develop a substantive engagement and communication strategy not only to maintain staff morale and collegiality but also the cooperative, integrated organizational culture that had been so assiduously cultivated in the years preceding the pandemic. Online organization-wide staff meetings were held to communicate developments and provide staff with the opportunity to ask questions. The gatherings were complemented by regular (usually weekly or bi-weekly) divisional staff meetings. A weekly news e-mail was sent to all staff. A battery of online events was organized for staff. Virtual staff seminars, usually lasting 1.5 hours, were organized and covered a wide range of issues. One set of seminars involved linking up with the main dispute resolution agencies in other Anglo-American countries to discuss and compare how each was responding to the pandemic. Other seminars involved connecting with external bodies such as Deloitte to explore how workplace conflict was addressed in countries such as Vietnam. Still others addressed matters such as well-being in the context of remote working. Various social events—online quizzes, for example—were also organized for staff. All in all, a dedicated effort was made to ensure that people continued to believe that they belonged to a supportive, purposeful organization even if they had to work alone at home.

Once the organization's remote-working regime was fully established, each division set about exploring how it could deliver services in a manner that did not require face-to-face interactions. This challenge was more burdensome for some parts of the WRC than others.

Adjudication

When the lockdown was announced in March 2020, the WRC had no option but suspend face-to-face adjudication hearings (*Industrial Relations News*, April 23, 2020). However, the prospect of not addressing any adjudication cases during the lockdown filled the team with foreboding: about 300 to 400 hearings would go unheard each month, which would no doubt cause disaffection among those involved in cases and lead to the reputation of the WRC being damaged; in the end, up to 2,000 hearings could not proceed because of COVID-19 restrictions in 2020. Thus, it was considered an imperative that a strategy be devised to deliver some type of adjudication service during the pandemic. A four-pronged strategy was quickly developed.

First, a concerted push was made to encourage—at times it came close to exhorting—the parties involved in cases to reach a settlement through telephone mediation. To enhance the attractiveness of this option, which all those lodging an adjudication case were offered, efforts were put in place to deliver mediation virtually (*Industrial Relations News*, May 21, 2020). In 1,600 cases filed for adjudication, the WRC contacted the parties to determine their willingness to accept virtual mediation. Most opted to wait for adjudication or for face-to-face mediation, with 36% proceeding to mediation; 85% were conducted by telephone, 14% face to face, and the remaining few virtually (*Industrial Relations News*, April 29, 2021).

Second, the team explored the possibility of using written procedures adjudication, where adjudication was conducted without a hearing, based on evidence supplied. Various pieces of employment legislation were viewed as providing the statutory basis for this resolution method: cases related to the payment of wages, holiday entitlements, and terms and conditions of employment were considered suitable for this method of adjudication, while unfair dismissals and equality cases were not. Overall, the written procedure method of adjudication was found to have worked well for less complex cases, although it has to be said that the legal profession was more welcoming of the procedure than were the employees or employers involved in cases (*Industrial Relations News*, April 29, 2021).

Third, conducting adjudication hearings by way of videoconferencing—virtual hearings—was considered another possible option, although it was recognized from the start that a lot of preparation would be needed to make this adjudication method a realistic possibility. The WRC did not possess the technology to conduct virtual hearings, and because none of the adjudication officers had experience with this resolution method, it was very much a step into the dark for them. More pressingly, although the WRC was satisfied that it had the powers to conduct hearings remotely, there was no explicit statutory basis for this adjudication method in any piece of employment law. As a result, it was questionable whether an adjudication officer could seek to resolve a case virtually without the consent of the participating parties. Finally, the great unknown was how the legal profession, employers, and trade unions, as well as others involved in cases, would respond to the prospect of virtual hearings. Thus, the WRC had work to do to make virtual hearings a viable option.

The first step taken by the adjudication team was to hold a consultation exercise to gather people's reactions and concerns about conducting adjudication virtually. Less than a month after lockdown, the consultation exercise, which was to last three months, was up and running. As the consultation exercise was proceeding, the WRC, with the help of its parent department, the Department of Enterprise, Trade and Employment (DETC), installed the technology platform WebX to conduct the proposed virtual hearings. Adjudication officers and administrative support staff were trained intensively in how to operate the technology. By the time the consultation period ended, the WRC was technically proficient at operating virtual hearings.

However, the 50 submissions to the consultation exercise checked the ambition of the adjudication team to fully launch this online service. Overall, the submissions provided only lukewarm support for virtual hearings, with the biggest concern being the potential compromise of procedural justice. A further view emerging from the submissions was that it would be preferable to establish clearer statutory grounds for the WRC to engage in remote adjudication. In light of those circumstances, the WRC considered it prudent to proceed with virtual hearings on a pilot basis only, focusing on relatively straightforward cases and where all parties involved had provided their consent.

Even then, it was difficult to persuade parties to use remote adjudication to settle their cases. The adjudication team estimates that 85% of offers for virtual hearings were rejected: evidently, people considered the option as too innovative and without proper legal foundations. But some virtual hearings did go ahead, and the issue that surprised the WRC the most was the labor-intensive nature of the entire process. Conducting virtual hearings involved as many as 25 additional tasks compared with doing face-to-face hearings, making organizing and operating them more burdensome. For example, staff had to be assigned to each party and the adjudication officer to troubleshoot technical glitches or lost connections. To address this problem, the WRC set up a dedicated concierge system to provide administrative support for virtual hearings—six additional staff were provided by the DETC to operate the system. Alongside these efforts to establish smoothly running virtual hearings, the WRC engaged with government legal counsel to provide the organization with unambiguous legal authority to conduct virtual hearings.

In September 2020, just six months after the lockdown announcement, a new statutory instrument came into effect, stating that parties could no longer refuse virtual hearings unless they would be "contrary to the interests of justice" (*Industrial Relations News*, November 12, 2020). If parties raised issues in relation to fair procedure in remote hearings, the presiding adjudication officer could take any steps deemed necessary, including adjourning cases to permit face-to-face hearings (*Industrial Relations News*, November 23, 2020). In the first three months of the operation of the new statutory powers, approximately 100 objections to virtual hearings were lodged—some citing IT-related problems and others the complexity of cases—and 60% of objections were successful (*Industrial Relations News*, April 29, 2021).

The senior management team recognized that no matter how successful the organization was in getting cases resolved through telephone mediation or by way of a written adjudication process or virtual hearings, there would always be complex cases requiring face-to-face hearings. So the last part of its four-pronged strategy was to continue with a limited number of face-to-face hearings to address cases that were considered difficult to resolve. These hearings were carefully organized to fully comply with the government's lockdown restrictions—for example, face-to-face hearings were restricted to 2.5 hours, and limitations were imposed on the number attendees per party (*Industrial Relations News*, August 23, 2020). The WRC considered it important to maintain restricted in-person hearings to uphold its reputation as being responsive and effective in addressing all types of employment-related disputes. But after the government tightened COVID-19 restrictions in autumn, face-to-face hearings were postponed. Although those hearings briefly returned in late November, they were postponed again in December. The level of consent to virtual hearings was described as disappointing, with less than 20% of the parties agreeing to them.

Adapting to the pandemic and getting virtual hearings up and running was challenging for the adjudication service. For example, the pandemic exacerbated tensions between the WRC and some adjudication officers employed on contract who complained about lack of communication and loss of work and income caused by constraints on holding hearings (*Industrial Relations News*, March 4, 2021; July 23, 2020). Yet by the start of 2021, conducting virtual hearings was the mainstay of the adjudication service. Adjudication officers and the backup administrative team by this stage had become accustomed to hearing cases remotely. A tight scheduling regime, which involved timetabling cases both to start earlier in the day and go later in the evening, alongside resolving cases expeditiously, led to the virtual hearing service becoming very efficient. An additional contributing factor was that the cases being heard were more or less the same as those heard before the pandemic. If COVID-19 had given rise to significantly different cases, then, inevitably, hearings would have been more protracted and thus the overall regime less efficient. Impressively, the adjudication team was able to address and conclude more cases under the virtual hearings regime than in face-to-face hearings.

The adjudication service become so proficient in operating virtual hearings that it was able, in the first nine months of 2021, to make significant inroads into the backlog of cases that had built up in 2020. A colossal amount of hard work over a sustained period plus considerable adaptability by all members of the adjudication team were considered the key factors behind this success. As the adjudication team slowly emerges from the pandemic, no fixed view has been formed on the desirably of continuing with virtual hearings. The team expressed an interest in operating a hybrid model that would involve introducing some virtual element into face-to-face hearings. Such a hybrid system was seen as making the deliberations in cases more comprehensive and thorough. However, the team was far from sanguine about being able to experiment with this hybrid model because the consensus view was based on the strong preference of government for a full return to face-to-face hearings.

Conciliation

Over the years, the conciliation service has prided itself on being a tightly integrated team capable of responding calmly and professionally to unanticipated external events. The team's composition has changed little in nearly two decades, and previous challenges such as managing the fallout from the 2008 financial crisis were seen as solidifying internal cohesion. Thus, when it was announced that the team would have to work remotely because of lockdown restrictions, there was a steely determination within the team to adapt the service to these challenging times. After a quick transition to remote working, the team set about organizing a virtual conciliation service. From the start, the team viewed virtual conciliation as a second-best option. Face-to-face meetings were considered a much better way of conducting conciliation because they enabled the conciliation team to foster closer relationships between disputing parties, more accurately assess the depth of animosities involved in a dispute, and more precisely gauge the possibilities for settlement (*Industrial Relations News*, April 29, 2021).

In setting up the virtual conciliation service, the team encountered several predictable challenges. For example, some team members who were unaccustomed to the software used for virtual meetings required extensive training. Like their colleagues in adjudication, the conciliation team quickly found that setting up and conducting virtual meetings was labor intensive. Initially, operating virtual conciliation sessions was not easy because participants were both hesitant and nervous about engaging with one another online. For instance, some trade union representatives were uncomfortable using online break-out rooms because of concerns about confidentiality being compromised. Over time, those problems eased but were not fully eliminated. Overall, the team views the operation of the virtual conciliation regime as a success. No backlog of cases built up as a result of online conciliation conferences, and the success rate for the service remained high, at over 80%. However, the team was confident that virtual conciliation will not become a permanent feature of the WRC's work and anticipated a full transition back to face-to-face engagements once the pandemic fully abates.

Information, Inspection, and Enforcement

The WRC's information, inspection, and enforcement services operate out of separate offices in Carlow, about 90 kilometers from the main WRC site in Dublin. We have already mentioned how enlightened improvisation allowed its information service, which operated via a call center at the Carlow offices before the pandemic, to be delivered virtually. After an initial period of intensified learning and adaptation, the information service operated online throughout the COVID-19 crisis in an unencumbered and broadly efficient manner. However, the same smooth transition to remote delivery cannot be said of the inspection and enforcement services. After the lockdown announcement, onsite WRC inspections ceased for several months—largely because organizations targeted for inspections were closed. Instead, the inspection team focused on reducing the large backlog of inspection cases that had accumulated. Once the backlog had been reduced, the team's work was dispersed over a range of different activities.

As a result of the government, unions, and employer bodies agreeing on a "return to work safely" protocol, some members of the inspection team collaborated with the Health and Safety Authority to conduct inspections to ensure that businesses were creating safe workplaces for their employees. This involved WRC inspectors receiving extensive training on verifying that any personal protective equipment used by organizations provided full protection and was not damaged. Other team members began conducting "desktop" inspections, requesting businesses to provide relevant files related to minimum wage payments and work permits for migrant workers. This method of inspection was considered unsatisfactory because it was effective only with larger firms that had the administrative capacity to keep well-managed files. But, of course, larger firms are more likely to be fully compliant with employment standards. Desktop inspection is a crude procedure for reaching organizations more likely to violate employment rules. Other members of the team devoted much of their time to devising smarter and more targeted ways of conducting inspections once "normal" business life resumed after the pandemic. New procedures such as online questionnaires and the adoption of new technologies were developed to improve inspections. The team was confident that a return to normal service will see it implementing its sectoral enforcement strategies, which had to be mothballed during COVID-19, in a more rigorous and effective manner. Overall, although the team was satisfied that they could not have adapted any better to the COVID-19 crisis, they did feel that the pandemic had an adverse effect on their work. The consensus view was that the team would fully revert to its established way of working after the pandemic ended.

COVID-19 and Patterns of Demand for Conflict Resolution

Data on patterns of demand for conflict resolution services are available for 2020. However, the data may not be the most reliable indicator of the effects of the COVID-19 pandemic on demand for the WRC's services or on patterns of workplace conflict. Workplace conflict and demand for services were "chilled" during the pandemic's first year and then varied as effects of the pandemic persisted and restrictions remained in place. New initiatives, such as the right to request remote work and the right to disconnect, may take time to affect workplace grievances. Changes to workplace regimes may also take time to solidify. A survey of private sector firms by Industrial Relations News and the CIPD found that the incidence of grievances in workplaces remained largely unchanged during the pandemic, while the incidence of bullying and harassment declined—a development possibly associated with the advent of remote working (Industrial Relations News, July 8, 2021).

Adjudication and Mediation

The volume of calls to the WRC's Infoline fell in 2020 by 3.5% over the previous year, but it was a slower rate of decline than seen in 2018. Levels of demand for other WRC services in 2020 were consistent with the chilling effect influencing employee behavior. There was a marginal fall in 2020 in complaints referred for adjudication—the first time that had occurred since 2016. The incidence of support for mediation in workplaces also declined from a low base. The incidence of mediation declined, reflecting the reluctance of disputants to opt for pre-adjudication, even when the pandemic had caused significant scheduling backlogs for hearings. The rate of decline, however, was less than that recorded in 2019—perhaps reflecting the efforts of the WRC to promote acceptance of pre-hearing mediation under pandemic constraints.

In assessing the impact of the pandemic on issues submitted for adjudication, there is some fluidity in baseline pre-COVID-19 patterns. A number of areas dominated pre-pandemic patterns of complaints: pay, hours of work, unfair dismissals, discrimination, terms and conditions of employment, and industrial relations/trade disputes. The pattern for 2020 is broadly consistent with the pre-COVID-19 pattern of complaints, except for a sharp rise in the share of redundancy-related complaints and a sharp fall in the share of equality and discrimination complaints. The rising share of redundancy-related complaints is largely attributable to a sizable number of complaints by employees about one employer, the retailer Debenhams Ireland (Workplace Relations Commission 2020: 20). Some 1,400 workers at Debenhams were issued redundancy notices following the company's liquidation in April 2020. In addition to undertaking industrial action in protest at the closure and the redundancy terms on offer—enhanced terms in a collective agreement with the Mandate trade union having been voided when the company went into liquidation—the workers union submitted multiple complaints to the WRC. The complaints sought compensation for the company's failure to provide information and engage in consultation, as required under the law governing collective redundancies (Mandate Trade Union 2020). The decrease in discrimination and equality complaints also evident in 2020 may reflect the inhibiting effect of the pandemic on such claims in circumstances where remote working had become widespread.

Prior to implementation of the right to request remote working, the WRC in November 2020 had issued its first remote working adjudication. The commission adjudicated in favor of an employee deemed to have been constructively dismissed by an employer who had failed to take adequate consideration of the elimination of risk in refusing to allow her to work mainly from home under a rotation agreement entered into with work colleagues (Industrial Relations News, January 28, 2021).

Conciliation and Facilitation

The pattern of demand for collective dispute resolution services can first be examined against the backdrop of trends in industrial conflict in the economy. The 21,700 working days lost in 2020 were significantly below the levels recorded most years since the economy recovered from the Great Recession, while working days lost in 2021 were the lowest on record (Central Statistics Office 2021b). Thus, the pandemic appears to have lessened or suppressed industrial conflict. The number of disputes referred to conciliation at the WRC in 2020 showed a sharp decrease of just under 25% compared with 2019 and with the general pattern of recent years. In fact, the figure for 2020 represented the lowest number of disputes referred for conciliation for nearly 50 years.

The issues involved in conciliation during 2020 were not much different from the pre-COVID-19 pattern. Pay, organizational issues, and industrial relations continued to rank highest and were well above all other issues referred for conciliation (Workplace Relations Commission 2020). Redundancy-related issues remained a small share (3%) of the issues in dispute between the parties to conciliation. This may reflect, in part, the wage supports introduced for companies affected by sizable decreases in revenue and orders. The low incidence of redundancy-related disputes may also have been influenced by the introduction of a special emergency measure in March 2020 that suspended an employee's right to seek redundancy if they had been laid off or put on short-time work as a result of measures to limit the spread of COVID-19.

The number of facilitation meetings chaired by the WRC increased marginally in 2019—facilitation activity during 2019 and 2020 included the commission's work in brokering a new public service pay agreement.

Inspection and Enforcement

Unlike the other services examined, inspection and enforcement activity is determined primarily by the WRC, although complaints influence inspections. The incidence of workplace inspections rose significantly in 2020 as a result of the WRC's role in supporting the return to work safely protocol that came into force in May of that year. Of all inspections carried out, 68% occurred under the protocol (Workplace Relations Commission 2020: 17). The number of prosecutions for breaches of employment legislation declined during the year.

The patterns of workplace conflict during the pandemic appear to be similar to pre-pandemic patterns. Post-pandemic patterns remain to be determined and may depend in large measure on the extent of remote working and the shape of the right to request remote working legislation. However, there is little reason to believe that the pandemic will transform patterns of workplace conflict.

The WRC did not pursue radical or opportunity-seeking strategies during the pandemic. No concerted effort was made to use the COVID-19 crisis to accelerate the introduction of new technological processes or reshape important features of work operations. The WRC's approach can be characterized as adaptation, problem solving, and consolidation. The pandemic was viewed as an unforeseen organizational shock requiring an immediate and systemic response. The focus was almost exclusively on devising solutions to problems and challenges generated by the COVID-19 crisis while maintaining internal cohesion and integrity. The senior management team considered themselves operating in an external environment replete with pervasive uncertainty. In those circumstances, the team viewed it as appropriate to adopt a risk-averse strategy and consolidate the organization around established corporate objectives without launching any new initiatives.

This posture was also reflected in the WRC's Strategy Statement 2022–2024, launched as pandemic restrictions were being wound down. The medium-term strategy recognized that the pandemic and associated changes in work and employment may have lasting effects and committed the WRC to providing an "appropriate mix of remote, hybrid and in-person services" (Workplace Relations Commission 2022: 4), yet the overall feature of the strategy is that it maintains a steady course focused on "resilience and continuity" (Workplace Relations Commission 2022: 3).

Indicative of this cautious approach was how the WRC retreated from its aspirations to develop human resources policies and working methods that were at least semi-independent from the Civil Service employment model. Thus, for example, the senior management team stated that the WRC intended to remain fully aligned with the Civil Service's policies and practices regarding transitioning out of COVID-19 restrictions and returning to "normal" working. It also stated that there would be no deviation from the wider Civil Service's policy on home and hybrid working after the pandemic had subsided. These statements contrast sharply with the pre-pandemic eagerness of the senior management team to introduce an open recruitment policy that would allow vacant positions to be filled from outside the Civil Service. However, COVID-19 dampened this eagerness, with senior managers now strongly believing that the organization will remain within the Civil Service's internal labor market. Being part of this internal labor market was seen as indemnifying the organization from people-management risks and uncertainties caused by COVID-19. For example, it could prevent potential demands for a radical remote-working policy from staff who had grown accustomed to and preferred working from home by stating that the organization did not have the authority to develop such policies independently from the wider Civil Service.

Underlying the risk-averse and cautious approach is a preference within the WRC for face-to-face methods of conflict management. Across the organization, whether in adjudication, inspection and enforcement, or conciliation, there is a strong consensus that resolving conflict virtually is a second-best alternative to in-person problem solving and dispute resolution. Therefore, while the WRC is likely to support some remote working or digital conflict management moving forward, the expectation—and, indeed, the desire—is that once the pandemic is fully under control, there will be a return to pre-COVID-19 ways of working. The pandemic will not prove transformative in how the WRC works and delivers its services.

Private Conflict Resolution During the Pandemic

To augment the assessment of how the WRC responded to the recession, it was considered worthwhile to examine the impact of COVID-19 on private forms of dispute resolution. The purpose was to uncover whether any developments were occurring that were at odds with the WRC experience. In examining private conflict resolution, a distinction was made between providers of mediation in individual employment grievances and interpersonal conflicts and providers of collective dispute resolution, although some providers offer services in both areas.

Private Mediation of Individual Employment Grievances and Interpersonal Conflicts

Data collected from 13 mediators on general mediation, including workplace mediation, suggest that a small decline (7%) in the incidence of mediation occurred from March 2020 to March 2021 (Kenny 2021: 9). In-person mediation could not be conducted in the early stages of the pandemic because of public health restrictions. A sharp rise was reported in telephone and subsequently online mediation. The main challenges reported by mediators concerned people's degree of familiarity with technology and access to broadband; mediators striving to maintain a balance of power between participants online by supporting parties to present themselves appropriately online; difficulties assessing the dynamics and reactions of people participating in online mediation; and maintaining confidentiality. In general, mediators reported positive experiences of online mediation and also reported similar feedback by participants (Kenny 2021).

Data on workplace mediation were obtained from a mediator with an extensive professional network and deep involvement in the main professional body in the field. The experience reported draws on the activities of established mediators and was broadly in line with that reported for mediation more generally. Regarding the demand for workplace mediation, little activity occurred during the early months of the pandemic. However, demand thereafter was seen to have quickly returned to pre-pandemic levels. While conflicts that had "smoldered on" before the pandemic again came into play, a new pattern was evident. This involved a concentration of mediation among workers in essential industries and services and concerning pandemic-related issues such as workplace safety, vaccination status, and issues surrounding people returning to workplaces after a period of working from home.

Established, experienced mediators sometimes saw a growth in demand for services among essential workers and involving those issues. Mediation commonly involved a combination of telephone and online activity, with online preparatory work supporting it, and in-person meetings when public health regulations permitted them. The reported experience both of mediators and parties to mediation was again generally positive. Ease of scheduling and less need for travel were seen as significant advantages for mediators and sometimes the parties. While mediators might find it more difficult to gauge the dynamics between the parties, for some parties to mediation, the online environment muted the negative emotions that might have arisen in face-to-face encounters, especially in cases involving bullying and related issues. The durability of mediation agreements reached online, however, was seen as less ensured because conflicts between parties might be triggered anew when they returned to working side by side.

The expectation is that various forms of hybrid workplace mediation would continue post-pandemic and become the norm. Because virtually no online mediation occurred before the pandemic—other than pre-adjudication mediation conducted by telephone by the WRC—this would represent a remarkable transformation of mediation practice.

A study of online dispute resolution (ODR) in Ireland in 2015, drawing on a survey of 214 mediators, described practitioners as "skeptics of the screen." Very few had used online technologies in their work, and a popular sentiment among practitioners was that ODR was not superior to face-to-face meetings (Boehme 2015).

Anticipating a Full Return to Face-to-Face Processes: Private Collective Dispute Resolution

To gain insight into patterns of private resolution of collective forms of workplace conflicts, a representative from Stratis, the largest consultancy in Ireland providing organizations with advice, guidance, and support for workplace conflict management, was interviewed. Regarding the consultancy's advisory activities, the representative was adamant that COVID-19 had nofc real impact: providing information and guidance proved to be as effective virtually as in person. However, he said that the pandemic had a significant adverse effect on the representative and advocacy roles of Stratis. Throughout the pandemic, nearly all forms of collective dispute resolution switched to being online. This method of conflict management was considered inferior to face-to-face engagement for three reasons. First, virtual forms of collective dispute resolution were viewed as excessively cumbersome. Unlike face-to-face problem solving, resolving disputes digitally required many more formal meetings—particularly lengthy meetings before and after formal sessions to address problems. Moreover, the adjourning of meetings and the need to reconvene sessions increased significantly under virtual collective dispute resolution. The Stratis representative also echoed the comments of the WRC's conciliation team about online forms of engagement being challenging for employers and trade unions alike. It took considerable time for both to become technologically competent and gain the confidence and trust to negotiate online.

Second, the actual process of deal making or problem solving was seen as being more difficult online. The Stratis representative stressed that the human contact that comes from face-to-face engagements across the table immeasurably improves the chances of successfully settling a dispute or problem. Virtual collective dispute resolution, he argued, deprives negotiators of those social interactions and, as a result, engagement in his experience remained cold and stilted. In addition to not being conducive to fostering meaningful, affective relationships, online platforms were viewed as squeezing out flexibility and informality from the dispute resolution process. The Stratis representative talked about it being "hard to read the room" virtually and lamented the inability to hold "corridor conversations" during online negotiating sessions with trade unions. Constraining the space for informal dispute resolution activity, often the key to successful deal making, was considered by the Stratis representative as a major shortcoming of virtual forms of collective dispute resolution—he talked about virtual conflict management having a process deficit. In this context, it is interesting to note that, although private dispute resolution arrangements in ten firms and public service agencies served by independently sourced panels and sole practitioners continued to function during the pandemic, only the three-person Internal Resolution Council at the Dublin Airport

Authority was able to conclude an agreement that addressed changes in pay, conditions, and work practices resulting from the collapse of airline traffic (Dublin Airport Authority and Fórsa Trade Union 2020).

Third, securing the formal acceptance of a proposed settlement to a dispute was considered more difficult under online collective dispute resolution. For the most part, the problem of "getting disputes over the line," in the words of the Stratis representative, was attributed to trade union officials and representatives finding it harder to maintain internal order and coherence among members. When dealing with any form of workplace conflict or unrest, trade unions place a premium on being tightly organized and disciplined internally. Not only do those attributes allow the union to project a united front to employers, but they also place trade union officials in a better position to sell a proposed agreement to rank-and-file members. According to the Stratis representative, virtual collective dispute resolution compromises the ability of trade unions to maintain internal organizational cohesion in conflict situations. In particular, because the pandemic required all interactions and communications between trade union representatives and rank-and-file members to be online, the opportunities to "disfigure" or "contaminate" such interactions increased dramatically. With the skillful use of social media platforms, specific groups or factions, normally opposed in one way or another to the union leadership, can discredit attempts at securing membership endorsement of a proposed agreement to a dispute.

The Stratis representative provided the example of a dispute involving Dublin Bus. After extensive online engagement, management and trade union representatives reached a proposed agreement to an ongoing dispute. All trade union representatives recommended that the membership accept the proposed deal, but their efforts were thwarted by a sustained and concerted social media campaign against the recommendation. In the end, the membership voted to reject the agreement. In other words, orderly forms of collective dispute resolution require the centrifugal pressures on internal trade union organization to be minimal. Online collective dispute resolution, however, created a permissive environment for those centrifugal pressures to flourish. Overall, the view of the Stratis representative was that employers and trade unions did their best to cope with the exigencies thrown out by COVID-19, but he was confident that when the pandemic subsided there would be a full return to traditional forms of face-to-face collective dispute resolution processes.

CONCLUSIONS

An influential argument is that COVID-19 will have a hysteretic effect on the labor market, with no return to pre-pandemic patterns of employment and ways of working. In particular, it is argued that the pandemic has released automation-inducing innovations and orchestrated a radical shift to remote working to the point that there will be no return to traditional forms of business or working life (Barrero, Bloom, and Davis 2021). However, our assessment of how the WRC has responded to the pandemic found little evidence of such hysteretic influences at play, at least in relation to public regimes dedicated to resolving workplace conflict. No part of the WRC viewed the pandemic as causing a permanent shift to new digital or technological conflict management procedures. Moreover, across the organization, a strong preference was expressed for a quick return to conventional face-to-face dispute resolution. Furthermore, the consensus view was that the pandemic would not result in a massive increase in remote working at the WRC. All in all, the considered view was that the organization is likely to revert to established ways of working. This is not to say that COVID-19 will not impact the activities of the WRC going forward. For example, as the pandemic subsides, the dark clouds of inflation are beginning to hover over many economies, including Ireland's. Rising prices could lead to a resurgence in robust collective bargaining as trade unions demand high pay settlements to maintain their members' standard of living. Far from seeing this adverse economic consequence of COVID-19 as a threat to its steady-state organizational equilibrium, the WRC will view it as a challenge requiring the use of tried-and-tested conciliation methods.

REFERENCES

Barrero, J.M., N. Bloom, and S.J. Davis. 2021 (April). "Why Working from Home Will Stick." NBER Working Paper No. 2873. Cambridge, MA: National Bureau of Economic Research.

Boehme, S. 2015. "Skeptics of the Screen: Irish Perspectives on Online Dispute Resolution. Master's thesis (unpublished). Maynooth University, Ireland.

Central Statistics Office. 2020a (May). "Business Impact of COVID-19 Survey Wave 3." Dublin: Central Statistics Office.

Central Statistics Office. 2020b (September). "Business Impact of COVID-19 Survey Wave 4." Dublin: Central Statistics Office.

Central Statistics Office. 2021a. "Industrial Disputes, Quarter 3, 2021." Dublin: Central Statistics Office.

Central Statistics Office. 2021b. "Pulse Survey—Our Lives Online: Remote Work, November 2021." Dublin: Central Statistics Office.

Chartered Institute of Personnel and Development. 2020 (June). The Impact of COVID-19 on Pay, Jobs and Employee Concerns, Dublin: Chartered Institute of Personnel and Development.

Dáil Eireann. 2022. "Joint Committee on Enterprise, Trade and Employment Debate, Wednesday, 2 Mar 2022." Dublin: Houses of the Oireachtas.

Department of Enterprise, Trade and Employment. 2021 (November). "Work Safely Protocol." Dublin: Department of Enterprise, Trade and Employment.

Dublin Airport Authority and Fórsa Trade Union. 2020. "Pay Stabilisation and Road to Recovery Agreement Between DAA and Fórsa Trade Union." Dublin: Dublin Airport Authority and Fórsa Trade Union.

Fórsa Trade Union. 2020 (August 12). "Largest Ever Employee Survey Reveals Huge Appetite for Remote Working." Fórsa Trade Union. https://tinyurl.com/mr2z7rus

Government of Ireland. 2021. "National Remote Work Strategy." Dublin: Government of Ireland.

Industrial Relations News. Various. Issues cited in text and published in Dublin.

Institute of Directors. 2022. "Director Sentiment Monitor for Q1 2022." Dublin: Institute of Directors.

Irish Business and Employers' Confederation. 2020 (October). "HR Update Survey." Dublin: Irish Business and Employers' Confederation

Irish Business and Employers' Confederation. 2021a (May). "Returning to Work Survey." Dublin: Irish Business and Employers' Confederation.

Irish Business and Employers' Confederation. 2021b (October). "HR Update Survey." Dublin: Irish Business and Employers' Confederation."

Kenny, T. 2021. "Adapting to Mediation Online: The Irish Experience." *Journal of Mediation and Applied Conflict Analysis* 7 (1): 1–19.

Mandate Trade Union. 2020 (August). *The Shopfloor*. https://tinyurl.com/3j3thx2j

National University Galway and Western Development Commission. 2020 (October). "National Remote Working Survey." Galway: National University Galway and Western Development Commission.

Workplace Relations Commission. 2020. "Annual Report for 2020." Dublin: Workplace Relations Commission.

Workplace Relations Commission. 2021. "Annual Report for 2021." Dublin: Workplace Relations Commission.

Workplace Relations Commission. 2022. "Work Programme 2022." Dublin: Workplace Relations Commission.

Chapter 8

Engaging Managers with Online Learning in a Context of COVID-19 Uncertainty: Challenges and Opportunities

Rita Neves
Paul Latreille
University of Sheffield

Richard Saundry
Peter Urwin
Fatima Maatwk
University of Westminster

ABSTRACT

As part of a wider research project to evaluate whether a training intervention to develop conflict competence in line managers improves workplace productivity, this chapter discusses the learnings from the pilot phase and the migration from face-to-face to online design and delivery in response to the COVID-19 pandemic. The training was provided online to 82 delegates across four organizations and consisted of six courses (with varying formats). Our data suggest varying levels of engagement, with a lack of time in pressured work environments being identified as a key constraint. The training was positively received, and delegates who engaged with the material reported finding it useful. This was confirmed by shifts in pre- versus post-assessment confidence levels on various managerial skills. Mode of delivery appears to matter, with an apparent trade-off between breadth and depth between one-day, largely synchronous delivery and multiweek, primarily asynchronous delivery. The study suggests a range of interesting and useful insights from an *in extremis* migration to online delivery, despite limited resources. Crucially, online delivery permits a range of new data to be collected, as well as providing important scalability benefits for both the training and research.

INTRODUCTION

Line managers play a key role in shaping experiences of work, including as implementers of human resource (HR) policies and practices (Bos-Nehles and Meijerink 2018; Bos-Nehles, Van Riemsdijk, and Looise 2013; Purcell and Hutchinson 2007). In so doing, they also impact employee outcomes such as affective commitment (Gilbert,

De Winne, and Sels 2011) and organizational engagement (Dromey 2014; MacLeod and Clarke 2009; Purcell 2010). Further, line managers have been found to be critical actors in debates about the strategic links between management practices and international productivity comparisons; data gathered over the past 20 years from the World Management Survey (for example, Bloom and Van Reenen 2007, 2011; Sadun, Bloom, and Van Reenen 2017) provides compelling evidence that poor management is one explanation for the United Kingdom's "long tail" of low-productivity firms.

However, growing evidence suggests that notwithstanding recognition of their central role and a tendency in recent years to devolve HR issues to the line (Saundry, Fisher, and Kinsey 2022), line managers often lack the skills and confidence to manage people effectively and to identify, address, and resolve difficult personnel issues, including conflict with and among employees. In the United Kingdom, Chartered Institute of Personnel and Development (CIPD) surveys of members have consistently highlighted a lack of trust in and significant competence gaps among line managers in resolving disputes informally and at an early stage (Chartered Institute of Personnel and Development 2007, 2008) and among senior leaders in handling difficult conversations and conflict management (Chartered Institute of Personnel and Development 2016). The contemporary emphasis on more robust approaches to the management of performance (Newsome, Thompson, and Cammander 2013) makes it more likely managers will find themselves having difficult conversations and in conflict with their subordinates. This suggests a need to focus on both the existence of managerial practices and the competences needed to enact them, including in relation to conflict management and skills, on which the broader literature is largely silent.

As Saundry, Fisher, and Kinsey (2022) note, there are three key aspects to what they describe as the "conflict competence problem." First, many managers are recruited or promoted on the basis of technical rather than people skills, and without the training necessary to navigate their new roles (Townsend, Wilkinson, Allan, and Bamber 2012). Second is a tendency for organizational development activities to center on strategic leadership training rather than core people-management competencies. And third, even when appropriate training is offered, it is rarely part of the core offer but instead an "added extra" that line managers may find difficult if not impossible to accommodate within busy schedules and pressing operational demands. Not surprisingly, line managers will often eschew more informal approaches to dealing with issues, preferring the certainty of formal process and drawing heavily on HR support and heuristics.

The above suggests that training programs designed to increase (line) managers' confidence and capacity in dealing with such issues could therefore potentially improve experiences at work and help boost employee engagement and improve productivity. However, there is limited robust academic research in this area that shows the effectiveness of training designed to improve conflict skills among line managers or about how such training could enhance wider interpersonal skills in the workplace, in the confidence of line managers, and, ultimately, in employee engagement and productivity. The ongoing Skilled Managers, Productive Workplaces (SMPW) project aims to fill this gap by providing a detailed evaluation of the impact on engagement and productivity of conflict competence training for managers.

To achieve this purpose, and with funding from the Economic and Social Research Council (ESRC) under its Management Practices and Employee Engagement call, we set up a workplace training intervention designed in partnership with Great Britain's Advisory, Conciliation and Arbitration Service (Acas), to develop the conflict resolution skills of line managers working in organizations in both the private and public sectors. This training was initially planned and developed for face-to-face delivery by Acas staff, with the intention of exploring classroom dynamics and establishing role-play exercises that could optimize the learning process. However, our pilot implementation coincided with the COVID-19 pandemic and the initial lockdown in the United Kingdom. Given the public health crisis and the climate of uncertainty that persisted over months, we eventually took the decision to reimagine the training for delivery online (see details below). For the pilot stage, we recruited four organizations of different sizes and working in different parts of the economy. This chapter discusses the implementation and evaluation of the pilot in the context of COVID-19, along with the learnings gained about what works.

DEVELOPING THE PRODUCT: THE MIGRATION ONLINE

As noted above, at the outset of the project, the plan was for the training to be delivered face-to-face by Acas staff using a well-established and pedagogically informed workshop format that had been deployed successfully on an extensive range of existing Acas courses. This involved the use of PowerPoint materials, a handbook for delegates, and a range of workshop activities—discussion, individual and group exercises, role play, etc. Our training intervention was designed by members of the research team with expertise in conflict resolution and management, in conjunction with selected senior Acas advisors at regional workshops in Manchester, Leeds, and London in late 2019 and was conceived as a one-day intervention. Using a mediative model, it drew on several existing Acas courses, including those on essential skills for line managers; having difficult conversations; managing conflict, discipline, and grievance; and managing under performance. The training also included new material. Workshop participants reviewed PowerPoint slides and a workbook, with discussion drawing on the extensive experience and expertise of Acas trainers to explore level, content, style, and utility of the proposed material. This was adjusted in response to feedback between the second and third workshops, with the final one in London also including Acas staff from their research and policy teams.

The overarching aim of the training was to develop the conflict competence of line managers—defined as the ability to anticipate, identify, and deal effectively and confidently with conflict and potential conflict situations—through a short, intensive focus on key skills, including listening, questioning, and reframing. Following the

Acas workshops, the resulting material was piloted by one of the team members at a proof-of-concept workshop for line managers in January 2020. The aim of this event was to secure feedback from an audience similar to our target group, with the (mostly positive) qualitative feedback used to make further minor modifications to the course, with a second line manager workshop scheduled for early April 2020.

The COVID-19 pandemic, however, meant all face-to-face events were initially paused and subsequently prohibited, with a lockdown announced on March 26, 2020, in the United Kingdom. Continued restrictions for meetings, social distancing, and other limitations made it clear by summer 2020 that our original mode of delivery was unlikely to be safe or practicable for some time and that many organizations would be working remotely for an extended and unknown period. Consequently, the decision was made to migrate the training online. This involved undertaking a rapid consultation of the pedagogic considerations for effective online delivery (see, for example, the recent rapid review by CIPD as featured in Wietrak, Rousseau, and Barends 2021), identifying and evaluating potential platforms to host the material, and revisiting the content in the context of an alternative mode of delivery and the move to remote working and managing.

After trialing several e-learning platforms, the team selected aNewSpring as the provider. As well as individual delegate licenses, aNewSpring offers a range of customization options (including branding), various templates, note-taking options, gamification elements, a calendar, the ability to turn learning blocks and lessons on and off (which supported a key element of our planned approach to customization and randomization for participant organizations), and opportunities for delegate discussion, direct messaging, and delegate–instructor interaction. It also includes integrated webinar and survey capabilities and is fully SCORM compliant, with native mobile and tablet apps for delegates. Given the steep learning curve entailed in moving online, an important consideration was that the organizational version purchased also included instructor onboarding and support.

Content was created by one of the project team in consultation with the remaining team members, and video content was shot with the help of a professional photographer/videographer who was part of the content lead's COVID "bubble." This was undertaken at a professional venue booked for the purpose on two occasions. Development of the content and how it was packaged was iterative, both in terms of the sequencing of material and how the various elements meshed in an online setting and as the capabilities of the platform were explored and learned. Along with the fundamental change to mode of delivery, changes to the exercises (which had to be capable of being delivered online) and support arrangements (in particular for the asynchronous elements) were necessary. We also experimented with assessing learner capability at the start and end of the training so as to assess progress, using multiple-choice tests and qualitative approaches for this purpose at different times.

One of the key advantages of moving online was the ability to track learner engagement in ways that were not possible in person; however, maintaining engagement was itself potentially more challenging. It was also possible to customize the course for different organizations and sectors—for example, using organization logos and changing simulations to fit with its context (such as an office or factory). It also became clear that customization could be extended to delivery—from a fully asynchronous version of the training with little or no instructor input to one that involved more synchronous delivery, including live webinars that brought delegates together at different times during the course (completed at the delegates' own pace within a specified window of time).

The course was divided into four modules designed to reflect the core issues identified through discussion with Acas staff and to move learners from basic skills to more complex approaches to conflict resolution. Each module had a similar structure and comprised three parts: lesson content containing a mixture of text, short videos, quizzes, and assessments (with feedback); simulated conversations and scenarios designed to test learning; and a final section outlining key learning points and offering learners an opportunity for reflection.

The first module focused on key questioning and listening skills needed to build good relationships and to explore potential causes for concern. It was followed by a module that explored the role of feedback, particularly in dealing with poor performance. In particular, it provided learners with a framework for planning and conducting difficult conversations. The course provided learners with micro-processes they could use to structure informal aspects of people management. The first two modules stressed the importance of early intervention and developing collaborative responses to workplace problems. The penultimate model examined decision making in conflict situations with an emphasis on the role of fact finding in developing responses to more serious instances of potential misbehavior and misconduct. The final module looked at more complex team-based conflicts and outlined an approach to resolution based on the typical structure of workplace mediation.

Delegates also had access to content in different formats, such as reading material, short videos, simulations of real workplace situations/dilemmas, podcasts (created with external experts, including Acas advisors), and complementary reading. A key feature of the training was the development of a tool kit—essentially a set of templates and other resources available to delegates at the end of the course—that was made available at the end of the course and could be used as part of learners' day-to-day practice, helping reinforce the learning and structuring it for use, such as a planner for having a difficult conversation with a staff member.

THE PILOT

As before, we first tested the material. This was initially done internally and with critical friends before recruiting organizations to take part in the study. The latter effort was initially compromised due to reluctance in committing to anything other than essential business activities and, for some in the private sector, the risk of bankruptcy in the context of the pandemic and economic and social disruption and uncertainty caused reluctance to participate. These pressures were especially acute for two of the main sectors targeted for the training interventions: hospitality and healthcare. Eventually, however, as the health crisis subsided somewhat in mid-2021 and restrictions were lifted, we were able to obtain participants by relying on Acas contacts and our own networks to contact and recruit participants. We secured four organizations for the pilot stage.

Each course in the training relied on customized material that reflected sector- and organization-specific challenges—for example, the setting (office-based, medical, etc.) and content (timekeeping, and so on) of the simulations. The content, modules, and corresponding activities were subject to adjustments from one course to the next (on a total of six iterations of the course across the four organizations) based on feedback from trainees (discussed further, below) and delivered over seven sessions.

Conflict competence was assessed using two self-developed instruments. At the start of the training, delegates were asked to consider a case study of an evolving conflict situation and asked to respond to ten multiple-choice questions (each with five options for answers) about how they would proceed as a situation unfolded. At the conclusion of the training, learners were then asked to take a quiz comprising ten additional multiple-choice questions, each considering a different conflict scenario and loosely linked to conflict handling styles. In broad terms, we would expect to see the training result in an improvement on delegate scores following the training.[1]

For the pilot, the organizations had a number of different dimensions and operated in various sectors—namely, (1) a large NHS trust (12,000+ employees, multiple sites), (2) a civil service organization (7000+ employees, multiple sites, but focused on one geographical subset), (3) a private bus company that employs 850 workers and is part of a larger travel group employing 30,000 across the United Kingdom, and (4) a public sector body (250+ employees, single location). Each of these organizations and their context is discussed more fully below.

In total, 82 line managers were enrolled across the four organizations and seven sessions. Although the training was primarily aimed at first-line managers, those enrolled included a number of managers with significant experience and seniority. Three of the organizations involved were public facing, meaning that line managers were potentially dealing with customers, clients, service users, and employees. Some of the learners enrolled in the course worked in a fast-paced environment, with high work pressure and little to no time available for training.

At the end of each course, data were collected directly from the learning platform, such as whether delegates initiated and completed the course, completed activities by type of activity, (in)correct answers to the quizzes and assessments, number of attempts for each multiple-choice question, time spent on each activity by each participant, and other criteria. These data were analyzed via descriptive statistics (detailed in the results sections below) and taken into account to adjust the course activities from one version to the next. A key feature of the different versions of the course was that we were able to experiment—in discussion with the organizations—with the mode of delivery. Thus, some versions were delivered in a single day with significant synchronous interaction, while others ran over a period of weeks and involved much less interaction (for example, an introductory webinar).[2] This enabled us to explore how levels of engagement and delegate responses varied and to assess whether such a flexible approach might work in the main stage of the project, responding to different organizational contexts and needs.

Delegates were asked to provide feedback on the course directly on the platform by answering open-ended questions. The answers were coded to identify key aspects that learners liked and disliked, covering issues such as design, content, and level, as well as with the level of interaction they had on the platform. The written answers were analyzed using a mix of content analysis and thematic analysis (Neuendorf 2018).

RESULTS

Results are presented in a case-study fashion, with some more in-depth understanding of the organizational context provided and combining both quantitative and qualitative data concerning engagement, impact, and delegate responses to the material.

Organization 1

This organization was recruited to the trial following prolonged engagement with Acas in regard to concerns about levels of conflict and poor employment relations. The organization was part of the civil service, highly unionized and, at the time the research was conducted, under extreme operational pressures related to COVID-19 and also to wider UK government policy. The work conducted by Acas had suggested that low levels of managerial confidence and capability in relation to personnel issues were a significant factor in driving employee grievances. Training and development within the organization tended to focus on complex operational issues, and there was an admitted lack of training in conflict management and resolution. The area of the organization in which the research was conducted was selected because it was seen as having particular problems with conflict.

In total, 24 managers took part in one of the three courses offered. These were customized courses, delivered exclusively online on three different days in mid-May 2021 (groups A, B, and C), and feedback from previous courses was incorporated into later versions. A one-day, synchronous model was used, with learners working either from home or in groups in the workplace. Managers were selected by the organization, given time off to attend the training, and expected to attend. The course began with an induction webinar that outlined the training and its place in research, identified key issues facing the learners, and introduced learners to the platform. There was also a short, lunchtime webinar to check on learners' progress and a final end-of-course webinar that gave learners an opportunity to ask questions and reflect on the course. The instructor remained online throughout and provided contemporaneous feedback to learners.

Overall, as Figure 1 shows, completion rates were high, with an 87% mean and 18 of the 26 learners completing 75% of more of the online activities. However, this is perhaps to be expected given the synchronous nature of the course.

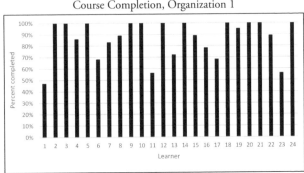

Figure 1
Course Completion, Organization 1

There was much more variation in the amount of time spent on the course (Figure 2), which could also reflect engagement, from just over 1 hour to just over 6 hours. There is little doubt that a number of learners "skipped through" content and were potentially combining online learning with other activities. Figure 3 provides a breakdown of the mean and median amounts of time spent on each activity. The median time spent on each module varied from 26 minutes (modules 1 and 2), 17 minutes (module 3), and 20 minutes (module 4). This suggests a reasonably stable pattern of engagement, with some drop-off toward the end of the course.

The test scores (Figure 4) were generally very high, which could be a result of high levels of capability. However, that could also suggest that learners were able to identify the expected correct answer when provided with multiple choices. Nonetheless, there was some evidence of improvement between scores in pre- and post-course tests and thus in terms of managerial skills.

Out of 24 learners, 14 had higher post-course than pre-course test scores. The mean pre-course score using our conflict competence scenarios was 85 (median = 85), which increased to 92 (median = 100) on the post-course instrument. The mean difference post-course to pre-course was 8 (median = 10).

In general, the managers involved in the training were happy with the course. They found it useful and relevant for their line of work, a good way to receive feedback on their own management skills and to know whether they are on the right track or need to change something. Some mentioned the course was in an area of training that managers at the organization, particularly at the entry level, would benefit from, although it was felt the training could also work as a refresher for some more senior managers:

> This was an excellent course [on]conflict management/resolution and difficult conversations—these are exactly the areas we need to learn about in [civil service organization]. I'm impressed that a course such as this is available. (Civil servant_17, course B)

> It has helped me to refresh some of the management skills required to carry out the management role. It has also been

Figure 2
Course Duration, Organization 1

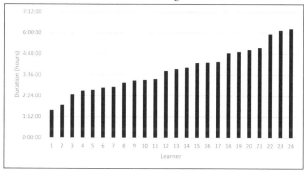

Figure 3
Activity Duration, Organization 1

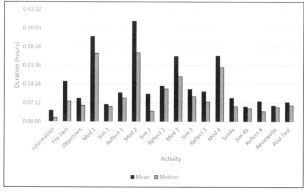

Figure 4
Test Scores, Organization 1

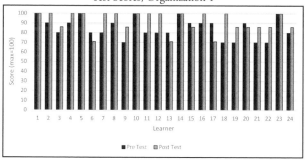

helpful in identifying embedded management behaviours that need to be avoided. (Civil servant_22, course B)

Learners commented that the course was useful for their role as line managers and something they could use in the future. They were also very positive about the interface, the content, and the use of video:

> I found the course very useful especially about how to manage conflict and giving feedback. I will use the skills provided to help with future management issues. (Civil servant_9, course C)

The feedback also suggested that real-time interactivity with tutors was a very helpful component of the course and that it made the course stand out from other online courses offered in the context of COVID-19:

> It is a good idea to have an individual as the "face" of the course rather than just an online training course. (Civil servant_7, course C)

However, some technical issues with Microsoft Teams compromised the interactivity in the first course:

> The problem we had with Microsoft Teams connecting was frustrating for the start of the course and I had a problem logging in at lunch which was frustrating, but I finally managed it. (Civil servant_5, course A)

This was largely resolved in groups B and C, with the webinar elements running more smoothly.

Some trainees suggested that a closer follow-up as the course progressed would have been useful:

> [It would be useful] if there is a way to guide people through this section by section. As I mentioned above I found it helpful (more engaging) to have a person overseeing the event and I know people work at different speeds but I would have preferred to check in after the first session and have a brief group discussion and confirmation that we were all on the right track. (Civil servant_7, course C)

> I think each session should have a "time completion" suggestion at the start. (Civil servant_10, course C)

Others mentioned the need for more group discussions among trainees and suggested that the scenarios worked during the course could be "live" examples taken from delegates:

> The contents of the course is useful [sic], perhaps making it a little more bespoke to current [civil service organization] issues would

> be extremely helpful going forward. Maybe some mangers [sic] wouldn't mind sharing experiences or cases that could be used, obviously not including specific details of cases or individuals […]. (Civil servant_2, course A)

Given the constraints imposed by the pandemic, the blended approach that combined learning at delegates' own pace with the live feedback of a tutor was welcomed. Learners were happy with the platform and mentioned its excellent usability and dashboard and navigation tools; it received good feedback even from those who dislike or usually find it difficult to work with information technology:

> It was very easy to navigate—and I'm a technophobe. (Civil servant_1, course A)

> Being able to conduct in your own time, so not rushing along to keep up with the rest of the group. (Civil servant_2, course A)

Overall, feedback was positive in terms of the content of the course. As pointed out above, less experienced managers appeared to be particularly positive, and there was general agreement that the content would be very suitable for newer line managers. More senior managers, particularly those in group B, felt that the material could have been made more challenging, especially for more experienced managers:

> The content is relevant to any line manager, but I think the multiple-choice answers when having role play "conversations" could be a little more nuanced—they seemed to be more directed at newer managers. (Civil servant_1, course A)

> It covers a broad range of issues and most are ones that I have come across at work, although some could be more challenging to appeal to more senior managers. (Civil servant_4, course A)

That said, even these respondents felt that the course was a useful refresher and, in some cases, confirmed and validated their approach to conflict issues. It is also important to note that after the second group, the course was revised to increase the level of challenge, which appeared to have a positive impact on delegate responses.

Organization 2

The second organization was a large, acute NHS trust. Its participation in the project was part of wider approaches to improve the management of conflict in the wake of highly publicized issues related to failures in the handling of discipline and grievance. Managerial capability was identified as being an area of concern and one that needed to be addressed. Managers who took part in the training course were drawn from patient-facing departments working under significant operational pressure. As a consequence, trainees received very limited (if any) protected time to complete the training.

In total, 20 managers were selected to take part, divided into two cohorts. Trainees were given three and a half weeks to complete the course and had complete freedom in managing their own learning. Two, hour-long synchronous webinars were offered: an introductory one (June 18 and 19) and another one at the end of the course (July 13 and 14), allowing trainees to engage with tutors and colleagues, share experiences, and provide feedback on the course. Approximately half of the learners attended these webinars—reasons given for nonattendance reflected the pressures of work. For example, one learner explained that they had just completed a double shift (because of staff shortages) and therefore needed to sleep.

Trainees had access to the platform until July 27 to follow up on any content and were able to complete the course until that date. The introductory webinar was a stark illustration of the challenges of management training in this context—attendance was patchy, and those who attended were doing so mostly from work, with a number of clinical staff in "scrubs." It was clear that learners were fitting the webinar into a very pressured schedule. There was also a sense of resistance from those present who stressed the difficulty in balancing this type of training with operational pressures.

This was reflected in engagement with the training. Out of the original cohort of 20 managers, 14 engaged with the online course, although three of those who did not start the online course did attend at least one of the webinars. Figure 5 provides details of the course completion data for the 14 learners who engaged with the course. As the figure shows, only four learners completed all activities—mean completion was 60% (median 58%). This was substantially lower than for organization 1.

Perhaps not surprisingly given the mixed engagement within this cohort, the time spent on the course also varied more widely than in organization 1—between just over 3 minutes (for a learner who completed just 5% of the course) to over 8 hours (Figure 6). The mean and median durations were around 4 hours, similar to organization 1, but it is interesting to note that if we focus only on the learners who completed all activities, the mean time spent on the course was 5 hours and 35 minutes compared to 3 hours and 34 minutes for organization 1.

Figure 5
Course Completion, Organization 2

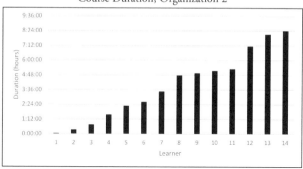

Figure 6
Course Duration, Organization 2

The pattern of activity for organization 2 had a similar structure to that of organization 1; however, there were one or two outliers, probably individuals not logging out when inactive (Figure 7). For that reason, the median values provide a more reliable indication of time spent on activities. Interestingly, the median for each module was substantially greater in organization 2 than in organization 1, with 43 minutes spent on each of modules 1 and 2, 22 minutes on module 3, and 30 minutes on the final module. Therefore, although engagement overall was more erratic, this cohort of learners spent more time on the core learning activities.

The varied engagement of this cohort also impacted on the completion of tests—in particular, one of the learners completed neither the pre- nor post-course tests while another five learners did not complete post-course tests (Figure 8). Of the learners who completed both tests, the mean pre-course score was 82 (median = 80), and the mean post-course score was 93 (median = 93).

Feedback from learners in organization 2 was again generally positive. They found the course relevant and noted that it provided a safe environment to practice and

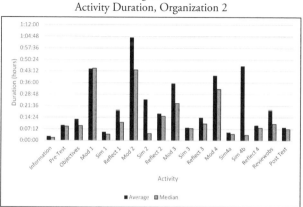

Figure 7
Activity Duration, Organization 2

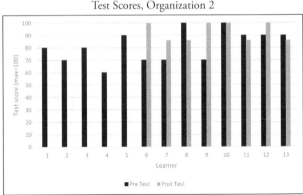

Figure 8
Test Scores, Organization 2

learn about having difficult conversations. They mentioned that they liked taking part and that they gained useful knowledge to help them in the future as line managers:

> I think that the course overall was good and has suggested a number of ways that I could approach difficult conversations. I think that this will help me going forwards. (Hospital manager_3)

> All aspects were relevant to my [day-to-day] work. I found the modules very interesting with lots of useful tips. I am happy that I was nominated to do the course. (Hospital manager_2)

> Whilst there were scenarios to practice—there is nothing like a bit of role play in a safe environment. (Hospital manager_7)

In terms of suggestions for improvement, the managers mostly highlighted the difficulties inherent in juggling the course with a high-demand work environment and thus having to take some of their personal time to complete it. They mentioned that they would like to review the course later and suggested setting specific milestones before group discussions took place:

> Whilst this is in [bite-sized] chunks, this could be done over the course of a day or set milestones to be achieved before a group discussion. (Hospital manager_7)

> Is there a way of re-accessing some of the course as a review? I would be interested in accessing the podcasts but they do not seem to be available as standalone recordings? (Hospital manager_3)

Delegates reported finding the content helpful in dealing with some of the challenges inherent to people management. Having feedback from the instructor and getting the information in a paced way were also described as positive aspects:

The topics were relevant to my day to day managerial work. (Hospital manager_2)

Yes, really great. I think completing in bite sizes and thoughts for the day a bonus. Liked the instructor feedback. (Hospital manager_7)

Organization 3

The third organization that volunteered to take part in the stage-one trial was a privately owned public transport company. Their interest in participating in the research was based on a perceived need to equip managers with the skills to resolve conflict at an earlier stage. HR practitioners in the organization explained that issues tended to escalate quickly into conflict, which could have a significant impact on the organization. Managerial capability varied, but there was no compulsory training in people management skills. Staff in the organization had worked under great pressure through the pandemic, and, at the time of the trial, operational pressures were intense. A similar model of delivery to organization 2 was used with an induction webinar, followed by learners being given four weeks to complete the training on their own time. No dedicated time was provided by the organization; however, participants were strongly encouraged by a senior manager with responsibility for HR to complete the training. Unfortunately, engagement was extremely poor. In total, 23 learners were registered for the course, but only seven started it. Among those who started, none completed more than 50% of the course, making any meaningful statistical analysis very difficult. Feedback from the organization suggested that the main reason for lack of engagement was the operational pressures faced by learners and the fact that it was impossible to provide dedicated time for course engagement and completion.

Organization 4

The fourth organization to take part in the trial was a medium-sized public regulatory agency. The rationale for their participation in the project was that it potentially addressed an important gap in their existing portfolio of management training and development. While important, conflict management was not seen to be a particular problem for organization 4, although levels of managerial experience among participating delegates were reported as varied in discussions with the organizational gatekeeper. In total, 14 managers took part in the course. At the time of the research, most staff were working remotely, which arguably provided an amenable context for online learning of this type. In addition, the organization's HR department played an active role in encouraging learners to complete the training and by ensuring that managers had the time they needed to do so.

As with the other three organizations, a customized version of the training was developed that included links to organizational policies and procedures. The structure of the training was similar to that used for organizations 2 and 3. The course started with a one-hour webinar, which was well attended, with engagement largely positive.

Learners then had five weeks to complete the online training on their own time. An end-of-course webinar was planned, but because of a family bereavement in the research team, it was postponed, and the organization subsequently decided that it was unnecessary. One significant change made to the design of the course was that learners could progress through the course only if they completed each block in order. Eleven of the 14 learners engaged with the course (Figure 9). Of those who started it, all completed at least 60% of the activities, with the majority (six) completing it fully. The mean rate of completion was 90% and the median was 95%—the highest of the three courses where delivery was asynchronous.

Course duration varied widely from just under 2 hours to 14 hours; however, as noted above, high duration may not necessarily reflect time spent learning actively. On average, learners spent a mean of 5 hours and 40 minutes on the course, while the median duration was 2 hours and 52 minutes, which is probably a closer reflection of true engagement (Figures 10 and 11).

The pre- and post-course test scores (Figure 12) showed a clear improvement—the mean pre-course score was 83% (median = 80%); that score increased post-course to 96% (median = 100%). Although two learners did not complete the post-course test, six learners improved their score, and the score of only one learner decreased.

Six delegates responded to the open-ended questions seeking feedback at the end of the course. Overall, they reported being happy with the course, finding it engaging, presenting relatable scenarios, and having credible information. The workload was considered manageable, and the coursework was perceived as having the right balance for a range of activities:

> I enjoyed the fact that the course was engaging. The fact that you had to interact with the course and think about the action you would take […] retained my interest, helped me to learn quicker and made the course more enjoyable. (Regulator_2)

> Like the scenarios and found them very relatable. The information flowed nicely. I liked it when you referred to your research and what it was telling you. Gave it credibility. (Regulator_1)

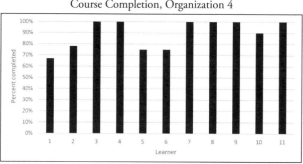

Figure 9
Course Completion, Organization 4

ONLINE LEARNING IN A CONTEXT OF COVID-19 UNCERTAINTY 153

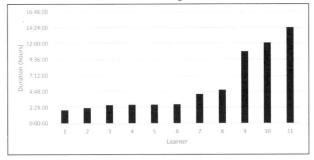

Figure 10
Course Duration, Organization 4

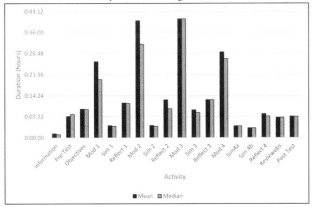

Figure 11
Activity Duration, Organization 4

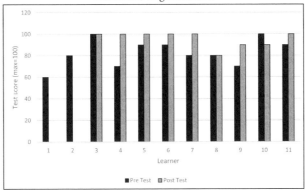

Figure 12
Test Scores, Organization 4

> I felt the course had a good balance in terms of reading, listening and activities. It was very manageable and didn't become onerous. (Regulator_3)

Participants reported finding the content relevant and helpful dealing with some of the challenges involved in people management, and, as in other participating organizations, having feedback from the instructor and getting the information in a paced way were also presented as positive aspects:

> I found that the course content was relevant to my needs as a line manager and provided the clarity of approach when it comes to dealing with issues. (Regulator_3)

> As a new Manager I found the content very relevant as there isn't any in house training. (Regulator_2)

In terms of suggestions for improvement, some managers showed interest in having a face-to-face version of the course, adding a section on giving positive feedback/praise, and breaking down the podcasts into bite-size elements:

> I do wonder if face to face role plays could play a part in the learning experience, as it is as close to real life practice as I am likely to get. (Regulator_2)

> I think it would also be good to have a section on giving positive feedback/praise. So often managers will say [...] good job or well done but the feedback is not specific so colleagues do not understand exactly what was [...] good, or how they did something was good/excellent. (Regulator_6)

CROSS-CASE COMPARISON AND ANALYSIS

The completion rates varied among the four organizations (Figure 13). As noted above, in organization 3, no learners completed the training, so Figure 14 contains the data for organizations 1, 2, and 4. There is little evidence that the differences outlined below reflect concerns over content or accessibility of the content—feedback was generally positive regarding these aspects. Of course, it could be argued that only those completing the course provided detailed feedback. However, feedback gathered through end-of-course webinars that included learners who had failed to complete the training did not suggest this was a particular issue. Instead, time and support appear to be the key factors determining levels of engagement. Organization 4 had the highest levels of completion but also the most conducive organizational context, provision of time, and a degree of expectation that managers would engage and complete the training. Although managers in organizations 1 and 2 were working under challenging conditions, high levels of completion were guaranteed in the former by providing dedicated time through a synchronous model.

However, attendance and completion are only one aspect of engagement, and a comparison of duration data (Figure 14) suggests that the compulsory synchronous model used for organization 1 did not necessarily translate to time spent and/or attention on the course itself, with the learners who engaged with the course in organization 2 spending most time on the course itself (when judged by median duration).

This is also reflected in the duration of specific activities (Figure 15). Therefore, one could conclude that while learners in organization 2 faced the most challenging context for learning, those who did engage with the course were prepared to commit a greater amount of time. One explanation for this finding could be that the very factors that placed managers under significant time pressure increased the relevance of the course objectives and materials.

Of course, time spent is a very crude measure of engagement, and ultimately the key measure is the impact on confidence in managing conflict. In this respect, the

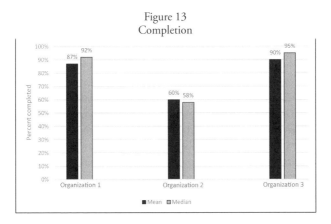

Figure 13
Completion

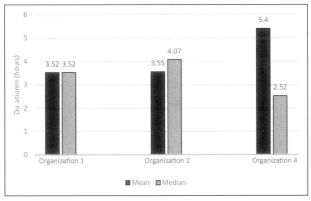

Figure 14
Course Duration

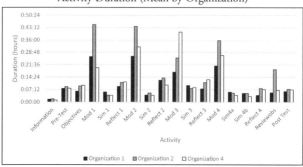

Figure 15
Activity Duration (Mean by Organization)

data from the pilot are encouraging. Over the sample of managers as a whole, test scores increased from a mean of 85 (pre-course) to 93 (post-course). Median values increased from 90 to 100.

The numbers are, of course, small, but two features are worth noting. The first is that delegates had high levels of confidence prior to the training (more than 80% reported being "conflict confident"). The second is that confidence levels were higher after the training in all cases except the private transport company, where no delegates completed the training. This is a striking finding, suggesting that a key benefit of the training is to increase manager confidence, even though training can sometimes alert learners to areas where their confidence was misplaced—essentially, the Dunning–Kruger effect (see Kruger and Dunning 1999).

These data also suggest that the compulsory synchronous model used in organization 1 does not necessarily deliver better results (Figure 16). There are two possible explanations for this: First, when delivery is asynchronous, those who engage are likely to be more committed to the course and, therefore, to some extent, the sample is self-selecting. Second, the data in relation to organization 4 tentatively suggests that completion is important—organization 4 had the highest completion of those that did engage and also the most pronounced improvement in scores.

In relation to internal barriers to completion, feedback suggests that neither course content nor technical issues represented a significant challenge. The course was viewed positively, and the style and design was seen as engaging and interactive. In addition, users did not report any technical challenges and found the platform easy and intuitive. There was limited evidence that users missed peer-to-peer interaction or interaction with instructors—where this was provided through webinars, engagement was inconsistent. In addition, the opportunity to use online discussion or receive feedback in real time from instructors was used by a very small minority of learners. Overall, the main barrier to completion and engagement appeared to be time and the extent to which employers were prepared to support, incentivize, or compel participation.

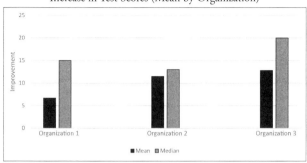

Figure 16
Increase in Test Scores (Mean by Organization)

DISCUSSION AND CONCLUSION

The pilot stage of this research project has reinforced the main premises on which it is based but also reflected a number of fundamental challenges. The way that the project has been positively received reflects existing research that points to line-managerial capability as a missing ingredient in the UK's productivity puzzle. Moreover, among those organizations with which the project team has engaged (both those that took an active role and those that did not), there has been support for the philosophy underpinning the content of the training intervention. In particular, anecdotal conversations with HR practitioners support the view that there is a need for a focus on what some may call "basic" or "soft" skills in contrast to the emphasis on relatively complex programs of leadership development that have dominated the human resource development landscape in the United Kingdom in recent years (Saundry 2020; Saundry, Fisher and Kinsey 2019). Such conversations also reflect a strand in the literature on the UK's performance (see, for example, Sadun, Bloom, and Van Reenen 2017). Crucially, managers often lack the skills they need to manage people effectively, and in particular to address and resolve problems and behaviors that could trigger conflict both with and among their staff (Hunter and Renwick 2009; Saundry and Wibberley 2014; Saundry et al. 2016; Teague and Roche 2012). Reflecting this need, feedback from participants suggests that the content of our intervention is highly relevant to the demands placed on line managers, and early findings provide tentative evidence that the training course has the potential to boost managerial confidence and skills in addressing and resolving conflict at work.

However, the impact of this (or any other) training intervention depends on the extent of engagement. The role of employer support for line manager development is clearly critical, and with organizations 1 and 4, higher engagement was certainly driven by greater organizational commitment and a willingness to provide managers with time to complete the course. Even with a no-cost intervention, it was clear that HR and organizational development practitioners did not find it easy to convince organizational leaders that such training is a good use of management time. This raises interesting questions about whether managers should be compelled to take part. While compulsion certainly guarantees engagement with online training, the quality of that engagement and its consequent impact is less clear. The experience of our pilot within organization 4 suggests that there is an optimal mix of expectation, support (by providing time to take the training), and incentives.

It could be argued that the extent and quality of engagement is also compromised or at least shaped by the online nature of the intervention. For example, role play is widely used in conventional face-to-face conflict management and mediation training. In addition, as outlined earlier, peer support and interaction is argued to have beneficial outcomes. Indeed, some of the feedback from learners in our intervention suggested that these elements are important. Our training attempted to address some of these issues by encouraging online discussion forums, using simulated role plays, and integrating webinars into the learning. However, the take-up of opportunities to interact with other learners was limited.

It is important to note that there are also multiple advantages of online training. First, the investment in an online product creates the potential for delivery at a greater scale and lower marginal cost than would be possible with face-to-face training. Second, training can be fitted more flexibly around existing work commitments—reducing disruption of managers and organizations—although there is the danger that organizations can use this format to avoid providing managers with time to train. Third, the use of tests, simulations, and scenarios is easier online and can be made more creative than in a traditional classroom setting. Fourth, online interventions can provide a more permanent resource for learners. This is particularly important in conflict resolution training, as conflict is unpredictable and, in many instances, by the time a manager needs to use their newfound skills, the necessary knowledge may be a distant memory. In our case, we also developed a "tool kit" of resources, including summaries, action templates, and other aids to which delegates would have access for 12 months after the training. Finally, we were able to track learner engagement and impact in ways not possible with in-person delivery.

There is, of course, a trade-off between online and face-to-face delivery, and it is certainly arguable that an in-depth conflict management training program using the best of both approaches would be likely to maximize impact on managerial behaviors. However, an underpinning premise of our research is that such training is not delivered at all in most organizations and therefore the counterfactual to online training is not face-to-face delivery but no training at all. This is particularly the case in the sectors on which our project focused—namely, healthcare, retail, and hotels and catering.

ACKNOWLEDGMENTS

This work was supported by the Economic and Social Research Council (grant number ES/S012796/1).

ENDNOTES

1. A concern with this scenario-based approach related to the potential for social desirability bias (see, for example, the review by Rumpal 2013). For the main stage of the project, an abridged and marginally adapted variant of Form B of the Rahim Organizational Conflict Inventory–II (ROCI II; Rahim 1983) has instead been deployed. It asks managers to respond to a series of statements concerning conflict and conflict situations, producing a score across each of five conflict management styles—collaborating, accommodating, competing, avoiding, and compromising. Preliminary findings suggest a shift from avoiding and competing styles toward more collaborative approaches.

2. The training can accommodate a range of delivery modes, including fully synchronous, fully asynchronous, and bichronous (i.e., a mixture; see Martin, Polly, and Ritzhaupt 2020).

REFERENCES

Bloom, N., and J. Van Reenen. 2007. "Measuring and Explaining Management Practices Across Firms and Countries." *Quarterly Journal of Economics* 122 (4): 1351–1408.

Bloom, N., and J. Van Reenen. 2011. "Human Resource Management and Productivity." *Handbook of Labor Economics* 4 (Part B): 1697–1767.

Bos-Nehles, A.C., and J.G. Meijerink. 2018. "HRM Implementation by Multiple HRM Actors: A Social Exchange Perspective." *International Journal of Human Resource Management* 29 (22): 3068–3092.

Bos-Nehles, A.C., M.J. Van Riemsdijk, and J. Looise. 2013. "Employee Perceptions of Line Management Performance: Applying the AMO Theory to Explain the Effectiveness of Line Managers' HRM Implementation." *Human Resource Management* 52 (6): 861–877.

Chartered Institute of Personnel and Development. 2007. "Managing Conflict at Work." London: Chartered Institute of Personnel and Development.

Chartered Institute of Personnel and Development. 2008. "Workplace Mediation—How Employers Do It." London: Chartered Institute of Personnel and Development.

Chartered Institute of Personnel and Development. 2016. "HR Outlook—Views of Our Profession, Winter 2016–17." https://tinyurl.com/55tep383

Dromey, J. 2014. *Meeting the Challenge: Successful Employee Engagement in the NHS*. London: IPA.

Gilbert, C., S. De Winne, and L. Sels. 2011. "The Influence of Line Managers and HR Department on Employees' Affective Commitment." *International Journal of Human Resource Management* 22 (8): 1618–1637.

Hunter, W., and D. Renwick. 2009. "Involving British Line Managers in HRM in a Small Non-Profit Organization." *Employee Relations* 31 (4): 398–411.

Kruger, J., and D. Dunning. 1999. "Unskilled and Unaware of It: How Difficulties in Recognizing One's Own Incompetence Lead to Inflated Self-Assessments." *Journal of Personality and Social Psychology* 77 (6): 1121–1134.

MacLeod, D., and N. Clarke. 2009. "Engaging for Success: Enhancing Performance Through Employee Engagement." Report. London: Department for Business, Innovation and Skills.

Martin, F., D. Polly, and A. Ritzhaupt. 2020. "Bichronous Online Learning: Blending Asynchronous and Synchronous Online Learning." EDUCAUSE. https://tinyurl.com/2s37fnm9

Neuendorf, K.A. 2018. "Content Analysis and Thematic Analysis." In *Advanced Research Methods for Applied Psychology Design, Analysis and Reporting*, edited by P. Brough. London: Routledge, 311–323.

Newsome, K., P. Thompson, and J. Commander. 2013. "You Monitor Performance at Every Hour: Labour and the Management of Performance in the Supermarket Supply Chain." *New Technology, Work and Employment* 28 (1): 1–15.

Purcell, J. 2010. "Building Employee Engagement." Policy Discussion Paper. London: Acas.

Purcell, J., and S. Hutchinson. 2007. "Front-Line Managers as Agents in the HRM-Performance Causal Chain: Theory, Analysis and Evidence." *Human Resource Management Journal* 17 (1): 3–20.

Rahim, M.A. 1983. "A Measure of Styles of Handling Interpersonal Conflict." *Academy of Management Journal* 26 (2): 368–376.

Rumpal, I. 2013. "Determinants of Social Desirability Bias in Sensitive Surveys: A Literature Review." *Quality & Quantity* 47 (4): 2025–2047.

Sadun, R., N. Bloom, and J. Van Reenen. 2017. "Why Do We Undervalue Competent Management? Neither Great Leadership nor Brilliant Strategy Matters Without Operational Excellence." *Harvard Business Review* 95 (5): 120–127.

Saundry, R. 2020. "The Impact of Covid-19 on Employment Relations in the NHS." Healthcare People Management Association. https://tinyurl.com/365wutj7

Saundry, R., V. Fisher, and S. Kinsey. 2019. "Managing Workplace Conflict: The Changing Role of HR." Acas Research Paper. https://tinyurl.com/4zsjtt46

Saundry, R., V. Fisher, and S. Kinsey. 2022. "Line Management and the Resolution of Workplace Conflict in the UK." In *Research Handbook on Line Managers*, edited by K. Townsend, A. Bos-Nehles, and K. Jiang. Cheltenham: Edward Elgar, pp. 258–269.

Saundry, R., D. Adam, I. Ashman, C. Forde, G. Wibberley, and S. Wright. 2016. *Managing Individual Conflict in the Contemporary British Workplace*. London: Acas.

Saundry, R., and G. Wibberley. 2014. "Workplace Dispute Resolution and the Management of Individual Conflict—A Thematic Analysis of Five Case Studies." London: Acas.

Teague, P., and W. Roche. 2012. "Line Managers and the Management of Workplace Conflict: Evidence from Ireland." *Human Resource Management Journal* 22 (3): 235–251.

Townsend, K., A. Wilkinson, C. Allan, and G. Bamber. 2012. "Accidental, Unprepared and Unsupported: The Ward Manager's Journey." *International Journal of Human Resource Management* 23 (1): 204–220.

Wietrak, E., D. Rousseau, and E. Barends. 2021. *Effective Virtual Classrooms: An Evidence Review*. London: Chartered Institute of Personnel and Development.

About the Contributors

EDITORS

Ariel C. Avgar is the David M. Cohen Professor in Labor Relations, Law, and History and senior associate dean for outreach and sponsored research at the ILR School at Cornell University. His research focuses on two primary areas within employment relations. First, he explores the role that employment relations factors plays in the healthcare industry. Second, he studies conflict and its management in organizations, with a focus on the strategic choices made by firms.

Deborah Hann is a reader in employment relations at Cardiff Business School. Her research focuses in two main areas: dispute resolution in the workplace and the real living wage as a form of civil regulation. She has undertaken research in conjunction with the UK Advisory, Conciliation and Arbitration Service; the Labour Relations Agency, the Civil Medication Council, and the Living Wage Foundation.

J. Ryan Lamare is the Reuben G. Soderstrom Professor of Industrial Relations in the School of Labor and Employment Relations at the University of Illinois Urbana-Champaign. His main research interests include the relationship between union and nonunion voice and politics, workplace dispute resolution in the labor and employment arenas, and international and comparative industrial relations.

David Nash is a reader in employment relations at Cardiff Business School. His research involves a number of international and UK projects, with a focus on employment regulation and workplace conflict resolution. He has undertaken research projects for the Living Wage Foundation; the Advisory, Conciliation and Arbitration Service; and the Labour Relations Agency.

CONTRIBUTORS

Greg J. Bamber is director of the International Consortium for Research in Employment and Work, Department of Management, and Theme Lead, Future of Work, Monash Data Futures Institute, Monash Business School. He has more than 200 academic publications, including many articles in leading refereed journals, and he has published influential books, including *International and Comparative Employment Relations: Global Crises and Institutional Responses* (co-editor). His interests and experience include artificial intelligence, the future of work, employment relations, organizational and technological change, high-performance work systems, smart workplaces, arbitration, dispute prevention and settlement, negotiation, logistics, international comparisons and transferability of management styles, people management and employment relations in aviation, agriculture, building, chemicals, distribution, and education, including universities, electronics, engineering, finance, healthcare, hospitality, infrastructure, manufacturing, mining, the public sector, railways, retailing, services, sport, tourism, telecommunications, and unions.

Martin Behrens is senior researcher at the Institute for Economic and Social Research (WSI) of the Hans Böckler Foundation, Germany. He also teachers Sociology at the Heinrich Heine University in Düsseldorf and currently serves as the deputy president of the Works Council at the Hans Böckler Foundation. Martin was educated at the University of Göttingen (master's) and at the ILR School at Cornell University (PhD). He was awarded his postdoctoral professorial qualification by the University of Göttingen in 2010. Between 2011 and 2020, he was co-editor of *Industrielle Beziehungen, The German Journal of Industrial Relations*, and served as a member of the executive committee of the International Labour and Employment Relations Association from 2015 through 2021. He has published widely in leading international journals in work, human resources management, and industrial relations, including the *British Journal of Industrial Relations, Industrial and Labor Relations Review, Industrial Relations, Socio-Economic Review, Comparative European Politics*, and Human Resource Management Journal. Current research interests include employee voice, trade union strategies, employer associations, and conflict management at the workplace.

Yashika Chandhok is a doctoral candidate and recipient of the Vice Chancellor's Doctoral Scholarship at Auckland University of Technology, New Zealand. She has a double master's in management, and her doctoral research focuses on understanding the role of culture and gender on the negotiation behavior of Indian women managers working in India and New Zealand. Motivated to understand negotiation behavior better by integrating the indigenous cultural lens, Yashika introduces the aspect of migration and intersectionality in her research. Her research interests expand into employment relations in international corporations, as well as small and medium-sized family businesses.

Denise Currie is a reader in human resource management at Queen's Management School. Her research interests lie broadly in employee relations. Specifically, she has interests in workforce conflict, cooperation and collaboration, well-being, and diversity and inclusion. She has contributed to numerous Irish, UK-wide, and international research projects examining the dynamics of workplace conflict and how it is resolved, alongside other projects that have examined various workplace issues in the health and social care sectors. She has published in leading journals, including the *British Journal of Industrial Relations, Industrial and Labor Relations Review, International Journal of Management Reviews, Industrial Relations Journal, Work, Employment and Society*, and the *International Journal of Human Resource Management*.

Gaye Greenwood describes herself as a "pracademic." A practicing mediator and academic for 23 years, Gaye is passionate about research informed practice. Her PhD research developed a collaborative sense-making model for practitioners and parties during negotiation, facilitation, mediation, or contexts where complexity and ambiguity influence interpretation. She advocates for a collaborative reflective sense-making/learning approach to conflict resolution. Gaye leads Greenwood Mediators in Aotearoa, New Zealand, providing mediation, facilitation, and negotiation coaching for interpersonal, family, workplace, healthcare, sport, recreation, employment, community, government, not for profit and, small to medium enterprises in our complex, ambiguous, changing world.

Paul Latreille is chair in management and director of strategic education projects at Sheffield University Management School. An economist by background, Paul researches the interfaces between applied labor economics and employment relations, focusing on the resolution and management of workplace conflict, including mediation/alternative dispute resolution and employment tribunals. With more than 100 research outputs, he has published extensively for both academic and policymaker/practitioner audiences, and co-edited the *Reframing Resolution* research volume on conflict management. Paul has also led or contributed to a range of funded projects for bodies including the European Commission; Ministry of Justice; Advisory, Conciliation and Arbitration Service; TUC; Low Pay Commission; and DTI/BERR/BIS. He is currently part of the team working on a large-scale Economic and Social Research Council–funded project evaluating the impact of a training intervention for line managers. Among other affiliations, Paul is a Research Fellow of the IZA, a Fellow of the Royal Society of Arts, Manufactures and Commerce, and a Fellow of the Learning and Performance Institute and serves on the UK Civil Mediation Council's Workplace and Employment Group.

Fatima Maatwk is a researcher and lecturer at Westminster Business School and a student partnerships lecturer at the Centre for Education and Teaching Innovation. She completed her doctoral research at Westminster Business School and her bachelor's and master's degrees in economics and business administration at Humboldt University, Berlin. In her role as student partnership lecturer, Fatima engages in research projects on partnership in higher education and pedagogies for social justice. In further research, she is investigating the effectiveness of diversity, equity, and inclusion management policies in both academic and nonacademic settings. Her research interests include social psychology, diversity and inclusion, decolonization, intersectionality, and cross-cultural and gender studies.

Rita Neves joined the Management School and the Centre for Decent Work as a research associate for the Economic and Social Research Council–funded project, "Managerial Competences, Engagement and Productivity: Developing Positive Relationships." Before that, she was a research associate at Sheffield Alcohol Research Group, Department of Public Health, ScHARR (University of Sheffield), where she investigated aspects of health inequalities in relation to employment. For her PhD, and as a member of the Research Network on Gender and Health Impacts of Policies Extending Working Life in Western Countries, she collaborated with different research centers around Europe, examining the mental health implications of unemployment in late career from a political economy perspective.

Katrina Nobles is the education and communications manager for the Scheinman Institute on Conflict Resolution at the Cornell University ILR School, focusing on educating the next generation of neutrals and practitioners on campus and in the workplace. She designs curricula, instructs professional programs, and facilitates discussions for organizational workplace conflicts. She also works with faculty and extension associates to coordinate programs, contracts, and grants. She has practiced mediation for several years, and prior to her employment at Cornell, Katrina was the Cortland County Coordinator for New Justice Mediation Services. During that time, she mediated hundreds of community, child custody/visitation, child support, and family disputes. She holds a master's degree in conflict analysis and engagement from Antioch University Midwest.

Erling Rasmussen is a former professor of work and employment at Auckland University of Technology (2007–2023) and is now the managing director of ER Publishing Limited. He has worked in employment relations in academia, the public and private sectors, and in several countries since the late 1970s and has undertaken research for government, businesses, and unions. Erling has published extensively on employment relations topics. He is an editor of the *New Zealand Journal of Employment Relations*, which is a genuine open-access journal, and he has co-authored several textbooks.

William Roche is a professor of industrial relations and human resources in the School of Business, University College Dublin (UCD) and honorary professor in the School of Management, Queen's University Belfast. He is a graduate of UCD and completed his doctorate at the University of Oxford, where he was Heyworth Memorial Prize Research Fellow of Nuffield College. He has written and edited ten books and published more than 100 peer-reviewed papers and book chapters. He has held visiting professorships at the University of South Australia, Adelaide; the University of Melbourne; and the Cyprus International Institute of Management. He was a Jean Monnet Fellow at the European University Institute, Florence. He is a member of the editorial boards of leading journals, including the *British Journal of Industrial Relations*, *Industrial Relations*, *Human Resource Management Journal*, and *Labour and Industry*. He is a member of the Chartered Institute of Personnel and Development (CIPD), for which he chairs the judging panel for the HR Excellence Award and is a member of the CIPD Quality Advisory Group. He is a member of international advisory panels for research programs and centers at the Manchester Alliance Business School and at the ADAPT program of the University of Bergamo.

Richard Saundry is a Principal Research Fellow at the University of Westminster, having previously held posts at the Universities of Leeds, Sheffield, Central Lancashire, and Plymouth. He is the United Kingdom's leading academic authority on the management of discipline, grievance, and workplace conflict. He is a co-author of *Managing Employment Relations*, the core Chartered Institute of Personnel and Development text for employee relations, and he edited *Reframing Resolution*. His work has been published in a wide range of leading international academic journals. He has held a number of research grants and is currently working on a major project funded by the Economic and Social Research Council investigating the links among conflict competence, employee engagement, and productivity. Richard has worked particularly closely with the Advisory, Conciliation and Arbitration Service (Acas) over the past ten years to shape policy and identify and evaluate innovative practice. Last year, he co-authored an Acas report that, for the first time, estimated the cost of workplace conflict to UK organizations.

Paul Teague is emeritus professor of management at The Queen's University Belfast. He has written widely on the themes of the employment relations consequences of deeper European integration, social partnership and employment performance, workplace conflict management, and human resources in the recession. He has published over 50 papers in top-tier journals on these themes.

Julian Teicher has degrees in economics and law from Monash University and a PhD from the University of Melbourne. In the early part of his career, he worked as an industrial relations officer for two unions—one in the maritime and power industries and the other in nursing. He was formerly head of the

Department of Management and director of the Graduate School of Business at Monash University and head of the Centre of Commerce and Management at RMIT University of Vietnam. His research is in two principal fields: workplace and human resources and public management and governance. He has published widely on such topics as conflict management, employee participation and industrial democracy, and employee voice and representation.

Peter Urwin is a professor of applied economics and director of the Centre for Employment Research at the University of Westminster. He has over 15 years of experience leading large-scale evaluations for a range of government departments. He is principal investigator for the Economic and Social Research Council–funded study, "Early Identification of Young People at Risk of Poor Educational and Labour Market Outcomes" and co-investigator on a large ESRC-funded study of managerial competences, engagement, and productivity. His research investigates issues of education and social mobility, equality and diversity, entrepreneurship, employment relations, and tax policy, with a focus on the use of advanced econometric techniques to capture causal impacts from policy interventions. Peter's academic and policy work includes over 100 publications.

Bernadine Van Gramberg is chair of the Academic Board at Federation University and a member of the University Council. She has more than 25 years of university governance and management experience. She also has experience in dispute resolution, industrial relations, human resources management, and public sector management. Bernadine's research has encompassed dispute resolution and public sector management. She has been widely published in peer-reviewed journals and has presented extensively at national and international conferences.

LERA Executive Board Members 2023–24

President
Dennis Dabney, Dabney Law LLC

President-Elect
Jim Pruitt, Kaiser Permanente

Past President
Paul F. Clark, Pennsylvania State University

Secretary-Treasurer
Andrew Weaver, University of Illinois Urbana-Champaign

Editor-in-Chief
J. Ryan Lamare, University of Illinois Urbana-Champaign

National Chapter Advisory Council Chair
William Canak, Middle Tennessee State University (retired)

Legal Counsel
Steven B. Rynecki

Executive Board Members
Peter Berg, Michigan State University
Sharon Block, Harvard Law
Andrea Cáceres, SHARE/AFSCME
Robert Chiaravalli, Strategic Labor and HR, LLC
Julie Farb, AFL-CIO
Eliza Forsythe, University of Illinois Urbana-Champaign
Ruben Garcia, University of Nevada, Las Vegas
Janet Gillman, Oregon Employment Relations Board
Beverly Harrison, Arbitrator/Mediator
John Johnson, Southeastern Pennsylvania Transportation Authority
Glenard Middleton, AFSCME MD Council 67
Deborah Moore-Carter, City of Baltimore
Deborah Mueller, CSEA Local 1000 AFSCME
Dionne Pohler, University of Saskatchewan
Jim Pruitt, Kaiser Permanente
Christine Riordan, University of Illinois Urbana-Champaign
Sean Rogers, University of Rhode Island
Christy Yoshitomi, Federal Mediation and Conciliation Service

UAW-Ford Labor Management Committee Trust

Powered By Our People
mycareer.ford.com

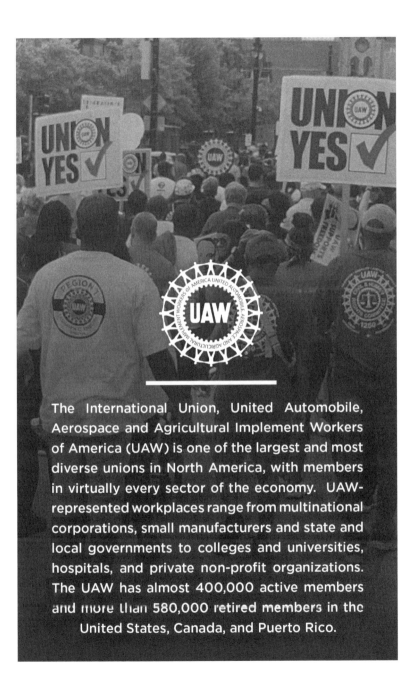

The International Union, United Automobile, Aerospace and Agricultural Implement Workers of America (UAW) is one of the largest and most diverse unions in North America, with members in virtually every sector of the economy. UAW-represented workplaces range from multinational corporations, small manufacturers and state and local governments to colleges and universities, hospitals, and private non-profit organizations. The UAW has almost 400,000 active members and more than 580,000 retired members in the United States, Canada, and Puerto Rico.

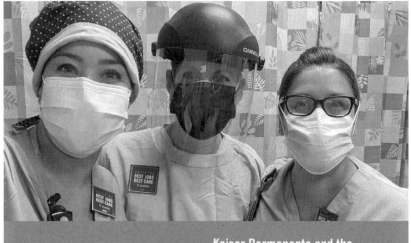

A *Better* WAY TO →→→→→→→ WORK

Kaiser Permanente and the Alliance of Health Care Unions thank all our managers, physicians and employees — including more than 50,000 union-represented workers — for 26 years of partnership.

Affordable, quality care. It started in California's shipyards and steel mills in World War II; today we continue that tradition across the country. Kaiser Permanente is America's largest non-profit health care delivery organization. Kaiser Permanente and the Alliance of Health Care Unions are proud to work together to ensure Kaiser Permanente is the best place to work and the best place to receive care.

In 2021, after tough negotiations, we affirmed our Labor Management Partnership in a new four-year agreement, which includes important new provisions committing to joint work on staffing, racial justice, and promoting the affordability of health care. The new national agreement covers more than 50,000 members of AFSCME, AFT, IBT, ILWU, IUOE, KPN AA, UFCW, UNITE HERE, and USW, in every market where Kaiser Permanente operates.

A FOCUS ON RESEARCH
ilr.cornell.edu/research

Cornell University's ILR School is the preeminent educational institution in the world focused on work, labor and employment. ILR-generated research – conducted by the largest number of full-time faculty members focused on work-related topics of any institution in the U.S. – influences public policy, informs organizational strategy and improves professional practice.

In the past year, ILR faculty and students have produced research on a diverse range of topics, including sexual harassment, remote work, fostering creativity in the workplace, migrant worker rights, the pitfalls of AI and the dangers facing workers in the global apparel and fishing industries.

We are also home to the Catherwood Library, The Kheel Center for Labor-Management Documentation & Archives, and over 15 centers and institutes focused on bridging the gap between research and practice.

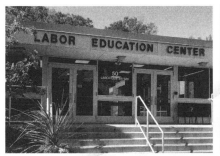

Leading the Way with LERA

Rutgers School of Management and Labor Relations (SMLR) is proud to partner with LERA through an established tradition of leadership and service to the association across executive, editorial and committee roles. Through our academic programs, research initiatives, and outreach programs, Rutgers SMLR is a leading source of expertise on the world of work, building effective and sustainable organizations, and the changing employment relationship.

Rutgers SMLR is pleased to continue our collaboration with LERA to offer a unique lens to explore the evolution of work and the Future of Work(ers).

RUTGERS
School of Management
and Labor Relations

smlr.rutgers.edu

Proud supporter of LERA

Forging new research frontiers since 1922

From the Hoover administration to the Biden administration, Princeton's Industrial Relations Section has been a hub for policymakers, companies, researchers, and activists seeking best-in-class data and research on the labor market and the relationship between industry and workers.

https://irs.princeton.edu
https://irs100.princeton.edu